How Much Is Your Business Worth?

A Step-by-Step Guide to Selling and Ensuring the Maximum Sale Value of Your Business

Frederick D. Lipman

PRIMA PUBLISHING

PRIMA PUBLISHING and colophon are trademarks of Prima Communications, Inc.

*"Caution Talks: Texaco-Pennzoil Case Makes Firms Careful about Merger Moves," appeared on April 15, 1986, in *The Wall Street Journal*. Article reprinted by permission of *The Wall Street Journal*, © 1986 Dow Jones & Company, Inc. All Rights Reserved Worldwide.

** "The Gambler Who Refused $2 Billion," May 11, 1987, by Stratford P. Sherman, reprinted with permission from *Fortune* magazine. © 1987 Time Inc. All rights reserved.

DISCLAIMER
This publication is designed to provide accurate and authoritative information (as of July 1996, except as otherwise noted) in regard to the subject matter covered. It is sold with the understanding that the author and publisher are not engaged in rendering legal, accounting or other professional services. Laws vary from state to state, and if legal advice or other expert assistance is required, the services of a competent professional should be sought.

The author and publisher specifically disclaim any liability, loss or risk, personal or otherwise, which is incurred as a consequence, directly or indirectly, of the use and application of any of the contents of this book.

Library of Congress Cataloging-in-Publication Data

Lipman, Frederick D.
  How much is your business worth? : a step-by-step guide to selling and ensuring the maximum sale value of your business / by Fred Lipman.
    p. cm.
  Includes index.
  ISBN 0-7615-0432-X
  1. Sale of business enterprises—United States—Handbooks, manuals, etc.
I. Title.
HD1393.4.U6L56   1996
658.1'6—dc20   96-610
                                                                    CIP

96 97 98 99 00 01 AA 10 9 8 7 6 5 4 3 2 1
Printed in the United States of America

How to Order:
Single copies may be ordered from Prima Publishing, P.O. Box 1260BK, Rocklin, CA 95677; telephone (916) 632-4400. Quantity discounts are also available. On your letterhead, include information concerning the intended use of the books and the number of books you wish to purchase.

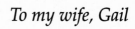

To my wife, Gail

Contents

*Reprinted from The Wall Street Journal, April 15, 1986. Reproduced with permission of *The Wall Street Journal.*

**Reprinted from *Fortune* magazine article by Stratford P. Sherman, May 11, 1987. © 1987 Time Inc. All rights reserved.

Acknowledgments

I want to acknowledge the helpful comments and editorial efforts of my partners at the Philadelphia office of the law firm of Blank Rome Comisky & McCauley—

Chapters 1 and 2: Fred Blume, Esq.; Chapters 3, 4 and Appendix 4: Alan L. Zeiger, Esq.; Chapter 5: Lawrence S. Chane, Esq. and Henry M. Kuller, Esq.; Chapters 7 and 12: Barry H.Genkin, Esq.; Chapter 8: Henry M. Kuller, Esq.; Chapters 9 and 17 and Appendix 5: Arthur H. Miller, Esq.; Chapters 10 and 11: Robert M. Broder, Esq. and Joseph T. Gulant, Esq.; Chapter 14: Arthur Bachman, Esq.; Chapters 15 and 16: Steve Dubow, Esq.; Chapter 18: Francis E. Dehel, Esq.; Appendix 6: Steve Dubow, Esq. and Abbott A. Leban, Esq.; Appendix 7: Kevin P. Cronin, Esq.

I absolve the editors from any responsibility for any errors in this book.

Helpful suggestions for this book were made by Seth Lehr of Legg Mason Wood Walker and my partner Fred Blume.

Jim Twerdahl, Chairman and Chief Executive Officer of Mayco Colors, Inc., was kind enough to permit me to use portions of his comprehensive buyer's due diligence checklist in Chapter 7. I also want to acknowledge the assistance of Kit Boyle, our librarian. Last but not least, I owe a special debt to Valerie Smith, who retyped the manuscript an unreasonable number of times, and to my personal secretary, Fran Ratcliffe.

Introduction

Maximizing the sale price of your business requires careful advanced planning, which should begin as early as five years before your target sale date.

Inexperienced business owners may think that it is simple to sell their businesses. They think they can just let it be known that the business is for sale, receive offers, sign legal documents, cash the buyer's check, and then golf for the rest of their lives.

Only one in ten business sales occurs this smoothly. The remaining nine out of ten may be plagued with at least one of the following problems, which can reduce, if not destroy, the value of your business:

- Key employees leave when you announce your decision to sell, taking important customers with them.
- Overvaluing your business can mean it takes so long to find a buyer that new well-financed competitors have time to establish themselves before your sale, thereby lowering the value of your business.

- Customers find out about your pending sale and seek out your competitors.
- Competitors find out about your pending sale and use this information to win away existing and potential customers.
- Suppliers who are important to your business start selling to your competitors when they realize that your business will be sold.
- In the course of their due diligence investigation, potential buyers discover your proprietary information and use it to start a competitive business.
- You and your top executives spend so much time involved with the sale process that the business itself begins to run downhill.
- Income taxes can consume more than 50 percent of the proceeds from the sale of your business.

Selling your business is an exit strategy and a method of diversifying your assets. Since most businesspeople have the overwhelming percentage of their net worth tied up in their businesses, a sale permits them to diversify their asset portfolios and avoid the risk of business failure.

Most business owners have little experience in the actual sale of a business, however. The skills that permit an entrepreneur to grow a business are not necessarily the skills that would permit him to sell the business successfully. There are also many costly traps for the novice selling a business.

There are six stages of selling your business, which are described in table 1.

The key to maximizing the sale price of your business is careful advance planning, which starts many years before your sale target date. The advance planning steps taken over a five-year period are discussed in detail in Chapters 1 through 6. These steps start with stage 1 and end with stage 3. The purpose of these steps is to enhance the value of your business and its appeal to potential buyers.

Table 1 Stages in the Sale Process

Stage 1	Stage 2	Stage 3	Stage 4	Stage 5	Stage 6
ADVANCE PLANNING (UP TO 5 YEARS FROM TARGET DATE)	ORGANIZATION (UP TO 1 YEAR FROM TARGET DATE)	PREPARATION FOR MARKETING	MARKETING	NEGOTIATIONS	FINALIZATION
• Assess objectives	• Finalize decision to sell	• Finalize marketing brochure	• Auction vs. negotiated process	• Selection of serious bidders	• Documentation
• Maximize valuation	• Ensure commitment from top	• Develop list of potential buyers	• Contact potential buyers	• Negotiation	• Closing
• Assemble advisory team	• Finalize advisory teams		• Buyer's due diligence		
• Draft marketing brochure					
• Eliminate deal killers and impediments					
• Protect the business					
• Minimize taxes					

Chapter 1 focuses on your motives for selling, which must guide the entire sale process, including your negotiation strategy. Unless you are experienced in selling businesses, you must also assemble a professional team of advisors in advance of the sale. Chapter 1 tells you how.

You must understand how your business will be valued so that you can maximize your sale price through steps taken prior to the sale. Those subjects are covered in Chapter 2.

During the presale years, you must identify and eliminate deal killers and other impediments to the sale. The elimination of deal killers may take many years to accomplish, and, consequently, you cannot begin too soon. Chapter 3 discusses these issues.

You must also give careful advance thinking to how you will protect your business during the sale. This includes maintaining confidentiality of both your decision to sell and your proprietary information. It is important that your key employees, customers, and suppliers do not become privy to this information earlier than necessary and that you do not inadvertently give potential buyers valuable proprietary information about your business. Chapter 4 tells you what you must do years before your target sale date to protect your business and proprietary information during the sale process.

Finally, you must take steps prior to the sale to minimize the taxes on the sale proceeds, including estate and death taxes, as well as federal and state income taxes. This is discussed in Chapter 5.

Businesses do not sell themselves. You must market your business and understand the motivations of buyers. You would not launch a new product line without careful study of the marketplace and a detailed knowledge of your customers' needs. This study might take several years.

The same careful study must be done prior to the marketing of your business. Chapter 6 tells you how to plan for the marketing of your business and discusses the pros and cons of using an investment banker or business broker. Chapters 5 and 6 describe stage 3 and prepare you for stage 4, the actual marketing of the business and the negotiations with the buyer, which are covered in Chapters 7 through 9.

Chapter 7 explains how to survive the buyer's due diligence process.

Chapter 8 provides a negotiation strategy for sellers, including the use of auctions to maximize the sale price.

Chapter 9 covers letters of intent, which may be more binding than you think.

Chapters 10 and 11 cover the structuring and tax issues to which you must be sensitive and teach you to think in "after-tax" terms.

If you are selling to a public-company buyer, Chapter 12 is must reading.

Chapter 13 explains the special problems of selling a public company. The sale of a control block of stock in either a public or a private company is also discussed.

Some entrepreneurs would prefer to sell their business to their key employees. Chapter 14 tells you how and explains the surprising tax benefits of selling to an ESOP (employee stock ownership plan).

Chapters 15 and 16 deal with notes and earnouts and the traps inherent to accepting these deferred payouts of the sale price.

Chapter 17 advises you on how to negotiate your employment or consulting agreement with the buyer.

The traps in the agreement of sale and closing (stage 6) are covered in Chapter 18.

Chapters 19 and 20 discuss two possible alternatives to selling your business: leveraged recapitalization and going public. Although neither alternative is possible for all businesses, it is important to understand these alternative exit strategies and their pros and cons.

The keys to a successful sale of your business are careful advance planning and a clear understanding of your motivations for the sale. Your motivations will dictate the manner in which you conduct the sale, your strategies for negotiation, and which alternatives you will consider. For example, if you believe that your business is going downhill, you may wish to promote a fast sale and price your business accordingly, and you may instruct your attorney to take somewhat higher legal risks to avoid delaying or interfering with a prompt sale.

A clear understanding of your motivations will also prevent you from suffering from seller's remorse, or at least alleviate the symptoms—and a substantial bank account always helps.

This book is intended to guide you through the sale process and around the traps inherent in that process. Every effort has been made to ensure that all information contained in this book is current as of July, 1996. However, there is no substitute for an experienced professional team of advisors, including a tax attorney, who should always be consulted to ensure that current statutes of the law and accounting principles are met in each specific circumstance. This book will help you pick such advisors.

PART 1

Advance Planning

CHAPTER 1

Preliminary Considerations

You should give consideration to all of the following items before seriously embarking upon the sale process.

UNDERSTANDING YOUR MOTIVES

It is important that you understand your motivation for selling your business. Your motivation will dictate the nature of your buyer and the structure of your transaction.

For example, if you are no longer interested in operating your business, you do not want to sell to a financial buyer or to have an earnout. An earnout is a provision in the agreement of sale that would measure the purchase price in whole or in part by the future profits of the business.

A financial buyer will typically not have the management in place to run your business and will expect you to remain to operate the business under a long-term employment or consulting agreement. You would not want to agree to an earnout unless you are in control of the business, since otherwise your final purchase price could be significantly reduced by poor performance of the managers installed by the buyer.

Understanding your motives to sell your business also avoids what is called "seller's remorse." In general, seller's remorse results from the significant change in lifestyle that the sale of your business can bring together with the emotional attachments that you have toward the business. Truly understanding your motivation will help you get through a very natural period of doubt and uncertainty concerning the wisdom of selling your business.

The following are some typical reasons for selling, which are usually a mix of personal and business:

- You are tired of working so hard and are ready to retire.
- You have no children who are interested in taking over the business.
- You have children who want to take over the business, but they are incompetent or you cannot stand them.
- New competitors are moving into your business area, and you do not have the capital with which to fight them.
- You would like to have enough money in the bank so that you can support your lifestyle for the rest of your life.
- You need more capital resources than you can acquire to grow the business.
- Your business is going downhill, and you would prefer to sell it before it reaches the bottom.
- You were just divorced, and you retained the second-best lawyer in town. Unfortunately, your spouse retained the best lawyer in town, and you owe your spouse a huge amount of money.
- Your partner just died, and you do not have enough life insurance to buy out your partner's family as required by your shareholder agreement.
- You just died, and you did not maintain enough life insurance to pay death and inheritance taxes.

The above are only the major motivations, and many other reasons may exist. At the beginning of the decision to sell your business, you may have one set of motivations, and by the time the process is through you may have dropped those motivations or added new ones.

What is important, however, is that you fully understand your motivations to sell your business and let those motivations continually guide the logic of your sale.

ASSEMBLING YOUR PROFESSIONAL TEAM

Your first step should be to assemble an outstanding professional team to advise you.

Most businesspersons select their professional team on the eve of their sale. This is far too late in the sale process. By selecting your professional team several years before the target date for your sale, you can obtain their guidance in the presale years as to methods of minimizing the obstacles. Your professional team will help implement the advance planning recommendations contained in Chapters 2 through 6.

M & A Attorney

The first person on your team should be an attorney specializing in mergers and acquisitions, an M&A attorney. This person may not be your regular attorney, who may be inexperienced in this area. You must carefully interview your attorney to be certain of his or her expertise. You should question your attorney as to how many mergers and acquisitions he or she has handled in the last three years and what size businesses they were.

If a public company is a potential buyer, does your attorney have securities law experience? Has your attorney ever handled the sale to a public company, where stock was part of the purchase price consideration?

If you do not get favorable answers from your personal attorney, look elsewhere. Most large corporate law firms maintain groups of attorneys who specialize in M&A. Select someone who not only is well experienced in M&A but also has good business sense and a good rapport with you.

The requirement that your attorney should have good business sense cannot be overemphasized. You will need to make delicate tradeoffs during negotiations, which require business and legal judgment from your lawyer. You need a lawyer who thinks like a businessperson but also has the necessary legal skills to protect you. It is a mistake to hire a lawyer who is a good scrivener but cannot properly translate legal risks into business risks and assist you in evaluating their importance.

During the sale negotiation, it is not unusual to request your attorney to play "bad cop" while you play "good cop." The "good cop–bad cop" negotiation strategy helps insulate you from the angry emotions of the buyer. This is particularly helpful if you expect to work for the buyer but is also useful if you want to maintain a distance from the give-and-take of the bargaining. Be certain that your M&A attorney can play the "bad cop" role but also knows when to stop playing it.

Be wary of attorneys recommended to you by an investment banker or business broker involved in your sale. These attorneys may be experienced in M&A, but they also may feel beholden to the person who recommended them. Carefully interview such attorneys to determine if they are sufficiently independent that they could recommend to you (1) to terminate the investment banker or business broker or (2) not to proceed with an agreement of sale that is against your interest but would result in a fee to the recommending investment banker or business broker.

Tax Attorney

In addition to an M&A attorney, you will need a tax attorney. This is true even if you have a good tax accountant. Unless the tax consequences of your sale are simple (which you cannot know in advance of its structuring), you will want to double-check any tax advice you receive with a second tax professional. Tax attorneys and tax accountants sometimes approach tax issues differently, and you should receive the views of both.

If your business is a C corporation for federal income tax purposes, one of the first questions to ask your tax consultant is what the tax consequences would be of changing to an S corporation. There are serious tax disadvantages to selling a C corporation, which are discussed in Chapter 11.

It is worthwhile to weigh the cost of changing to an S corporation five years prior to your sale target date versus staying a C corporation for the same five years and suffering the adverse tax consequences when you sell. This, of course, does not apply if you have a C corporation that is qualified under Section 1202 of the Internal Revenue Code, which is discussed more fully in Chapter 11 under the heading "Fifty Percent Exclusion."

Accountant

It is generally not necessary to select a new accountant in order to sell your business. Most accountants can perform this task.

Some business owners use their accountant to negotiate the business terms of the sale. Caution should be exercised in doing this. Inquire how many sales transactions your accountant has previously negotiated as well as their size and complexity. Discreetly inquire from other clients of your accountant as to whether they were satisfied. You must be discreet, since you do not want to announce to the world your decision to sell your business.

Your accountant and your personal attorney may be losing a significant portion of their revenues if your business is sold. Be sensitive as to how important your fees are to them.

> **TRAP WARNING** Be careful in using any accountants or lawyers with an economic interest in killing your sale. Have a heart-to-heart talk with them before engaging them, and, in case of doubt, look elsewhere.

Investment Banker or Business Broker

As early as five years before your sale target date, you should consider obtaining advice from an investment banker or business broker. The advice should primarily cover the following areas:

- an estimated value of your business as it currently exists and the factors that affect that value (see Chapter 2)
- the likely buyers for a business such as yours

You should seek this advice even if you intend to sell the business yourself and do not expect to retain an investment banker or business broker.

The purpose of this advice is to help guide you in the growth and development of the business during the years prior to the sale target date. If negative factors about your business are identified by the investment banker or business broker, you should take steps to eliminate them to the extent possible.

For example, if you are advised that you have a weak management team, you should consider strengthening your management structure during the years prior to sale. Likewise, if you are advised that your overdependence on a single customer will materially reduce your ultimate sale price, you can make efforts to diversify your customer base in the years prior to sale.

The investment banker or business broker you select as an advisor need not necessarily be the same one you choose to sell your business (see Chapter 6). You should select your investment banker or business broker based upon their familiarity with your industry and the quality of their advice.

CHAPTER 2

Maximizing the Sale Price

The following are methods of valuing your business, along with techniques to maximize that value.

UNDERSTANDING THE METHOD OF VALUING YOUR BUSINESS

You can increase the value of your business if you understand how buyers are likely to value it. Likewise, by understanding the valuation method, you may be able to remove assets from your business prior to sale that do not affect the valuation, thereby effectively increasing the total sale consideration you ultimately receive.

An appraisal of your business, which specifies the primary valuation methods and factors, should be sought from a qualified appraiser well in advance of the expected sale date. Such an appraisal could cost as little as $5,000 to $10,000. Select the appraiser by reputation and personal recommendation.

In general, an appraiser from an investment banker or business broker with *actual* experience in selling businesses in your industry is the most valuable. What is important is not so much an appraisal of what your business is currently worth but rather an understanding of the primary methods of valuation and valuation factors. Someone who actually sells businesses in your industry is best qualified to provide this information.

If you cannot find anyone with such experience, look for appraisers who are members of recognized appraisal groups that require an examination. The prestigious American Society of Appraisers and the somewhat newer Institute of Business Appraisers (typically certified public accountants) are examples of such groups. The Institute of Business Appraisers does not require any specific valuation experience, in contrast to the more rigorous requirements for the American Society of Appraisers, which requires five years of experience for the designation accredited senior appraiser and two years for the accredited member designation.

These different professional requirements usually are reflected in the cost of the appraisal, with members of the American Society of Appraisers generally charging significantly higher fees.

Appraisal

Appraisal is an art—not a science.

Take all appraisals with a large grain of salt. The larger your business, the less likely that the appraisal will be accurate in assessing your business's total valuation. Businesses that are worth more than $5 million to $10 million tend to attract financial as well as strategic buyers. The presence of financial buyers tends to drive up the price.

No one can accurately predict what you are worth to a particular strategic buyer. The strategic buyer may find that the value of your business to them far exceeds the result of any standard valuation formula. Your customer list, sales force, and market identification may blend so well with the market direction of the strategic buyer that a high sale price can result.

The balance of this section presents some of the more common methods used to evaluate a business.

Businesses worth less than $1 million tend to be valued using the rule-of-thumb formulas and the asset accumulation methodology discussed below.

Buyers of businesses worth $5 million or more tend to use the EBITDA (Earnings Before Interest, Taxes, Depreciation, and Amortization) method combined with a comparable transaction analysis. If there are no significant earnings, a discounted cash flow methodology will be used. It is not unusual for the investment banker to also use a discounted cash flow analysis to double-check the valuations obtained using the EBITDA or comparable transaction method.

Caution should be exercised in using any formula to value your business. Every business is unique. The following formulas can give you a very misleading picture of your value because they are not tailored to your particular business. There is no substitute for an appraisal performed by a competent investment banker or business broker.

However, even the best appraisal cannot take into account the value of your business to a specific buyer. For example, a strategic buyer who can lay off all of your back office employees might be willing to pay an absurdly high price for your business because of the cost savings of the layoffs. Without knowing the pro forma effect of combining your business with the business of a specific buyer, any appraisal becomes little more than an educated guess.

Rule-of-Thumb Formulas

Potential buyers have a variety of rule-of-thumb methods for valuing businesses, depending on the nature of the business. For example, vending machine businesses are typically valued based on the number of locations. Cable TV businesses are typically valued based on the number of subscribers. The accounting income shown by these businesses is only of secondary importance to the buyer, since the buyer will change the business to conform to the buyer's model, thereby making your financial results irrelevant.

Rule-of-thumb valuation methods are more typically used for smaller businesses (usually valued at less than $5 million), particularly where there is a perception that the financial information is not completely reliable. However, rule-of-thumb formulas are occasionally used for larger businesses as well.

If you are in a business that uses these rules of thumb (e.g., vending machine locations or cable TV subscribers), consider increasing your locations or subscribers prior to sale. Thus, by understanding the valuation method for your business, you can increase the likely sale price.

Some valuation experts have criticized this method of increasing valuation because it ignores profitability. They argue that a cable TV system, which is valued at $2,000 per subscriber, can easily add new subscribers by cutting prices or giving away free services. Adding new subscribers at a loss per subscriber should not, they argue, increase the value of the cable TV system.

Some common sense must be used to increase the value of businesses that are valued on a rule-of-thumb basis. If our hypothetical cable TV system can cause new subscribers to sign up by cutting prices and still have the lowered "teaser prices" cover the additional costs of these new subscribers, adding new subscribers is a good strategy. However, if the cable TV company cannot charge prices to new subscribers that will cover the incremental costs of these new subscribers (except for a very short period of time), it is not a good idea to add subscribers by reducing overall profitability.

There are many rule-of-thumb formulas for valuing specific industries. The following are examples:

Insurance agencies	1 to 2 times annual gross commissions
Real estate agencies	.2 to .3 times annual gross commissions
Restaurants	.3 to .5 times annual gross sales
Travel agencies	.05 to .1 times annual gross sales

Buyers do not apply these rules of thumb universally, since they ignore the profitability of the specific business.

First find out the formula for valuing your business. Then attempt to maximize the elements of the formula for the year in which your business will be valued and, if possible, prior years. Typically, this is the year prior to sale.

EBITDA Method

There are a number of businesses that are valued by buyers based upon accounting earnings or income. Indeed, one of the most common methods of valuation is the so-called EBITDA method. This involves the determination of your accounting earnings before interest, taxes, depreciation and

Example	
Revenues	$10,000,000
Cost of sales	8,000,000
Gross profit	2,000,000
General and administrative costs	500,000
Depreciation	100,000
Amortization	50,000
Interest expense	250,000
Total expenses	900,000
Net income before taxes	1,100,000
Income taxes (40%)	440,000
Net income after taxes	$660,000
Calculation of EBITDA	
Net income after taxes	$660,000
Interest	250,000
Income taxes	440,000
Depreciation	100,000
Amortization	50,000
EBITDA	$1,500,000

amortization, and multiplication of the EBITDA by the relevant multiplier to obtain a business valuation.

The following is an example of the EBITDA method:

Your EBITDA is then adjusted to remove expenses and revenue that will no longer be carried forward into the new business. These adjustments can be quite substantial for a closely held family business.

Most closely held businesses are operated to minimize income taxes. As a result, excessive compensation and perquisites may be provided to the owner and his family in order to reduce taxes. The excessive compensation and perquisites are really forms of disguised dividends.

The true cost of replacing the owner and his family with a high-level executive usually results in a substantial addition to the EBITDA.

Some buyers will subtract from the adjusted EBITDA any required yearly capital expenditures.

Multipliers

The adjusted EBITDA is then multiplied by a multiplier to obtain an overall valuation for the business. The multiplier typically ranges from 4 to 6 times adjusted EBITDA, particularly for financial buyers. However, the multiplier has gone below 4 and substantially above 6, depending upon whether it is a buyer's market or a seller's market for the sale of businesses. A multiplier above 6 is more typical for strategic rather than financial buyers.

Appendix 1 contains an example of a multiplier of 9.8. Multipliers of 20 or more are not unheard of for strategic buyers of companies with strong market niches.

The multipliers are derived from comparable company valuations, including the multipliers applicable to public companies in the same industry. For example, if a public company in your industry has a total market valuation (based on its stock price) of 10 times its EBITDA, this multiplier could be the starting point in determining the appropriate multiplier.

This multiplier would then be discounted by the fact that your company was smaller and had less market dominance.

Many business owners incorrectly assume that the multipliers applicable to larger companies in the industry apply to their smaller company. The multipliers for less dominant companies in an industry are significantly smaller than for dominant companies.

A further discount to the multiplier may be applied to reflect the lack of liquidity of your stock in the hands of the buyer (that is, if there is no public market for your stock).

General

If your business has long-term debt, the overall valuation of your business will be reduced by the market value of this debt. The market value can be greater or less than the principal amount of the debt. For example, long-term debt that bears an interest rate below current interest rates for comparable maturities will have a market value less than its principal amount.

Businesses that are likely to be valued on the EBITDA basis should consider methods of increasing their accounting income during the one or two years prior to sale. This requires advance planning.

TRAP WARNING Many businesses have inventory cushions. This is an illegal method of minimizing taxes by underreporting your ending inventory. The result of underreporting your ending inventory is to increase your cost of sales, which in turn reduces your taxable income. Many businesses that have an inventory cushion find that whatever savings they had in taxes over the years by underreporting their taxable income are partially or completely offset by the fact they never get paid by the buyer for their inventory cushion. The seller merely gets paid for the inventory that was reported. It is not usually possible to eliminate an inventory cushion in one year. Several years are required for this purpose.

For each $1 that you increase your EBITDA during the valuation year, you should arguably receive an additional $4 to $6 in sale price.

Discounted Cash Flow Method

Under this method of valuation, you look at future cash flows projected from the operations and discount them in accordance with time and risk factors. The higher the risk, the higher the discount factor.

The discounted cash flow method begins with a projection of revenues and operating profit. These projected financial results are then adjusted for nonrecurring and nonoperating items of income and expense and are reduced by taxes. The projected operating profit estimates after taxes are then further adjusted by adding back depreciation and amortization and deducting net investments in working capital and capital expenditures.

At the end of a given period, typically five or ten years, a "terminal" or "residual" value is calculated for the business. This terminal or residual value is then combined with the discount cash flows to produce an overall valuation for the business.

The two most common methods of calculating residual value are the perpetuity method and the multiplier approach. The perpetuity method capitalizes the final year's projected cash flow by a discount rate as if it were an annuity. The multiplier approach applies a multiplier to the final year's cash flow. Because the residual value is typically a large figure, the underlying assumptions in the calculation must be carefully examined.

The net equity value of the business, including the residual value, is then determined by deducting the market value of interest-bearing debt and adding the market value of nonoperating assets that remain in the business. An example of this calculation is contained in the Discounted Cash Flow Valuation figure.

Discounted Cash Flow Valuation (In multiples of 1,000)						
	Year 1	Year 2	Year 3	Year 4	Year 5	Terminal Value
Revenues	$30,000	$45,000	$50,000	$55,000	$62,000	
EBIT	3,264	3,825	4,322	4,884	5,519	
Income taxes (cash basis)	1,110	1,301	1,469	1,661	1,876	
Net operating income	2,154	2,524	2,853	3,223	3,643	30,358
Cash flow adjustments						
Plus: Depreciation	1,392	1,800	2,034	2,298	2,597	
Less: Net change in working capital	(405)	(731)	(168)	(204)	(244)	
Capital expenditures	(1,966)	(3,675)	(4,161)	(4,398)	(4,697)	
Free cash flows	1,175	(82)	558	919	1,299	
Net present value at 12.0%	1,049	(65)	397	584	737	17,226
				Total corporate value		$19,928
				Less: Market value of debt		12,528
				Shareholder value		$ 7,400

Obviously, a cash flow ten years from today is not worth the same amount to the investor as a current cash flow. Thus, the formula tends to give little current value to cash flows that are too far in the future.

Discount Factor

The discount factor applicable to the cash flows is arrived at by using various formulas, one of which is the capital asset pricing model. The capital asset pricing model sets the discount rate at the weighted average cost of equity and debt capital.

The capital asset pricing model estimates the future cost of the corporation's equity through a multifactor equation and then determines the after-tax expected future costs of the corporation's debt. The final step is to compute the weighted average cost of capital, which is the weighted average cost of both equity and debt.

The weighted average cost of equity is computed by using the following equation: $re = rf + B(rm - rf)$, which can be defined as follows:

re = expected future cost of equity

rf = risk-free rate of return

B = the beta factor, which is a measurement of market risk, with the value 1 equaling a normative risk (One court has defined the beta factor as "the nondiversified risk associated with the economy as a whole as it affects this firm.")

rm = the market risk premium for this particular business

The rm factor, together with the beta factor in the equation have the effect of discounting the future cash flows by the risk of their nonoccurrence. The greater the risk of the projected cash flow not occurring, the higher the expected future cost of equity.

Your historical financial results are only relevant to this discounted cash flow method to the extent that they give credence to the projections of future cash flow. However, if your business is likely to be valued by this method, assets that do not contribute to your cash flow can be safely removed from the business without affecting its valuation.

Comparable Company Method of Valuation

The comparable company method of valuation typically involves comparing your company to the market capitalization and multiples of certain financial criteria (such as net income, projected net income, earnings before interest and taxes, earnings before depreciation, amortization, interest and taxes, revenues, and book value) of comparable public companies. Market capitalization refers to the public trading price of the stock multiplied by the number of outstanding shares. Thus, if a comparable public company had a public trading price of $20 per share and there were two million shares outstanding, the overall market capitalization of that comparable public company would be $40 million.

The market capitalization method of valuation contains a number of limitations. The trading price of shares of a public company does not normally reflect any control premium unless the company is expected to be sold shortly. Consequently, the public trading price may significantly understate the overall value of the comparable public company in a sale situation where a control premium is paid for the shares.

In addition, it is difficult to compare a publicly held company with a privately held company. Shares of public companies typically trade at a price that reflects the liquidity available to shareholders, which is not available to shareholders of a privately held company. As a result, privately held companies tend to sell at a discount compared to comparable publicly held companies.

Comparable Transaction Method of Valuation

Where information is available on the sale of comparable companies (whether public or private), this information is very valuable in assessing the value of your company. However, great care must be taken in using this information, since every company is unique, and there may be significant differences between your company and the so-called comparable company.

One of the major problems with this method is the lack of sufficient information to be able to judge how "comparable" another company is to yours. For example, your company may have one customer that accounts for 15 percent of your sales—a negative factor. You may not be able to determine if the so-called comparable company has this same negative factor. Therefore, information on the sale price of the comparable company may be difficult to assess and should be taken with a grain of salt.

Asset Accumulation Method

This method involves accumulating the going concern value of each of the specific assets of your business. This includes off-balance-sheet assets, such as customer lists, product market identification, value of your trained work-force, and so on, in addition to your balance-sheet assets. In computing going concern value, three standard appraisal methods are utilized:

- cost approach
- income approach
- market approach

The replacement cost of certain off-balance-sheet intangible assets may be utilized to value them on the theory that the buyer would have to pay replacement cost to duplicate these assets. For example, if the buyer were to start your business from scratch, the buyer would have to incur costs until a trained management team and workforce could be assembled. These costs could be considered to be the value of your management team and workforce. A similar value could be applied to value your other intangible assets.

The value of your balance-sheet and off-balance-sheet assets is then combined to calculate the total value of your entire business. The major advantage of this valuation method is that if you eliminate specific assets from the sale (for example, accounts receivable), you can easily adjust the total sale price. This valuation method is more typically used in valuing smaller businesses than midsized and larger businesses.

Asset liquidation value serves as a minimum valuation figure, regardless of whatever other valuation method may be used. Thus, if the rule-of-thumb formula for your business is 1 times annual sales, and your liquidation value is higher, you should receive the liquidation value.

Other Valuation Formulas

A myriad of other valuation formulas are used today.

If your business is asset intensive, some have suggested that your business value is equal to your hard assets plus goodwill. "Hard assets" refer to the total fair market value (which can be replacement cost) of your fixed assets and equipment, leasehold improvements, accounts receivable, and inventory. Your "goodwill" is your discretionary cash for one year, that is, the amount of cash you received as salary and dividends.

Another formula used for smaller businesses focuses on the seller's discretionary cash per year and multiplies this figure by 2.2727 to arrive at a sale price.

None of these formulas or the many others currently in use are universally applied. What is important is that you understand the particular valuation formula most likely to be applied to your business.

MINIMUM VALUE FORMULAS

The minimum value of your business is the higher of (1) its value to service acquisition debt or (2) its liquidation value.

Acquisition Debt Value (Leveraged Buyout Analysis)

If your business produces positive cash flow before interest, taxes, and depreciation amortization (EBITDA), that cash flow can service (that is, pay interest and principal) a certain amount of acquisition debt for the buyer. The amount of acquisition debt that can be so serviced is the minimum value for your business, particularly to a financial buyer.

For example, assume that the excess cash flow of your business (EBITDA) is $500,000 per year, and that, based upon current interest rates, that $500,000 is sufficient to pay the interest and principal due on $3 million of bank debt, which matures over a five-year loan term (exclusive of the balloon principal payment in the fifth year, which can be refinanced). The minimum value of your business would be $3 million, particularly to a financial buyer.

There is a limit to the amount of debt senior lenders will provide for a given business without an equity component. Therefore, once that debt limit is reached, your cash flow must be sufficiently high to be able to attract equity investors.

In this sense, you can determine the minimum value of your business using a leveraged buyout analysis (see Chapters 14 and 19).

Liquidation Value

Some businesses are worth only the liquidation value of their assets. Liquidation value refers to the price that would be received in an orderly liquidation, not in a fire sale. These businesses are typically not producing positive cash flow and do not have prospects of doing so.

SPECIFIC FACTORS THAT AFFECT VALUATION

Let us assume that your business has an identical EBITDA to one of your competitors, and in your industry, businesses generally sell for 5 times EBITDA. Should both businesses sell for the same price? Not necessarily.

EBITDA is merely the beginning of the valuation process. There can be specific favorable and unfavorable factors to your business that increase or decrease the multiplier of 5. The following are some examples:

Factors Increasing Valuation	Factors Decreasing Valuation
1. Strong customer relationships at all levels.	1. Weak customer relationships and frequent turnover.
2. Proprietary products or services.	2. Lack of proprietary products or services.
3. No single customer accounts for more than 5% of revenues or profits.	3. A single customer accounts for over 15% of revenues or profits.
4. Strong management team (important mainly to financial buyers).	4. A weak management team (so-called one-man-show syndrome).
5. Excellent employee turnover and relations.	5. Poor employee turnover and relations.
6. Consistent revenue and earnings trends.	6. Inconsistent revenue and earnings trends.
7. Plant and equipment in good repair.	7. Plant or equipment has been neglected and requires significant repairs.

These specific valuation factors will affect all of the valuation formulas, not just the EBITDA method.

You must analyze the strengths and weaknesses of your business and be prepared to point out the strengths and acknowledge the weaknesses, which the buyer will probably discover in its due diligence process.

RECENT SALES OF BUSINESSES

Appendix 1 contains examples of recent sales of businesses of all types and sizes with a sale price of between $10 million and $1 billion.

Appendix 2 contains examples of recent sales of businesses whose sale price ranges from $500,000 to $10 million. Appendix 3 contains examples of recent sales of businesses whose sale price ranges from $100,000 to $500,000. Appendices 2 and 3 use the abbreviation "SDCF" to refer to the seller's discretionary cash flow, which is the equivalent of EBITDA plus the owner's salary and non-business-related expense.

The information in Appendices 2 and 3 has been supplied by BIZCOMPS, which collects information from business brokers throughout the United States. BIZCOMPS also supplies similar information on businesses sold for less than $500,000. The address and phone number of BIZ-COMPS are Jack R. Sanders, P.O. Box 711777, San Diego, CA 92171; 619-457-0366.

Other computerized databases include the following:

- *Mergerstat Review,* an annual publication of merger and acquisition transactions published by Houlihan, Lokey, Howard & Zukin Investment Banking Firm
- Lotus One Source—U.S. M&A database (a CD-ROM-based computer database containing information from the IDD U.S. Mergers and Acquisitions and Compustat Research databases)
- Securities Data Company's Mergers & Corporate Transactions online computer database

INCREASE YOUR NET BOOK VALUE

Regardless of what valuation is placed on your business, some buyers will not, at closing of the sale, pay more cash for your business than its net book value. Any excess of the sale price over the net book value is deferred. Net book value refers to your total assets less your total liabilities as reflected on your financial statements. This is the same figure as your shareholder equity as reflected on your financial statements. The balance of the purchase price is then deferred.

The theory of some buyers is that your net book value or shareholder equity approximates the liquidation value of your business. The buyer does not want more than that amount invested in cash on the acquisition at closing.

The seller's counterstrategy should be twofold: (1) to use different accounting methods in preparing your balance sheet than you use in preparing your tax returns so as to maximize net book value and (2) to reflect undervalued assets on a pro forma statement of your adjusted net book value or shareholder equity.

Your accountant will typically choose accounting principles that minimize your taxable income for tax purposes. However, it is not necessary to use these same principles for financial reporting purposes.

For example, you may use accelerated depreciation of your equipment for tax purposes to reduce your taxes. However, you should use straight-line depreciation of equipment in preparing the financial statements given to the buyer, with a footnote disclosing the different depreciation method for tax purposes.

The effect of using straight-line depreciation will typically significantly increase your net book value, since your equipment can be reflected at a high book value. Other accounting changes can be suggested by your accountant to increase your net book value.

It is preferable not to adopt new accounting methods on the eve of a sale. Therefore, good advanced planning should include adopting such accounting methods many years before sale.

After you have exhausted using favorable accounting methods to increase your net book value, you should supplement your financial statements with a description of written-off or undervalued assets and add the value of these assets to your net book value or shareholder equity on a pro forma basis. These off-balance-sheet assets can add significantly to your value.

For example, you may in the past have purchased $1 million worth of machinery that has been fully written off through depreciation charges. The machinery may still be worth $500,000, but it does not appear anywhere in your financial statements. Add this $500,000 to your net book value as shown on your financial statements in a column called "Pro Forma Adjusted Net Book Value" or (alternatively) "Pro Forma Adjusted Shareholder Equity." You may have purchased land years ago for $100,000 that is now worth $500,000. The $400,000 appreciation should be added to your pro forma net book value or shareholder equity.

Many businesses expense small tools, that is, they run the cost of tools through the income statement and do not capitalize them as an asset. Under some accounting conventions, a small tool could be one costing less than $500. Determine the market value of these small tools and increase your pro forma net book value or shareholder equity by this figure.

Comb through your business assets to be certain that you have reflected them all at their market value.

REMOVING UNPRODUCTIVE ASSETS FROM YOUR BUSINESS

Once you understand the method most likely to be used to value your business, consider removing assets from the business prior to sale that do not affect its value. Each dollar of asset value that you can remove from the business prior to sale without affecting the buyer's valuation is an additional dollar in your pocket. This is an excellent way of increasing your overall sale consideration.

For example, if you owe your business money, your debt is an asset of the business. However, if the buyers use the EBITDA or discounted cash flow valuation method and do not include interest income on the debt in computing your valuation, they have assigned a zero value to your debt. Accordingly, you should be able to remove your debt from the company (or forgive it) prior to the sale without affecting the buyer's valuation. The same may be true of life insurance on your life and your automobile, which is not necessary to operate the business.

However, rather than waiting until you are negotiating with the buyer to remove these assets, it is wiser to remove them at an earlier time so it never becomes a point of negotiation with the buyer.

MAKE YOUR FINANCING ASSUMABLE

If you receive bank or other financing for your business, you can make your business more valuable to a buyer by inducing the lender to agree in advance that the financing will be assumable if your business is sold. This is particularly valuable if you have long-term indebtedness at favorable interest rates and terms and is less valuable if your indebtedness is all short term. The buyer's ability to assume long-term financing will increase the value of your business to the buyer.

Most lenders will resist assumability clauses in the financing documents unless they are properly hedged. For example, the bank may require the potential buyer to have a minimum net worth or satisfy other financial tests set forth in the financing agreement in order to agree to permit the automatic assumption of the debt by a potential buyer and may require you to remain liable on the debt.

BIGGER IS GENERALLY BETTER

Larger businesses tend to sell for higher multipliers of EBITDA (for EBITDA valuations) and lower discount rates (for discounted cash flow valuations). You cannot analogize a business worth less than $5 million with a business in the same industry worth more than $50 million. The business worth over $50 million always sells for a higher multiplier and lower discount rate. Likewise, you cannot analogize a business worth $50 million with one worth $500 million in the same industry.

This is understandable, since buyers prefer larger sized businesses, which are more dominant in their field, and financial buyers are typically not interested in businesses worth less than $5 million.

What this suggests is that a good way for you to build your valuation prior to your target date is to yourself engage in strategic mergers. By "building up" your business during the presale years through mergers and other acquisitions, you will be a much more attractive target when it comes time to sell.

CHAPTER 3

Eliminating Deal Killers and Impediments

Once you have made a decision to sell, you should immediately examine your business, with the help of your M&A attorney, to determine whether you have deal killers or other impediments to a sale. These deal killers or other impediments may require many years to resolve successfully. Hence, it is important that you start many years before your sale target date.

DEAL KILLERS

The following are typical examples of deal killers if the resulting contingent liability is large in relation to the value of your business:

- environmental liabilities
- litigation liabilities
- tax liabilities resulting from misclassification of employees as independent contractors
- unfunded pension obligations and multiemployer pension plan liabilities
- product warranty obligations of unreasonable scope or length

No buyer is going to assume these liabilities willingly if they are of a material indeterminable amount. Even if you do not require the buyer to assume these liabilities, they may still prevent the sale of your business.

For example, if the property on which your plant is located is environmentally contaminated, the purchase by the buyer of the property subjects the buyer to environmental liability as the owner. This is true even though the buyer did not cause the pollution.

If your business has large, unresolved litigation liabilities, the buyer may be concerned about purchasing your assets because, at least under some state laws, liabilities can be imposed upon the buyer even though the buyer never agrees to assume them. This is particularly true if the buyer continues the same business under the same name and products of the business caused personal injury.

Many businesses misclassify employees as independent contractors. The resulting liability for payroll taxes, interest, and penalties can, if this practice is carried on long enough, create a very large contingent liability.

The existence of large, unresolved contingent liabilities that could potentially exceed your assets may indicate that your business is insolvent. If so, a sale of assets to the buyer at less than its fair market value could be legally challenged by creditors in the future.

It is, of course, possible to wait to resolve these deal killers until a buyer is found. However, by the time you clean up your environmental contamination, or even get a firm estimate on the cost, the buyer may have disappeared. Therefore, it is wiser to handle these issues prior to the potential sale of your business.

If you cannot get rid of the deal killers prior to the sale of the business, it may be possible to set up escrow arrangements for the protection of the buyer and nevertheless proceed with the sale. These escrow arrangements would typically require objective proof of the largest amount of the contingent liabilities, and the buyer would undoubtedly require that same amount of the sale proceeds to be escrowed.

If you handle your deal killers prior to the sale, it is likely that much less money will need to be spent to resolve these contingencies than the buyer would require in an escrow. By waiting until the point of sale to handle these problems, you will create a high escrow to give the buyer a significant margin for error in its estimate of the cost of cleaning up your problems. Therefore, it behooves you to clean up these problems prior to sale.

There are some deal killers that cannot be escrowed away. These must be resolved well before you proceed with the sale of your business.

OBTAIN AUDITED OR AUDITABLE FINANCIAL STATEMENTS

It is advisable to obtain an audited financial statement for at least the year in which your company will be valued. This is typically your last full fiscal year.

It is also advisable to obtain an audit for the two prior years as well. This is especially true if your business will likely be valued on an EBITDA basis, if your business trends are important to the buyer, or if you may sell to a public company.

An audited financial statement provides the buyer with a greater assurance of your financial results. This is particularly true if your auditor is a larger international auditing firm. However, even if your auditor is a one-person office, that audit report is better than giving the buyer an unreviewed financial statement or a so-called compilation report.

Using a prestigious auditing firm tends to reduce the buyer's due diligence. It also creates a certain aura about your company that is conducive to a sale.

Large buyers are particularly enthralled by a prestigious auditing firm, since their own audits are usually performed by these firms. They incorrectly view the auditing firm as having some liability to them if the financial statements are wrong. In most states, your auditor has no such liability unless he or she was negligent and actually knew that you intended to furnish the financial statements to the buyer. However, you need not mention that fact to your buyer.

If you normally use a good regional accounting firm, there is probably no necessity to change auditors on the eve of sale.

Your decision to save money on an audit may reduce the number of potential buyers for your company, particularly public company buyers.

Even if you do not obtain an audited financial statement, you should at least obtain an auditable financial statement for the three years prior to sale. An auditable financial statement permits you to complete the audit retroactively at the time of sale.

Public Company Buyers

Public company buyers will generally require audited financial statements from your company if the acquisition is significant (over 10 percent) to them in terms of assets or income or if their investment and advances to your company exceed 10 percent of their total consolidated assets. Your audited financial statements are also required for poolings (see Chapter 12) when the public company issues more than 10 percent of its stock to you.

If any of these tests yield a result greater than 10 percent but less than 20 percent, one year of your audited financial statements is required by the SEC (Securities and Exchange Commission). If the impact is over 20 percent but less than 40 percent, two years of audited financial statements are required. If the impact on assets or income is over 40 percent, three years of audited financial statements are required. These requirements are softened for buyers that are small-business issuers. In addition, the SEC is currently considering some relaxation of these rules for all buyers.

Since the public company buyer must abide by these SEC rules, your failure to obtain an audited financial statement can be a deal killer.

It is not a good idea to go to your brother-in-law's auditing firm. The SEC requires that your auditing firm be independent as defined in their rules.

MAKE YOUR ASSETS TRANSFERABLE

Some of your most valuable assets may be nontransferable without the consent of a third party. For example, most leases are not transferable without consent of the landlord. Neither are most licenses, such as those for patents, trademarks, and other intellectual property.

Good advance planning would suggest that you attempt to make these leases and licenses assignable to a buyer of your business well in advance of the actual sale. If you wait until the agreement to sell your business is signed, the lessor or licensor may well demand additional consideration from you since they are aware that you need their consent to consummate the sale.

However, if you obtain such consents in the normal course of negotiating or administering the license or lease, the landlord or licensor will be less likely to try to negotiate additional consideration, since you are not "under the gun."

Some sellers seek to avoid these consents by selling the stock of their business or by using direct or triangular mergers. This works only if the lease or license does not contain a "change-of-control" clause and if the buyer is willing to engage in a stock purchase or reverse merger (see Chapter 10). A change-of-control clause in a lease or license is a clause that treats a change in control of your company as a direct assignment of the lease or license.

Most lessors and licensors will resist any blanket permission to transfer your lease or license unless you remain liable for the performance by the transferee. Even then they may not agree in advance to the transferability of the lease or license. This is particularly true if the lease or license has nonmonetary obligations on your part that will not necessarily be performed satisfactorily by an unknown transferee (for example, a clause in a license requiring the licensee to promote sales of the licensed product).

At a minimum, you should attempt to have the lessor or licensee agree not to withhold their consent to a transfer unreasonably.

SIMPLIFY CORPORATE STRUCTURE

Some businesses are organized with an unusually complex corporate structure. The complexities of the corporate structure can delay and sometimes impede the sale of the business. It is best to have an M&A attorney review your corporate structure to determine if there are methods of simplifying it to facilitate a potential sale.

AVOID BURDENSOME LONG-TERM COMMITMENTS

If you expect to sell your business within a year or two, you should carefully consider the effects on the sale of entering into long-term contracts that will have to be assumed by the buyer. For example, a five-year contract tying you to a particular supplier may make your business less valuable to a potential buyer. Likewise, committing your company to purchase very expensive equipment shortly before the sale could also reduce the value of your business to a potential buyer and impede the sale.

ELIMINATE IMPEDIMENTS TO POOLING ACCOUNTING

If you sell your business to a publicly held company for a significant premium over your book value, the publicly held company may well want to use pooling accounting to reflect the acquisition. Pooling accounting requires you to accept stock of the publicly held company as the sole consideration for all or substantially all of your stock or assets.

If the publicly held company cannot use pooling accounting, they may lose interest in your company or significantly lower the purchase price. This is because the public company's acquisition of your business in a nonpooling (so-called purchase accounting) transaction may result in a large amount of goodwill on their balance sheet and higher depreciation and amortization charges, all of which will depress their future earnings. In addition, the public company may wish to reflect your preclosing income in their income statement, and this can be accomplished only if pooling accounting is available.

Pooling accounting is not available to the public company buyer if, for example, you have done any of the following within two years prior to initiation of the plan of combination:

- paid extraordinary dividends
- purchased stock back for your company's treasury (with certain exceptions)
- recapitalized your company to create a new class of stock

This list is not exhaustive, and you should carefully read Chapter 12, which discusses pooling accounting in more depth.

You cannot determine whether a public company will or will not be the ultimate buyer for your business. Nor is it possible for you to predict with certainty that you would not be willing to accept stock in that public company as the purchase price.

Many potential buyers for your business may not be currently publicly held but may be considering a public offering in the near future. These potential buyers may also want to acquire your company in a pooling transaction in order to avoid depressing their future earnings to be reflected in a public offering prospectus. For each $1 that the buyer's earnings are reduced by virtue of a nonpooling acquisition, the overall valuation of the buyer's business in a future public offering could be reduced 15 to 30 times that amount.

Therefore, you should take care not to engage in transactions that create an impediment for a pooling transaction within two years prior to your sale target date.

CHAPTER 4

Protecting Your Business

You must give careful advance thinking to how you will protect your business and your proprietary information during the sale process. You must begin thinking well before your target sale date.

MAINTAINING CONFIDENTIALITY OF YOUR DECISION TO SELL

The process of selling your company can last from several months to several years. It is important that you maintain confidentiality of your decision to sell throughout the process.

The sale of your company may have adverse effects on your key employees, customers, and suppliers. Competitors may use your decision to sell as a tool to obtain your customers. It is best that your decision to sell not be publicly disseminated until absolutely necessary.

There are at least three methods to maintain the confidentiality of your decision to sell:

- Limit the information to trusted advisors, such as attorneys, accountants, investment bankers, or business brokers.

- Require your professional advisors to approach only potential buyers who are approachable on a "no-name basis" and who will likely maintain the confidentiality of your sale's decision once your name is revealed.
- Require potential buyers to sign confidentiality agreements.

It is important that your professional advisors institute their own internal procedures to protect the confidentiality of the sale process. For example, you may receive a bill from an attorney that specifies exactly what legal services the attorney performed for you and contains the following notation: "Advice concerning sale of your business." Once that bill is submitted to your bookkeeping department for payment, you have effectively blown your confidentiality, since your accounts payable clerk now knows your secret.

Early in the process your professional team should use a code name for the project that will not cause suspicion. The use of terms such as *consultation concerning project X* merely invites suspicion. It is better to use a code name that does not invite suspicion, such as *business planning* or a similar nondescriptive name.

Secretaries of your professional advisors must be brought in on the secret, since they may be talking to secretaries at your place of business. Require your professional advisors to sensitize their own secretaries to avoid having them inadvertently disclose your sale intentions.

At some point in the sale process, you will no longer be able to maintain the confidentiality of your decision to sell. The ideal is to maintain such confidentiality until the closing of your agreement. However, that is not always possible. Leaks may occur, and rumors may be started.

Long before it is no longer possible to maintain complete confidentiality, you must plan how and to whom the disclosures will be made. It is important that you control the process.

For example, key employees will have to be informed of the secret at an early stage, since serious buyers will want to talk with them. How to give incentives to key employees is discussed later in this chapter.

In addition, you may wish to personally visit a few key customers before making any general announcement. You must carefully think through when and how you will approach such customers.

PROTECTING YOUR PROPRIETARY INFORMATION

Maintaining your decision to sell as confidential is not sufficient. You must also make advance plans as to how you will protect the confidentiality of proprietary information of your business from potential buyers who are performing due diligence. Your proprietary information includes customer lists, trade secrets, methods of marketing, and so on.

There are three methods of maintaining the confidentiality of proprietary information:

- Give potential buyers only enough information to permit them to make a purchase decision, but no more.
- Require potential buyers to sign confidentiality agreements.
- Require buyers to agree to refrain from hiring your key employees.

Several methods can be used to limit the information available to what potential buyers absolutely need. For example, if names and addresses of your customers are sensitive information, the potential buyer may initially be satisfied with obtaining the list of the top twenty-five customers without receiving their actual names and addresses. Rather, the list could identify each customer with a code name (e.g., customer A), indicate the state in which the customer was located, and specify the amount of revenues attributable to that customer during the last fiscal year. Your customers' zip codes could also be revealed without stating their actual name or address.

Obviously, at the time of signing the agreement of sale, and certainly no later than closing, the buyer will want the actual names and addresses of the customers.

There are unscrupulous potential buyers who use the due diligence process to gain valuable information concerning your business. These buyers do not really intend to purchase your business and are using the due diligence process as a vehicle to obtain a competitive advantage. Sometimes you can identify such unscrupulous potential buyers by carefully checking them out.

It is important that you require each potential buyer to sign a confidentiality agreement, which creates a monetary deterrent for using your proprietary information (e.g., liquidated damages) as well as entitles you to injunctive relief and which includes a clause restricting the hiring of employees. See Appendix 4 for an example of a confidentiality agreement.

TRAP WARNING It is crucial to restrict potential buyers from hiring past, present, and future employees of your business for some period of time—at least one year. Hiring your employees is a simple way of gathering sensitive information about your business. Indeed, as key employees are interviewed by potential buyers during the due diligence process, they may be overtly or subtly solicited for employment with the potential buyer. From the potential buyer's point of view, it is much cheaper to hire an employee to capture a portion of your business than to pay you for the business. Be certain that the potential buyer agrees not to hire employees even if they are solicited by the employee.

SPECIAL PROBLEMS OF SELLING TO CUSTOMERS, COMPETITORS, AND SUPPLIERS

Selling to a customer, competitor, or supplier creates unusual confidentiality problems.

For example, unless you have a proprietary product, you would not want a customer to know your profit margins. They can use this information to reduce the price they pay to you in the future. Therefore, unless you have a method of disguising this information, or a proprietary product, you should refuse to discuss this information prior to closing with a customer.

A competitor would love to know your customer list and the prices they pay, among other things. You should refuse to supply this information prior to closing, whether or not the competitor signs a confidentiality agreement. If you provide such information and the competitor uses it unfairly, you will probably never be able to prove that the competitor ever breached the confidentiality agreement.

Suppliers can also be troublesome buyers, although not as troublesome as customers or competitors. However, you generally would not want a supplier to know your customer list, your resale markup on your purchases from the supplier, or what you pay to competing suppliers, unless the supplier could not possibly harm you with that information.

Occasionally, the problem of selling to customers, competitors, or suppliers is handled by giving the information to an investment banker for the buyer, with the written agreement that it will not be disclosed to the customer, competitor, or supplier until after the closing. However, this can still be a dangerous solution because of your inability to *prove* that the investment banker intentionally or inadvertently leaked the information.

INCENTIVES FOR KEY EMPLOYEES

Potential buyers will want to speak to your key employees prior to signing the agreement of sale as part of their due diligence. Therefore, your decision to sell the company will be brought to the attention of this group of persons at some point in the process.

It is important that these key employees be incentivized to help promote the sale. If they are not incentivized, their natural tendency will be to become concerned about their job security and their future with your company. Moreover, these key employees will begin to think about the full implication of your decision to sell and the effect it will have upon their lives and their futures. This may cause them to think about other possible alternatives for their careers.

Whatever bond you may have created with your key employees through the chemistry of your leadership may also change once you have announced your decision to sell.

The incentivization of your key employees must be both affirmative and negative:

- affirmative, to align the employees' interest with yours in the implementation of the sale
- negative, to disincentivize the employees from leaving or becoming potential competitors

The affirmative incentives usually consist of some form of termination bonus equal to a meaningful percentage of the employee's base salary. Typically, anywhere from 50 percent to 100 percent of the base salary should be paid.

The bonus should be payable only in the event of sale.

This affirmative cash incentive can be created immediately, before the potential buyer commences his due diligence with these key employees.

Other types of affirmative incentives must be implemented earlier. One example would be a stock option granted at an early point in time that could be exercised only in the event the company is sold or goes public.

The advantage of a stock option granted several years before the potential sale occurs is that there is no charge against the income of the business for the grant of the option or its exercise, provided that on the grant date the option price is at least equal to the fair market value of the stock at that time.

The disadvantage of a cash termination bonus equal to a percentage of base salary is that in the year of sale your earnings are reduced by the amount of the bonus. This reduction may or may not be important to the buyer.

In contrast, the exercise of the stock option that had been originally granted years previously does not reduce your year-of-sale earnings. This is true even though the employee could exercise the stock option at a price significantly below the current market value of your stock.

A cash termination bonus is simpler to implement than a stock option plan and should be used in situations where the reduction in the year-of-sale earnings is not material or is unimportant to this buyer.

Negative incentives could take the form of an agreement not to compete or engage in other hostile acts in relationship to your company. It may not be possible to obtain this type of agreement on the eve of the sale of your company, since it requires a voluntary act by the employee to execute such a noncompetition agreement and some special consideration under state law to make it enforceable.

Therefore, it is necessary to obtain a noncompetition agreement from a key employee several years before your sale decision and preferably when the employee is hired. To make such a noncompetition agreement enforceable, you should seek counsel from attorneys specializing in this area. Many state laws require some form of special consideration to be given to the employee for this purpose if the agreement is signed during the course of employment. For example, in some states you might be able to implement this type of agreement at the same time you are implementing your normal increases or bonuses.

The length of time of the noncompetition agreement should be kept sufficiently short so that there is no difficulty in having a court enforce it. Typically one year is sufficient to protect a buyer and will usually be enforceable if the scope of the limitation is reasonable under the circumstances.

Another alternative is to work out a severance plan for employees that requires them not to compete with the company during the period of the severance payments. Severance payments to less important employees can be limited to one or two weeks, whereas the payments to key employees can last as long as one year.

CHAPTER 5

Personal Considerations

Personal tax considerations should be foremost in planning the sale of your business. Advance planning pays off handsomely in minimizing the following taxes.

MINIMIZING ESTATE AND DEATH TAXES

Long before the target date for the sale of your business, you should consider methods of minimizing estate and death taxes on the transfer of sale proceeds to the next generation.

These taxes can be higher than your income tax. The combined federal and state income tax rate can be as high as 43 percent; in contrast, estate and death taxes can be as high as 60 percent.

The time to do estate planning to minimize these taxes is in the years prior to the sale of your business. It is preferable to make gifts of rapidly appreciating property, such as the stock of the corporation that owns your business. The gift has the effect of preventing the appreciation of stock from being taxed in your estate at death. One common method of minimizing these taxes is by making annual lifetime gifts to your children and grandchildren to take advantage of the annual exclusion. The annual exclusion permits gifts having a value of $10,000 per donee each year ($20,000 if you have a spouse and so elect) without using your lifetime exemption.

You can make gifts above the annual exclusion amount ($10,000 to $20,000 per donee each year) without paying any gift taxes during your lifetime. This can be accomplished by using your lifetime exemption, which at present permits $600,000 of taxable gifts ($1.2 million for married couples) to be made without paying any gift tax.

To the extent that you make gifts above the annual exclusion plus the lifetime exemption, you will pay a gift tax. However, the elimination from your taxable estate of the future appreciation of the stock that you give away (plus the amount of the gift tax you pay) may result in sufficient estate and death tax savings to be justified.

Before making gifts for which you must pay a gift tax, you should carefully weigh future estate and death tax savings against the following disadvantages: (1) you lose the use of the amount of gift tax you must pay (including interest), and (2) if the stock you gifted would otherwise have been retained by you until your death, there are higher capital gains taxes, which must be paid by your children and grandchildren on their sale of the stock. If you would have otherwise kept the stock until your death, your children and grandchildren would, for federal income tax purposes, have received a step up in their tax bases to an amount equal to the fair market value of the stock on the date of death (or alternate valuation date) and therefore would not pay any long-term capital gain tax except on postdeath appreciation.

Discounts

The value of your stock gift may be significantly discounted by the "minority interest discount" and a "lack of marketability discount" if the stock is of a closely held corporation. The minority interest discount reflects the fact that the minority shares of a closely held business do not have the ability to control the business.

While the discount depends on the facts and circumstances of each situation, the combination of the minority interest discount plus the lack of marketability discount can result in total discounts of up to 50 percent of the fair market value of the stock on the date of the gift. It is important, however, that the gift not be on the eve of the sale of the company. Rather, the gift should be made over several years prior to the sale.

Gifts of stock of the corporation owning your business should be made sufficiently before the sale so that you can obtain the benefit of a very low valuation for the gifts. This permits you to transfer a greater percentage of your wealth to the next generation while minimizing the estate and death taxes.

For example, if you sell the stock of the corporation that owns your business for $1 million and you give away 10 percent of the stock on the eve of the sale, it is likely that the value of the gifted stock will be $100,000. However, if three years before the sale you funded a trust for your children with 10 percent of the stock, it is likely that you will be able to sustain a substantially lower valuation for the same stock gift. Thus, by making gifts at an earlier point in time, you can increase the percentage of your wealth that can be transferred to the next generation without tax.

If you make gifts of stock, you should contractually retain the right to force the donees to sell the stock if you decide to sell your shares. These contract rights are sometimes referred to as "drag-along" clauses.

Family Partnerships

The selling shareholder should also consider forming family limited partnerships to reduce estate and death taxes. A limited partnership could be formed in which you would be the general partner and your family would be the limited partners. Stock of your corporation would be given to the limited partnership as a gift.

As general partner, you would continue to control the stock owned by the limited partnership and would have full voting rights and the ability to sell the stock. Your family would hold limited partnership units. It is arguable that the limited partnership units might permit a further discount on the value of the gifted stock over and above the minority interest discount and the lack of marketability discount.

Family limited partnerships do not work with Subchapter S corporations. Instead, you can divide the stock of your Subchapter S corporation into voting and nonvoting stock and give the nonvoting stock to your family.

Recently, limited liability companies (particularly ones formed in Nevada, a low tax state) have been utilized instead of limited partnerships. In contrast to a limited partnership, a limited liability company affords greater protection for family members against personal liability for debts of the limited liability company and does not require a general partner who is personally liable for such debts.

Charitable Foundations and Charitable Remainder Trusts

If you are charitably inclined, you should consider establishing a charitable foundation or charitable remainder trust and funding it with a portion of the stock of your corporation. The advantage to you is that when the stock is sold, the charitable foundation or charitable remainder trust does not pay any federal or state income tax on the gain resulting from the sale.

In addition, your gift of stock to the charitable foundation or charitable remainder trust produces a federal income tax deduction on your personal tax return. To the extent that you cannot absorb the tax deduction in a single year, your charitable deduction can be carried forward for the next five years.

The charitable foundation permits you to control future charitable gifts by using the gross sale proceeds without diminishment by income taxes. You and/or members of your family can be the trustees of the foundation. However, no portion of the funds can benefit you or your family—except indirectly by relieving you of your future personal charitable obligations.

The charitable remainder trust permits you and your family to receive an annuity for a term of years or for their lives from the trust. At the end of the term of years or upon the death of the noncharitable beneficiaries, the remainder is paid to a charity or charities designated in the trust instrument or chosen by the trustees (which could include you and/or members of your family). Since the charitable remainder trust does not pay federal income taxes on the sale proceeds, the income produced by the gross sale proceeds is approximately 30 percent higher than the income you would have received had you personally sold the stock to the buyer and paid a 30 percent tax on the gain (28 percent long-term capital gain plus an assumed rate of 2 percent state income taxes).

The major disadvantage of both the charitable foundation and the charitable remainder trust is that you lose the ability to receive any portion of the sale proceeds from the stock that you have given away (except that you can receive an annuity from a charitable remainder trust), and hence you have lost ownership of a portion of your wealth. In addition, your income tax deduction for the gift to the charitable foundation or charitable remainder trust will be equal to the fair market value of your stock only if distributions are made from the charitable foundation directly to public charities within fourteen months after the stock is given to the charitable foundation, or if the charitable remainder trust may make distributions only to public charities.

General

It is not recommended that you give away so much of your wealth that you have to depend on your children for your future. Saving estate and death taxes is not a sufficient reason for jeopardizing your lifestyle.

It is best to make gifts of assets that are passive assets, i.e., assets that are not critical to your business. For example, if you lease business real estate from yourself or from a separate partnership that you control, give away a minority interest in that real estate or partnership.

Another ideal asset to give away is life insurance on your life that has cash value.

Any wealth transfer of an appreciating asset (such as stock of your corporation) should be accomplished sufficiently prior to the actual sale date so that a low valuation for the gift can be obtained, thereby permitting you to maximize the amount of the wealth transferred.

An excellent time to make gifts of stock is right after a leveraged recapitalization (see Chapter 19). If you engage in a leveraged recapitalization, your business will have taken on a substantial amount of senior debt, and you will have withdrawn a substantial amount of equity, thereby depressing the value of your stock.

MINIMIZING STATE INCOME TAXES

A number of states, including California and New York, have very high personal, state, and local income taxes.

The sale of your business will generate income to you that will be taxed at the state and local level.

Currently state and local income taxes are deductible for the purpose of computing your federal income tax. However, even after the benefit of the federal income tax deduction, state and local income taxes can still be a significant amount.

For example, if you are a resident of New York City and are in the 39.6 percent federal income tax bracket, and you sell your business for a gain of $10 million, the combined state and city taxes you pay can exceed $4.6 million (even after considering the benefit of your federal income tax deduction for the state and city taxes). If you are a New York City resident, New York state and city income taxes on the gain can exceed 12 percent of the gain.

One method of avoiding these taxes is to consider changing your state of residence prior to the sale. For example, both Florida and Nevada have no state personal income tax. If the businessperson in the previous example were to have moved to Florida prior to the sale, she or he could probably save enough taxes, by virtue of the shift of residence, to purchase a significant-size house or condominium in Florida.

You do not necessarily have to change your place of employment in order to change your residence. You should change your voter registration address, your driver's license, and your bank accounts to Florida. You can still work and have your business in New York. You should take care to examine the state laws at the time you make your decision, since some states, such as New York, California, and Ohio, are tightening up on this method of avoiding state income tax.

This procedure is not for everyone. It does not make sense to change your residence to Florida or Nevada unless you would actually enjoy living in Florida or Nevada. The residency change should fit in with your lifestyle and not be driven solely by tax motivations.

In addition, certain states are beginning to crack down on changes of residency to avoid state income taxes. Check with your tax attorney before you attempt this maneuver.

CHAPTER 6

Marketing Your Business

The effective marketing of your business requires you to understand the thinking of potential buyers and characteristics they would find appealing. You must learn to think like a buyer. Many business owners are abysmally ignorant of their competitive position in their own industry. Yet this is very important to buyers and a key to effectively marketing them.

During the years prior to your sale target date, you must learn as much as possible about the competitors in your industry—both their strengths and their weaknesses. Potential buyers would expect you to understand your strengths and weaknesses vis-à-vis your competition. Therefore, it is essential that you become more knowledgeable about your competition.

You must also become an expert about your markets and customers. Do you have a special niche in the marketplace? Is your market growing, flat, or declining? If the latter two, what are you doing in order to diversify your markets?

A useful step is to try to prepare a marketing brochure five years prior to your sale target date. See where the weaknesses are in the description of your business.

During the years prior to the sale target date, grow your business in a manner to eliminate these weaknesses and improve your strengths. The maximization of the ultimate sale price depends upon how successful you are.

SHOULD YOU USE AN INVESTMENT BANKER OR BUSINESS BROKER?

It is possible to sell your business yourself. A few business owners do so successfully, particularly those whose businesses have values of less than $1 million. It is also possible to sell your home yourself; some homeowners do so successfully.

However, business owners who do not have significant experience in selling a business should consider hiring a reputable investment banker or business broker. This is particularly true of businesses having a value of more than $1 million.

A business broker is used for smaller businesses, usually those below $10 million in total value. Some business brokers specialize in selling businesses worth less than $1 million. An investment banker is used for larger businesses, with the minimum size depending upon the size and prestige of the investment banking firm.

The larger New York Stock Exchange firms (Goldman Sachs, Merrill Lynch, etc.) will typically not handle transactions below $50 million to $100 million. Local and regional investment banking firms will usually handle transactions in which the consideration is at least $5 million to $10 million or more. Transactions between $1 million and $10 million are usually handled by either larger business brokers or smaller investment banking firms.

The advantages of using an investment banker or business broker are as follows:

- An investment banker or business broker experienced in your industry has a greater knowledge of potential buyers for your business than you do.

- Even if you know one obvious buyer for your business, an investment banker or business broker may be able to find one or more other prospects, thereby permitting an auction to occur, which tends to maximize the sale price (see Chapter 8).
- The investment banker or business broker can help screen your potential buyers and prevent you from wasting your time on financially unqualified buyers.
- An investment banker or business broker can assist you in maintaining the confidentiality of your decision to sell by soliciting buyers anonymously.
- An experienced investment banker or business broker can devote a significant amount of time and attention to selling your business and has better methods of contacting potential buyers than you do.
- An experienced investment banker or business broker can assist in negotiating the sale, smoothing rough spots, and protecting you from unrealistic demands.

Some business owners foolishly refuse to obtain an investment banker or business broker because they know at least one potential buyer for their business and do not want to pay a commission on the sale to this buyer. It is far wiser merely either to exclude this one potential buyer from the commission arrangement or to provide for a lower fee and to use the investment banker or business broker to seek out other purchasers.

The disadvantage of using an investment banker or business broker is that you have to pay a fee based upon a percentage of the sale consideration. In the case of business brokers, for businesses worth less than $500,000, the fee can be 10 percent or even more. The high commission percentage is the result of the relatively low valuation for the business and the fact that the business broker has certain fixed costs of marketing the business. For businesses worth less than $500,000, for which you are unable to negotiate a fee lower than 10 percent, you might consider using a business broker only as your last resort.

For larger businesses, the fee is usually based on the so-called Lehman Formula: i.e., 5 percent of the first $1 million, 4 percent of the next $1 million, 3 percent of the next $1 million, 2 percent of the next $1 million, and 1 percent on the rest of the sale consideration. These commission percentages are usually negotiable.

In some cases, you may also have to pay a fixed consulting fee, which is due without regard to whether the business is sold. This is particularly true if your investment banker or business broker intends to prepare a brochure to describe your business in order to better market the business to potential buyers.

Finding an Investment Banker or Broker

How do you find a reputable and experienced investment banker or business broker? You should start with recommendations from an experienced M&A attorney.

If other companies in your industry have been sold recently, inquire as to whom they used for the transaction.

TRAP WARNING Make your inquiries discreetly and indirectly so that you do not tip off competitors, customers, suppliers, or employees that your business is for sale.

Obtain recommendations from trusted friends and business acquaintances who can keep a secret. Your accountant can also be a good source for referrals.

You should ask all potential investment bankers or business brokers about their experience in selling companies in your industry. Some investment bankers or business brokers represent only buyers. Try to obtain the names of persons whom they have previously represented in selling their businesses and seek to interview these persons. Take care not to identify yourself as a potential seller.

There are many persons who call themselves investment bankers or business brokers who are either inexperienced or disreputable. Unemployed executives who have an MBA degree may call themselves investment bankers even if they have never sold a business. There are a number of investment bankers and business brokers who are less than reputable.

In some states, such as New York, business brokers must be licensed. However, state licenses are no guarantee of either competency or reputability.

Once you have selected the investment banker or business broker, you must negotiate an agreement with them setting forth the terms of the arrangement, including the transaction fee. You will need the help of your experienced M&A lawyer to negotiate this agreement. There are many pitfalls.

TRAP WARNING State laws may require you to pay a commission once a ready, willing, and able buyer is located and signs an agreement, whether or not the transaction closes, unless you have a specific agreement to the contrary. In effect, you may be legally liable to pay a commission for aborted sales. The fee agreement should be in writing and be specific that no fee is due unless and until the sale closes.

There are many other issues involved in negotiating an agreement with an investment banker or business broker. Here are some examples:

- If a purchase price is payable in installments, the fee should be paid in similar installments and should not all be paid when the sale closes.
- If the deferred payments to you are reduced by indemnification claims of the buyer, the fee payments should likewise be reduced.
- If the purchase price is payable in whole or in part in stock, try to pay the fee in stock in the same proportion.
- Some forms of agreement require you to pay a commission on the amount of your long-term debt assumed by

the buyer. Since the assumption of long-term debt does not necessarily put money into your pocket, you should resist paying a fee on such debt assumption

You must control whom your investment banker or business broker approaches as a potential buyer to purchase your business. Advance approval of such approaches helps you control the sale process and preserves confidentiality of your decision to sell.

TRAP WARNING Be very careful how you approach direct competitors. Do so very carefully and on a no-name basis. Otherwise, your competitors may use your sale decision as a competitive weapon.

SELLING THE BUSINESS YOURSELF

If you decide to sell the business without an investment banker or broker, you must maintain the confidentiality of your decision to sell in two ways: by not specifically identifying your business in letters to prospective buyers and in advertisements and by designating your attorney, accountant, or a friend to be the initial contact person with potential buyers.

To discover buyers, you might consider having your attorney, accountant, or friend do the following:

- Consult investment bankers and business brokers who represent potential buyers.
- Advertise in trade journals.
- Advertise in business papers, including *The Wall Street Journal*.
- Send letters to companies that you think would be interested in your business.
- Send letters to companies that have the same SIC code as yours.

PREPARE A MARKETING BROCHURE

Whether you use an investment banker or business broker to sell your business or sell it yourself, prior to commencing the selling of your business you should have a marketing brochure, which should contain a description of your business, including a package of financial information.

The marketing brochure will be a key selling tool and should be carefully prepared. If you prepared a marketing brochure many years before the target date, you will just need to update your existing brochure.

A good marketing brochure will take several months to prepare. Your attorney, accountant, and other advisors will be helpful in its preparation. It is important to highlight the strengths of your business and to present the weaknesses in the best possible light. You must take care to identify off-balance-sheet assets and assets that your balance sheet undervalues. (See Chapter 2.)

If your business has favorable special valuation factors (see Chapter 2), emphasize these in the brochure. You should also discuss customer relationships and market identification. Your competitive strengths should be carefully noted and explained.

The marketing brochure should not be provided to a potential buyer until appropriate confidentiality agreements have been executed. (See Chapter 4.)

A well-prepared, detailed, and thoughtful market brochure will reduce the buyer's due diligence and expedite the sale.

SETTING THE SALE TARGET DATE

There are some business owners who wait until they are too old or too sick to sell their business. Some let their executors sell their business after their death.

A great deal of energy is required to market your business properly. Your active participation is necessary in the sale process. Who better can market your business than you?

If you wait to sell until you lack the energy to run the business, potential buyers will sense your weakness. Potential buyers also like to purchase a business from an estate that is under pressure to sell.

To maximize the sale price, you must attract financial buyers, if possible, to compete with strategic and other buyers. A financial buyer will generally want you to continue to operate the business until new management can be trained.

All of these considerations dictate that your sale target date should be several years before you really have to sell. Of course, no one knows when their health will fail them. Therefore, unless you have trained management that is to carry on without you, prudence would dictate a target date that will make it likely that you can actively participate in the marketing of your business.

PART 2

Preliminary Negotiations

CHAPTER 7

Surviving the Buyer's Due Diligence

Few buyers will purchase a business without conducting an extensive investigation, generally called "due diligence." The key to surviving the buyer's due diligence is understanding what areas of your business the buyer is likely to investigate and being prepared for that investigation.

Due diligence has similarities to the dating process prior to marriage. If you really want to get married (i.e., sell your business), you'd better dress well and otherwise look as attractive as possible for your date. You want your date (i.e., the buyer) to fall in love with you.

That does not mean that you should hide your defects. The buyer will probably discover them anyway. Rather, once the buyer falls in love with you, your defects become less important. Therefore, it is important for the buyer to fall in love with you before you reveal your defects.

If you have a major defect, consider at least hinting at (but not discussing in depth) the defect early in the due diligence process. While the buyer is flattering you about what a wonderful business you have is a good time to be modest and mention your major defect very obliquely and casually and without detail.

It is very important that the buyer not feel that he was misled by you when the true extent of your major defect is revealed. The buyer must at all times have confidence in your integrity. Who wants to marry a liar?

DATA ROOM

In larger sale transactions, it is customary to maintain a data room in which all relevant documentation about the seller can be inspected by the potential buyers. It is preferable to have this data room off of your premises to maintain confidentiality and prevent interference with your operations. Your M&A attorney's office is an ideal site.

SPECIFIC DUE DILIGENCE

A recent publication for buyers lists the following four general due diligence rules for buyers:

- Do wine and dine customers, employees, and competitors.
- Talk to outsiders.
- Read upside down.
- Don't fall in love.

The first two rules should alert sellers to the scope of the investigation they will face. The third rule, "read upside down," suggests that sellers keep their desks clean and require that their key employees maintain clean desks during the due diligence process.

The final rule for buyers, "don't fall in love," suggests that this is exactly what the seller should seek.

The intensity and breadth of the due diligence process surprise unprepared sellers. It is important that you anticipate what the potential buyer is likely to look for.

Here are some of the many questions that must be answered by the seller during the due diligence process:

- What makes the company and/or its principal products unique?
- Where or how is the company positioned against competition?
- What is the company's place in the industry (rank, recent growth history, reputation, etc.)?
- What principal advertising messages has the company used successfully and unsuccessfully in the past?
- Are there any major developments in the company, competitive companies, or the industry that could have long-term effects on the company?
- Are there any legal, moral, social, or ethical issues with regard to the business or the industry that could have future impact?
- Generally, how is the business regarded by customers, competitors, vendors, the press, and the industry at large?
- In detail, what has industry growth during the past five years been, and what is the outlook for future years? Attach trade association, published data, and government data if available.
- Does the company give key customers Christmas gifts or other presents? Does the company's management entertain extensively? (Be sensitive to clues that indicate inappropriate gifts.)
- What are some major new accounts sold during the past year, and why did they take on the line?
- What are some major accounts lost during the past two years, and why are they no longer customers?
- Who is responsible for product development?
- What long-range plans are under consideration?
- What limitations exist in product development (people, capital, technology, outside vendors, tooling time, etc.)?

- What technology or proprietary knowledge is significant to the business?
- What companies possess similar or related knowledge?
- Is the company dependent upon outside resources for any of its technology? If so, describe what and upon whom dependent.
- What resources has the company dedicated to improving product and process technology? What plans are in place (timetables, budgets, etc.)?
- What quality control systems are in place, and what management tools monitor their performance?
- What are the purchasing terms (payment terms, shipping, payment of duties, etc.) for each vendor?
- Are foreign purchases made in dollars? If not, in what currency? Are there exchange rate sharing agreements? Does the company hedge foreign purchases?
- Who owns tooling for component parts, packaging, etc.?
- Are tooling costs amortized in piece part prices, or are they purchased and depreciated?
- Is the company a licensee for any brand names, patents, technology, etc.?
- Are any vendors critical to success? What contingency plans are in place in case a vendor cannot supply for any reason?
- Are any materials used ones that could become in short supply?
- Who has principal purchasing responsibility? Is anyone else involved?
- How is inventory financed?
- How did the book inventory vary from the computer reports and from the physical? That is, what adjustments were made?
- What kind of computer hardware is used? Describe fully, including age, lease agreements, special features, etc.
- What software packages are used?
- How customized are the software packages? Are they written in a commonly used language?

- Does the company have the source code for the software?
- Have vendors been in business a long time, and do they have a large number of similar users?
- What are the sales trends by month for the past two years? Are there seasonal patterns? Are sales affected by major shows or promotions? Does the industry have its own sales cycle? Are sales affected by competition?
- How is sales forecasting done? By whom? How formally? How often? How is it reviewed and validated? How accurate have forecasts been? Does the forecast drive purchasing and production, or are they driven by other decisions?
- What are standard payment terms by division, product line, channel of distribution, etc.?
- What nonstandard terms are granted? When? Why? Who approves them?
- Are reserves for returns or other after-sale adjustments made?
- Are standard, actual, or estimated costs used in estimating and general reporting? How often are standards updated? Who sets the standards?
- How are promotional budgets determined? Evaluate each advertising and promotion account by year in total and as a percentage of sales.
- How are expenses budgeted and controlled? Evaluate all G&A expenses from year to year and as a percentage of sales. Note significant increases or reductions.

The following are suggested to buyers in performing their due diligence among your key employees:

- Ask each key manager what major problems are faced
    by his or her department
    by other departments
    by the company as a whole
    by the industry
- Ask each key manager to list the company's strengths.

- Ask each key manager to list the company's weaknesses.
- Ask each key manager to describe outside threats to or vulnerabilities of the company.
- Ask each key manager to describe the company's major opportunities as it moves forward, especially under new ownership.
- Ask each key manager to assess the risks faced in a change in ownership.
- Ask each manager to evaluate the impact of the current owner/top manager no longer serving in the present role or being as active. What will future relationships be like?

CHAPTER 8

Avoiding Negotiation Traps

The effectiveness of your negotiating strategy plays a major role in your ultimate success in selling your business. The following are suggestions to enhance your negotiating position and to avoid negotiation traps.

TYPES OF BUYERS

One way of classifying potential buyers is by whether they are considered financial buyers, strategic buyers, or neither. If you expect to work for the buyer after the sale, it is particularly important that you understand the buyer's culture and motivations.

Financial Buyers

A financial buyer is a purchaser who is motivated solely by financial considerations in acquiring your business and who is not engaged in a business that could be integrated with yours or could otherwise strategically benefit from the acquisition. The financial buyer looks only to your projected financial results and is uninterested in any synergy with an existing business. Financial buyers typically finance their business with money from institutional investors who are looking for large returns over a five-year period. These institutional investors typically are interested in exiting at the end of the five-year period through a sale or public offering.

However, it is not always true that a financial buyer will pay less than a strategic buyer. If capital is very available, as in the late 1980s, financial buyers may have pressure from their investors to consummate transactions and to show a financial return. This pressure can cause a financial buyer to outbid a strategic buyer at times when capital is overly plentiful.

Since the financial buyer does not have any business with which your business has synergy (other than the ability in the case of the consolidator to lay off your back office personnel), you will typically get a lower valuation from a financial buyer.

The presence of financial buyers in the marketplace permits a broader range of potential buyers for your business and tends to set a floor on the price of your business.

You should take great care in selling to financial buyers who have received their capital from an institution and are still private. These buyers tend to use a portion of the purchase price as "equity" for purposes of their balance sheet. For example, they may offer you $10 million for the business but only permit you to receive $6 million in cash, with the remaining $4 million subordinated to their institutional lenders on a long-term note. Effectively, you have $4 million added to the equity base of the buyer, since their institutional lenders will treat your $4 million note as equity. You are at risk because if the buyer defaults to its institutional lenders your note will never get paid.

Today, many financial buyers are also strategic buyers because they have a portfolio company engaged in the same business.

Strategic Buyers

A strategic buyer is willing to purchase your business because of the synergy with its existing business. For example, if your products have penetrated a particular market that the strategic buyer would also like to penetrate, the strategic buyer may acquire your business to achieve that market penetration.

The strategic buyer must compute how much it would cost to penetrate the same market. A strategic buyer might be willing to pay you a much higher figure than your earnings would indicate based upon the cost savings to them of market access that your business gives them.

Your financial results are less important to strategic buyers because they are interested in the financial results of their business combined with yours. The strategic buyer tends to take a longer view of their investment than the financial buyer and is less concerned about exiting in five years.

An example of a strategic purchase is the recent acquisition by IBM of LOTUS Development Corp., which gave IBM access to the huge software inventory of LOTUS.

Some strategic buyers express interest in your business in order to discover important competitive information. You should take care with strategic buyers to prevent so-called fishing expeditions.

Other Buyers

Some buyers, sometimes called special-purpose buyers, are neither financial nor strategic buyers. For example, a father may purchase a business for his son or daughter. A businessperson who previously sold a business may decide to purchase another business.

Regardless of what category your buyer is in, it is important to understand your buyer's motivations. Doing so will help you to structure your negotiations with the buyer better and maximize your chances for a successful sale.

NEGOTIATION STRATEGY

It is important that you do not become the principal negotiator for your company. That is why you have a team of
professional advisors.

The reasons for not becoming a principal negotiator
for your company are as follows:

- Typically, you will have less experience than your professional advisors in negotiating such sale transactions.
- You will want to remain above the "trench warfare" that
sometimes occurs in negotiations.
- The principal negotiator for your potential buyer will probably be a second- or third-level management person or
their lawyer. You do not want to put yourself at their level.

There are two types of negotiators:

- A cooperative negotiator is a negotiator who recognizes
mutual problems and comes up with cooperative, creative solutions.
- A competitor negotiator is a negotiator who puts demands on the table indicating that if his or her demand is
not met the negotiation will be over.

If competitor negotiators are attorneys for the potential buyer or second- or third-level managers, it is possible
to handle them by going over their heads. However, if they
are CEOs of potential buyers, you have a serious problem,
and it may be smart to look elsewhere to sell your business.
This is especially true if you are going to have an employment agreement and you are reporting to a CEO who is a
competitor negotiator.

You should consider using your investment banker or
business broker as the lead negotiator. If you have selected an
experienced M & A lawyer, that person may also be a good
choice to negotiate the sale. Be certain that your attorney has
good business sense as well as good technical abilities.

ESTABLISHING A SALE PRICE

Sam Goldwyn, the legendary Hollywood producer—the same Sam Goldwyn who allegedly uttered the immortal lines "any man who goes to a psychiatrist ought to have his head examined" and "a verbal contract isn't worth the paper it's written on"—was negotiating a deal one day with a certain actor.

The actor declared, "I'm asking fifteen hundred a week." Snapped Goldwyn, "You're not asking fifteen hundred a week. You're asking twelve, and I'm giving you a thousand."

If you are not really interested in selling your business unless you receive a ridiculously high price, set a ridiculously high price.

On very rare occasions you might actually receive it. At worst, you will just drive off potential buyers. Since you are presumably not really interested in selling anyway, this is not a great loss.

Some potential sellers establish a sale price that is not realistic and assume that this provides them with the flexibility to negotiate a high price. In general, an unrealistically high sale price merely drives away potential buyers. If you believe that the highest price will be obtained by having competing buyers (such as at an auction), it is not in your interest to discourage potential buyers. Moreover, your "high-ball" price merely encourages buyers to offer you "low-ball" prices in return.

You are not required to set a sale price for your business. You may just wait for offers from buyers.

Your value to a strategic buyer may be significantly higher than your value to other possible buyers. For example, in valuing your business, the strategic buyer may consider what it would cost them to reproduce your customer base and skilled workforce, and the cost savings to them may make your business extremely valuable. Occasionally you might receive offers from strategic buyers that exceed your wildest dreams. Therefore, it is not normally in your interest to establish a sale price since your value may depend upon who is making the offer.

If you must establish a sale price for your business, it is recommended that it be set at the highest level that could be justified by any of the valuations you have received (see Chapter 2) plus at least an additional 20 percent to give yourself some bargaining room. You will need the help of an investment banker or business broker to compute that valuation, since the value can be higher for one buyer than another, as previously noted.

If your motivation in selling is to obtain a specific amount of money that will keep you comfortable for your lifetime, it is a judgment call as to whether to reveal that information to the buyer. If that amount of money is less than the maximum amount you can reasonably ask for the business, it may be a good negotiating plan, in appropriate circumstances, to reveal to the buyer both the price you want and the reason you have established that price. However, you should not reveal that information until late in the negotiations, when you are comfortable that the buyer is serious. The advantage of revealing that information is that it creates credibility for your asking price, since you have tied the figure to your future lifestyle, thereby indicating to the buyer the importance of the asking price to you personally.

If you own real estate that is leased to your business, you have to make a decision as to whether you want to sell the real estate or continue to lease it to the buyer. In some businesses, the primary value of the business is in the real estate. Therefore, when setting a sale price for your business, you should make it clear whether or not that price includes the real estate and, if not, what your lease terms will be. There have been many negotiations where the buyer was willing to overpay for the real estate to make up for the fact that the seller was unhappy with the price offered for the business.

Dos and Don'ts for Effective Negotiation Strategy

The following are some general negotiation suggestions:

- Use questions to establish the buyer's needs, to clarify issues, and to advance creative alternatives.
- Listen carefully to the buyer's lawyer. Evaluate the information you have received before you respond.
- Be open-minded about your strategies and tactics. Carefully choose the words you use to be sure they are essentially neutral. The way you use them will determine how successful you are in establishing a positive climate. Don't use them as fixed rules that determine who will be the winner. Instead, use them to move the negotiation forward toward a mutually satisfactory solution.
- Be sensitive to the meaning of the buyer's gestures. They give you valuable information about the progress of the negotiation, even if the buyer is trying to manipulate you.

The following are various buyer negotiation strategies and possible seller counters:

Buyer's Strategy	Seller's Possible Counters
Buyer starts by making a "low-ball" offer.	Don't rise to the bait. Counter high and wait it out.
Buyer sends someone who has to answer to others for most decisions.	Find out how and when employee will get approval from superiors. Try to meet head person alone. Ask how negotiations are expected to be successful with this approach.
Buyer presents demands as unalterable.	Change focus to other issues. Bring in associates to strengthen side. Suggest mediators and arbitrators.

(continues)

Buyer's Strategy	Seller's Possible Counters
Buyer pretends to be personally insulted, even if the seller hasn't done anything to deserve it.	Deny attempt to personalize. Ask forgiveness. Call a caucus.
Buyer takes an unexpected approach while maintaining original objective.	Spring surprises in return. Delay in taking action.
Buyer leaves the room and stops the negotiation.	Cut off the negotiations temporarily. Start at preparation stage again. Call a recess. Spring surprises in return.
Buyer pretends a matter is already settled and agreed on in hopes that the other side will go along.	Reject this ploy. Get others to verify that no such matter was settled.

The Public Offering Alternative

If there are only one or two potential buyers, you might consider the public offering alternative to gain leverage in your negotiations. If your company can qualify for an initial public offering (IPO), see if you can get a letter of intent from a potential underwriter. The letter of intent is typically a nonbinding letter expressing the willingness of the underwriter to participate in your IPO.

The letter of intent shows that you have an alternative to the sale of your company. It strengthens your bargaining position.

Moreover, the letter of intent demonstrates to the potential buyer that once the buyer has acquired your business, the buyer can do its own IPO or, if the buyer is already public, do a spinoff of some of your stock to its public shareholders.

Conducting an Auction

It is generally agreed that an auction produces the highest price for a business. Generally, you need two or more bidders to conduct an auction. However, an auction can be conducted with only one bidder if the auction is a closed auction, i.e., no one knows who else is bidding.

To induce potential buyers to bid at an auction of your business, you must assure them that the business will be in fact sold to the highest bidder and that the auction will be conducted fairly.

If you have not made a decision whether or not you really want to sell your business, you will not be able to hold an auction effectively. Likewise, if you favor one bidder over another and want to give your favored bidder the last bid, it is unlikely that you will be able to induce other potential buyers to participate in the auction.

The most suitable businesses for an auction are businesses with good financial results and a strategic market position. If neither of these characteristics is present, the auction may not be as successful but should still be considered if there are competing buyers.

The auction must be conducted by a person in whom bidders have confidence and pursuant to written rules and procedures that are uniformly applied to all bidders. Your investment banker or attorney can fulfill this role.

Bidders are generally turned off by open auctions, i.e., auctions where their bids are disclosed to all other bidders, and by auctions in which there are innumerable rounds of bidding.

To induce bidders to participate in your auction, bids should be submitted in writing and maintained in confidence. Cutoff dates for bids should be advertised and adhered to.

It is preferable from the seller's point of view to have at least two rounds of bidding, with the second round of bidding confined to the highest two bidders. If there are more than four bidders, you may wish a third round of bidding.

It is essential that you provide all bidders with the same form agreement of sale, which will be prepared by your counsel. Each bidder should be requested to state any changes in the form agreement of sale when they submit their bid. In determining who is the highest bidder, the legal terms must be considered along with the price.

For example, suppose one bidder bids $15 million and a second bidder bids $14.5. If the $14.5 bidder is willing to cut off any indemnification rights against you after the closing, but the $15 million bidder is unwilling to do so, you may consider the $14.5 million bid to be higher. As noted in Chapters 11 and 18, the important question is how much will you be left with after the sale is completed and any indemnification rights of the buyer have terminated.

To make the bids meaningful, the agreement of sale should provide for a forfeitable deposit on signing and eliminate any due diligence out. Otherwise, the high bidder could use the auction as a vehicle to postpone making a final purchasing decision to the prejudice of the seller, who has lost the other bidders.

The form agreement of sale should contemplate a quick closing after the signing. If the sale to the high bidder does not close quickly, the other bidders will have lost interest by the time the seller realizes the sale to the high bidder will not be consummated.

WEEDING OUT POTENTIAL BUYERS

It is important that you quickly weed out potential buyers with the following characteristics so that you do not waste your valuable time:

- The buyer is merely on a fishing expedition.
- The buyer does not have a strong commitment at the CEO level to purchase your business.
- You always negotiate with second- and third-level management, never the CEO.
- The buyer has no prior record of making acquisitions.
- The buyer does not have the financial resources to acquire your business.
- The buyer's culture is not acceptable to you, and you want to continue to run the business.

CHAPTER 9

Letters of Intent: A Recipe for Litigation

A letter of intent (also called an "agreement in principle") is a document signed by both the buyer and the seller that expresses the intention of the parties for the sale of the business but is not legally binding. The purpose of the letter of intent is to set forth the major business terms of the transaction and to confirm in writing these terms to prevent any misunderstanding. Typically the letter of intent will state that it is not legally binding and that the only legally binding document is the definitive agreement of sale. Appendix 5 contains a sample letter of intent.

The problem with letters of intent is that sometimes they are legally binding even though the parties say that they are not. For example, the $11 billion judgment against Texaco, Inc. in the Getty merger was based upon a letter of intent signed by Getty with Pennzoil that was not supposed to be legally binding. The reason the $11 billion judgment was obtained against Texaco (the ultimate buyer) rather than Getty's shareholders (the seller) was an indemnification agreement Texaco had executed with Getty that protected Getty against suits by Pennzoil. This famous case and its repercussions are discussed in the articles at the end of this chapter.

Another problem with the letter of intent is the fact that many securities lawyers believe that a public company buyer must disclose a proposed material acquisition once a letter of intent is signed. The public disclosure of the letter of intent with your company effectively tells the world about your decision to sell sooner than you might prefer.

A final problem with letters of intent is the tendency of the lawyers for the buyer and seller to use the letter of intent to negotiate terms. This may result in expensive and protracted negotiations over the words of a document that is not intended to be legally binding. It also holds up the drafting and execution of the final agreement.

Therefore, it is preferable to avoid a letter of intent and proceed directly to the final agreement.

GETTY LETTER OF INTENT

The most dramatic example of the sometimes binding nature of letters of intent is the jury verdict in Texaco-Pennzoil involving the battle for the Getty Oil Company.

Pennzoil had prepared a five-page single-spaced memorandum of agreement that was signed by Gordon Getty, as sole trustee of the Sarah C. Getty Trust; Harold Williams, as president of the J. Paul Getty Museum; and Hugh Liedtke, Pennzoil's chairman. That memorandum of agreement spelled out in considerable detail the terms of the transaction and provided for approval by the Getty Oil board. After lengthy meetings and negotiations, the Getty board rejected the terms of the transaction as spelled out in that memorandum. Ultimately, Pennzoil and the Getty Oil board agreed on a proposal that contained some revised and, from Getty's standpoint, improved terms. Although the Getty board clearly voted to reject the terms of the initial memorandum of agreement, at the trial there was conflicting testimony as to whether the Getty board ever voted on approving the memorandum of agreement with revised terms.

The jury returned an $11 billion verdict against Texaco based on its finding that the Getty Oil Company, the Sarah C. Getty Trust, and the J. Paul Getty Museum, which controlled about 11.8 percent of that stock, had entered into a binding agreement with Pennzoil pursuant to which Pennzoil was to become a three-sevenths owner of Getty Oil. The jury found that the "agreement in principle" between the parties was binding even though no definitive agreements had been reached, and even though the parties contemplated negotiating and entering into such agreements.

In reading the subsequent articles on the Getty letter of intent, remember that the $11 billion judgment would have been the responsibility of the seller's major shareholders but for the indemnification agreement executed by Texaco.

Caution Talks: Texaco-Pennzoil Case Makes Firms Careful About Merger Moves; Just What Is an Agreement Stirs Much Uncertainty; a Risk in Shaking Hands—but the Precedent May Fade[1]

Earlier this year, Michel Zaleski consummated a day and a half of tough negotiations by doing what he always does upon reaching an agreement in principle. "I looked the guy in the eye, stuck out my hand and said, 'Let's shake on it,'" the New York investment banker recalls.

But across the table, the opposing attorney looked back askance. "We can't do that," he told Mr. Zaleski, with an uncomfortable smile.

As Mr. Zaleski pulled back his hand, he could feel the Texaco chill. "I never thought a handshake was anything more than a moral commitment," he said. "But now people are afraid to make even a moral commitment for fear someone will use it against them."

1. Reprinted from *The Wall Street Journal*, April 15, 1986. Reproduced with permission of *The Wall Street Journal*.

Four months after a Texas jury delivered an $11.12 billion verdict against Texaco Inc. for thwarting Pennzoil Co.'s agreement in principle to buy part of Getty Oil Co., the largest civil-damage award in history is casting a long, cold shadow across American business. Deal makers say the huge verdict, by undermining time-honored assumptions on Wall Street about what constitutes an enforceable agreement and what doesn't, is forcing people to be much more cautious.

"The lesson learned is that the most general of writing can be construed as an agreement," says Jay Grogan, an attorney who researched the Texaco case for his Dallas law firm of Jackson, Walker, Winstead, Cantwell & Miller. "It's really pretty scary."

Adds another Dallas lawyer, Robert Profusek of Jones, Day, Reavis & Pogue: "Today, an agreement is in the eyes of the beholder."

This "post-Texaco" climate of uncertainty is having a chilling effect on bidding competition. Some companies, accustomed to vicious bidding wars in the mergers and acquisitions market, have grown gun-shy in the wake of the Texaco verdict, especially when a potential target has entered any type of agreement with a third party. Some boards of directors, meanwhile, have had to grudgingly accept lower bids for their companies' assets rather than risk being sued for breach of contract by an angry bidder.

"No longer can we say, 'We stole a deal fair and square,' " says Alen E. Rothenberg, a San Francisco investment banker. "Now, there's a new constituency out there. In addition to shareholders and employees, now we have to worry about rejected suitors."

By discouraging companies from aggressively competing for acquisitions, the Texaco verdict has provided management, in effect, with a new lockout tool. For example, in a news conference two days after directors of Eastern Airlines agreed to sell the carrier's assets to Texas Air Corp. for what many analysts termed a very low price, Eastern's chairman, Frank Borman, dismissed the possibility that a rival bid for Eastern could succeed "even if someone offered more." He added, "You probably have heard of Texaco and Pennzoil."

Lawyers and investment bankers also say the Texaco case is one of several factors—including cost—that have hastened the pace of deal making. These observers note that "letters of intent" and "agreements in principle" are becoming less common today as negotiators try to reach final terms faster to freeze out any higher bidders or interlopers.

"Now, instead of relying on a handshake and two months of due diligence, the lawyers fly in immediately, lock the door, and sign everybody up in a few days with conditional outs," says Michael Halloran, a securities lawyer for Pillsbury, Madison & Sutro in San Francisco.

Much of the Texaco chill, however, may be due to psychological overreaction. The case didn't make any new law in the areas of contracts and fiduciary duty; it determined only that an agreement existed between Pennzoil and Getty and that Texaco had wrongly interfered with it. "That's an important distinction legally, and most business people don't understand it," says Mr. Profusek, the Dallas attorney.

Moreover, many legal experts consider the case an aberration whose significance they expect to be whittled away on appeal. Daniel J. Good, a mergers and acquisitions specialist with E. F. Hutton & Co., says, "The most sophisticated legal talent on Wall Street are incredulous that this decision was decided on the facts."

Many companies say the case has had no effect on their business practices. International Business Machines Corp., for example, says its standing policy, spelled out in its Business Conduct Guidelines, remains unchanged. The guidelines instruct IBM sales representatives that letters of intent, additional agreements "and the like" are "usually not firm orders" and are thus fair game for competing bids.

Other judges, meanwhile, have already signaled disagreement with the thinking in the Texaco verdict. Last month, Nebraska's Supreme Court, in a 4–3 decision, overturned a lower-court judgment against the Minneapolis-based commodities giant, Cargill Inc., for thwarting a merger agreement between its rival, ConAgra Inc., of Omaha, NE, and MBPXL Corp., a Wichita, KS, meatpacker. The case, which closely resembled Pennzoil's suit against Texaco, focused on the question of whether Cargill had "tortiously interfered" with ConAgra's written agreement to buy MBPXL by offering a higher price for the meatpacker's assets.

But in contrast to the Texaco case, the Nebraska high court rejected the notion that a merger agreement could be used to lock out interlopers. The court held that MBPXL's directors acted in accordance with their fiduciary responsibility, as stipulated in Delaware law, by reneging on the ConAgra agreement in favor of Cargill's higher bid. Board of Directors, wrote the court's majority, cannot use agreements to "infringe on the voting rights of shareholders or chill the bidding process."

After the decision, ConAgra's chairman, Charles M. Harper, said the company's shareholders "would be much better off if we were in Texas, where a contract is a contract."

The ConAgra-Cargill case, in fact, probably better reflects prevailing legal doctrine on contractual interference than the Texaco verdict does. In a major decision in January 1985, the influential Supreme Court of Delaware ruled in the case of *Smith v. Van Gorkam* that directors can be held personally liable if they approve a takeover agreement at an undervalued price. The Van Gorkam decision suggests that a board's obligation to shareholders may well supersede an agreement with a suitor.

Says J. Tomilson Hill, a mergers and acquisitions specialist at Shearson Lehman Brothers Inc.: "The Texaco decision hasn't changed a board of directors' fiduciary responsibility with respect to price—a basic tenet of both Delaware and [federal] securities law."

Nonetheless, the Texaco case has clearly affected some recent agreements. Texas Air's $600 million proposed acquisition of Eastern stands out as a case in point. After Texas Air's takeover announcement, at least two other carriers were said to have considered offering higher bids for Eastern: Pan American World Airways and Braniff Inc.

Although a Pan Am spokesman said the Texaco verdict didn't figure in the carrier's decision not to bid on Eastern, one Braniff official close to Jay Pritzker, whose family holds a majority stake in Braniff, says Mr. Pritzker would have made a bid but was dissuaded by, among other impediments, his concern that Mr. Borman's public invocation of the Texaco case indicated that the two parties wouldn't tolerate any interlopers.

"The Texaco case was used as a negotiating tool to stop the bidding process," observes this official, who declined to be identified, "and it was used to the detriment of shareholders."

In the Eastern Airlines case, one key union, the machinists, refused to agree to new labor concessions unless Mr. Borman resigned. The board wouldn't go along with that and instead signed with Texas Air. But insiders critical of the pact say Eastern should have sought a higher bid once it became clear that all three of the company's unions were willing to take sizable wage cuts if Mr. Borman resigned. Mr. Borman hasn't resigned, but Eastern's pilots and flight attendants agreed to new wage concessions; its machinists have refused.

Some industry analysts say the ultimate deterrent to other suitors was economic, not legal. The Texaco case "was a factor," says Robert J. Joedicke of Shearson Lehman Brothers, but with $2.5 billion of debt and severe labor problems, "Eastern was not an outstanding candidate for a takeover."

The Texaco case also affected a recent bidding war between two jet-engine makers, Pratt & Whitney, an East Hartford, Connecticut, unit of United Technologies Corp., and Rolls-Royce Inc. of Greenwich, CT, a unit of Rolls-Royce Ltd.

In December, the Greenwich-based United Parcel Services of America Inc. ordered 20 refitted Boeing Co. jets, starting a competition between Pratt and Rolls for the $400 million engine contract. At first, according to a source privy to the negotiations, Rolls seemed in the lead, but then Pratt made price concessions. United Parcel gave Pratt a handshake agreement for the order.

While lawyers were writing the final contract, however, Rolls came back with another bid, some $25 million below

Pratt's price. At that point, Pratt representatives raised the Texaco decision in a conversation with executives of United Parcel, and the Pratt accord sailed through, the source says.

Spokesmen for Rolls, Pratt, and United Parcel declined comment.

In another recent transaction, the closely held Miraflores Co. of San Francisco declined to entertain potentially higher bids for its assets after entering into a preliminary takeover agreement with Guest Supply Inc., based in New Brunswick, NJ. Although the two companies had exchanged letters explicitly stating that their merger agreement was non-binding, advisers to Miraflores, a supplier of hotel amenities with 1985 revenue of $7.1 million, recommended against considering subsequent bids for fear that Guest Supply might sue.

"In the Texaco case, even though the parties were not legally bound to go forward, pulling out at the last minute offended the jury's sense of justice," Miraflores' chairman, John Chapman, contended. "That turned out to be more important than the law."

If nothing else, most lawyers agree that the Texaco verdict is a chastening reminder of how capricious the legal system can be. "The Texaco case is a textbook illustration of the dangers of ever getting involved in the American judicial system," says Rodgin Cohen, an attorney with the New York law firm of Sullivan & Cromwell. "The courts can do wild and unpredictable things."

Insofar as the Texaco verdict has contributed to an increasingly prevalent lockout mentality, it may be costing shareholders money. Companies that try to limit bids are less likely to receive the fullest price. In 1983, for instance, the family that owned a large stake in Stokely–Van Camp Inc. tried to buy the company for $55 a share. An unsolicited suitor, Quaker Oats Co., launched an offer, however, and eventually bought Van Camp for $77 a share.

Ultimately, the principal issue raised in the Texaco verdict—whether a director's fiduciary responsibility to seek the highest price takes precedence over contract law—may have to be more clearly resolved in the courts before many deal makers will feel comfortable entering bidding wars. Utilicorp United Inc. is asking a Houston federal court to do just that.

In a suit against Energas Co., of Amarillo, TX, the utility is contending that Energas unlawfully interfered in January with Utilicorp's preliminary agreement to buy Trans Louisiana Gas Co., of Lafayette, LA. Utilicorp is arguing that TransLa's directors repudiated their agreement, just two days after it was reached, to take a higher offer from Energas. Each side has accused the other of trying to either duck or exploit the Texaco verdict by "forum shopping" for a favorable court.

An Energas spokesman, who says the case belongs in Louisiana courts because the target company is situated in that state, charges Utilicorp with trying to "capitalize on the hysteria following the Texaco verdict" by bringing suit in Texas.

Utilicorp's president, Richard C. Green, Jr., counters that both the suit and the Houston venue have "substantial merits," but he concedes that "clearly, the Texaco-Pennzoil example was there and seemed to be the best path to follow."

The Gambler Who Refused $2 Billion; Pennzoil's J. Hugh Liedtke, Fighting Texaco, Made a Historic Bet[2]

The whole amazing story is beyond anyone's previous experience in business or law. Pennzoil's celebrated suit arose from Texaco's takeover of Getty Oil, which allegedly wrecked a planned Pennzoil-Getty deal. A Texas jury decided in November 1985 that Texaco owed Pennzoil $10.5 billion—the largest award in history. A higher court later reduced it to $8.5 billion, but by mid-April interest and penalties had brought it up to $11 billion. Texaco offered to pay Pennzoil around $2 billion if Pennzoil would drop its claims. Pennzoil Chairman J. (for John) Hugh Liedtke—in what must be the biggest turndown of cash

2. Reprinted from *Fortune* magazine article by Stratford P. Sherman, May 11, 1987. © 1987 Time Inc. All rights reserved.

ever—looked that ten-figure sum in the eye and said no. The next day Texaco filed for bankruptcy protection, the biggest company ever to do so.

Liedtke (pronounced LID-key), the man who turned down Texaco's $2 billion settlement offer, in mid-April still held out his hand for more. Asked by *Fortune* whether he is the greediest man in the world or simply in need of psychiatric help, Pennzoil's barrel-bellied chief executive chuckled and replied, in a voice so gravelly and deep you practically have to drill for it, "Maybe both." Then he adds, "I don't think 'greed' is fair, I really don't." Liedtke, 65, refuses to accept what he calls a "shotgun settlement" on Texaco's terms. "Pennzoil is unmoved by Texaco's dramatic gesture," he says. "Maybe now we should sit back awhile and see how they like bankruptcy—the euphoria should wear off in about a week. We will not take an unreasonably low settlement, whether it takes six months or four years."

This pugnacious gambler may never have expected to pocket the whole $11 billion, but Liedtke still insisted on a settlement in the $3 billion to $5 billion range—roughly twice as much as Texaco's equally intransigent leaders would pay.

The man who runs Texaco is adamant that his company has done nothing wrong. "I am interested in settling this thing," says James W. Kinnear, 59, a trim, personable marketer who became Texaco's chief executive only last January. "But I believe we are absolutely right under the law."

That obstinate attitude is reminiscent of John K. McKinley, 67, who was Kinnear's predecessor and got Texaco into this bind. Combined with the arrogance for which Texaco is famed in the oil patch, stubbornness contributed to the devastating series of setbacks the company has suffered in courts from Delaware to Texas to Washington, D.C. McKinley, an overbearing Alabamian who looks like Lyndon Johnson, failed to take Pennzoil's suit seriously enough at first and then lost big. He and Kinnear reluctantly tried to settle the case, but their efforts accomplished nothing. Now the company, long criticized for flat-footed management, will be run under the cumbersome rules of Chapter 11 bankruptcy, perhaps for years. Only three units, accounting for 4% of Texaco revenues, are in Chapter 11, but since they are the parent company and finance units, their uncertain prospects cast doubt on all Texaco operations.

The inability of Liedtke and Kinnear to reach a compromise for so long proved horribly costly. The day after Texaco's bankruptcy filing, the market value of Pennzoil's stock dropped $631 million, prompting outraged shareholders to wake Liedtke in the middle of the night with angry phone calls to his home. Texaco's stock, already priced far below estimates of the company's intrinsic value, fell a bit further. Security analysts believe that if asset-rich Texaco had paid a settlement as high as $3 billion instead of going bankrupt, relieved investors would probably have pushed Texaco's market value up by more than $3 billion. Kinnear does not think much of that argument, and he is sticking to his guns: "Whatever we offer now will be less than our last settlement proposal."

For all the allure of a timely settlement, none seemed likely as long as the leaders of the two companies refused to sit down and negotiate seriously. For months, backed up by squads of expensive lawyers and investment bankers, they did little more than lob unacceptable proposals at one another like hand grenades.

When Liedtke and Kinnear individually discuss their negotiations, one likely reason for their lengthy impasse emerges: these men genuinely do not seem to understand or respect one another enough to communicate effectively. Both talk; neither listens. For 16 months Texaco threatened to file for bankruptcy if pushed too hard. Liedtke pushed anyway, and Texaco eventually made good its threat.

Asked why he continued to push, Liedtke offers this story: "When my daughter Kristie was a little girl, she'd threaten to hold her breath until she died if she couldn't have her way. She'd turn red and scare her mother and me half to death. On our pediatrician's advice, one time we just let her hold her breath till she keeled over. She never did it again. She has a very sweet disposition now." Counters the exasperated Kinnear: "The truth is he was holding our head under water. You better hold your breath."

Liedtke and Kinnear have almost nothing in common to help bridge the $2-billion-wide gulf that divided them. Liedtke is an entrepreneur and a rebel who named his first major company, Zapata Petroleum, after the famous Mexican revolutionary. Kinnear, by contrast, is an Annapolis-trained company man who toiled in Texaco's rigid bureaucracy for 33 years before winning his place atop it just six years before his mandatory retirement. Liedtke's suits don't always fit; Kinnear dresses for success, Texaco style, with French cuffs and a tie clip. Each man is convinced he is fighting for a principle and the other fellow is wrong.

The bankruptcy filing came on a Sunday, after days of intense settlement negotiations in Houston between Texaco and Pennzoil. Kinnear, whose earlier offers had reportedly been somewhere around $500 million, finally made his top offer of about $2 billion if Pennzoil would acknowledge that amount as full settlement of the court's award. "Texaco was in a hostage situation," says Frank Barron, a Cravath partner. "It's analogous to paying ransom to kidnappers. You don't do it because the kidnappers deserve the money but because you want the hostage back."

Liedtke refused the offer, and Kinnear returned to White Plains for a Texaco board meeting on Saturday. That day Liedtke sent a counteroffer to Kinnear by corporate jet, using Pennzoil's pilot as courier. Liedtke says he offered to settle for something between $3 billion and $5 billion. The next day he flew to New York for meetings with Kinnear. But, relates Joseph Jamail, chief lawyer for Pennzoil in its suit against Texaco, "They filed for bankruptcy while he was still in the air. It kind of made him wonder whether they were talking in good faith."

Liedtke says he had to turn down Texaco's $2 billion offer. Having won $11 billion, he argues, he has a fiduciary duty to Pennzoil's stockholders to collect as much of that money as possible. His advisers told him that a settlement in the $3 billion to $5 billion range would be fair. If he were to accept a settlement much smaller than his advisers have suggested, says Liedtke, Pennzoil's shareholders might have grounds for a successful lawsuit.

Kinnear and his fellow Texaco board members—who include such business heavyweights as former IBM chairman Frank Cary and Capital Cities/ABC chairman Thomas Murphy—have a similar problem. Texaco shareholders have already filed 15 suits against them, arguing that the directors should be liable for an act—the Getty takeover—that resulted in an $11 billion judgment against the company. A settlement with Pennzoil could give those suits extra power by appearing to be an admission of wrongdoing by directors, and the dollar amount of the settlement might be seen as a measure of the damage done to Texaco's shareholders. Says Frank Barron: "That possibility never entered into the board's deliberations."

Tulsa-born Liedtke, a big friendly galoot with a face as droopy as a basset hound's, definitely does not look or talk like a wizard of high finance. But be warned: the blood in his veins is Prussian, and this good old boy is a graduate of Amherst, where he majored in philosophy, and of Harvard Business School and the University of Texas Law School. He is smart, tough, unconventional, and lucky—a combination that makes him a fearsome adversary.

Liedtke got lucky early in life. After navy service on an aircraft carrier during World War II, he settled down to practice law in Midland, Texas, which sits atop one of the biggest pools of oil in the continental U.S. According to Robert Green of Merrill Lynch, who had been Liedtke's Amherst roommate and is now Pennzoil's lead investment banker, Liedtke quickly tired of the divorces, estate cases, and wills that constituted the bulk of his practice. So Liedtke teamed with his younger brother, William, also a Midland lawyer, to invest modest sums in oil exploration.

In 1953 they joined with George Bush—now vice president of the United States—to form the exploration company called Zapata. They invested $2,500 each, raised $1 million, and had the good fortune to drill one successful well after another, amassing Texas-size fortunes while still in their early 30s. Though they severed their business ties in 1955, Liedtke and Bush remain good friends. "George isn't a wimp, I can tell you that," says Liedtke. "I think he'd make a whale of a president."

Liedtke was a corporate raider and bust-up artist decades before those terms were invented. His first big move was a friendly takeover of South Penn Oil Co. in the early 1960s. Once part of the Standard Oil trust, South Penn made the popular lubricating oils sold under the Pennzoil brand name. The company owned plenty of valuable assets but produced paltry profits. The brash young Liedtke figured South Penn would do better if he were running it. When Liedtke arrived on the scene, the company was controlled by J. Paul Getty, the oilman then called the richest American. Getty installed Liedtke as chief executive, and a few years later Getty sold out to him. Liedtke merged the exploration business into South Penn and renamed the company Pennzoil.

His fascination with hidden asset values led Liedtke into the fight with Texaco. In late 1983 he noticed that shares of Getty Oil Co. were selling for considerably less than the per share value of Getty's vast reserves of oil and gas. Liedtke started buying. Soon he formed an alliance with Gordon Getty, one of the late J. Paul's sons. A gifted musician and an amateur businessman, Gordon headed a family trust that owned 40% of Getty oil.

He and Liedtke cooked up a deal that would greatly increase Getty's market value. Early in 1984, Pennzoil and Getty Oil announced a detailed agreement in principle for Pennzoil to buy three-sevenths of Getty's shares for $3.9 billion, or $112.50 per share, $40 more than the market price of a month before. Several days later, however, Getty accepted a Texaco offer to buy all of its shares for $125 each, a price later raised to $128. The total came to more than $10 billion, a record at the time. Pennzoil sued, arguing that Texaco had illegally interfered with a binding contract between it and the Getty interests. Far from being intimidated by the lawsuit, Texaco's McKinley went ahead with the purchase.

In retrospect he should have been much more cautious. Martin Lipton, the renowned takeover lawyer who represented the Getty Museum—a principal owner of Getty Oil—had insisted that Texaco indemnify the Getty interests against lawsuits arising from the deal. Texaco management considered the risks and agreed, scarcely imagining how vast the consequence would be. When the Texas jury ruled in Pennzoil's favor to the tune of $10.5 billion, Texaco had no one with whom to split the bill. And while Texaco, along with many objective observers, regards that damage award as absurdly high, the company did not present its own theory of damages during the original trial. To advocate a different way of figuring damages, the company's lawyers reasoned, would only dignify Pennzoil's claim.

The Texas appellate court that reduced the damage award nevertheless sustained the jury's verdict. As of mid-April, Texaco still intended to appeal to the Texas Supreme Court and then, if necessary, the U.S. Supreme Court. But neither tribunal was obliged to hear the case. G. Irvin Terrell, an attorney with Baker & Botts, one of Pennzoil's law firms in Houston, estimated that exhausting the appeal process could take as little as nine months if neither court accepts the case, or as long as 18 months if both do. Some independent lawyers and security analysts think presenting appeals to both courts could take much longer, perhaps three or four years.

The only way Texaco could escape the judgment entirely would be to win on appeal—possible but unlikely. At worst, if Texaco refused to settle it could end up having to pay Pennzoil the whole $11 billion it owed the day it went into bankruptcy—also unlikely. But as of mid-April each of those extremes represented a serious risk for one of the two warring CEOs, and an opportunity for the other. Since neither man had won a decisive advantage, settlement still seemed in the interest of both. Although the sum of roughly $2 billion that divided them seemed impossibly large, the financial risks each man faced if he did not settle were even larger. Splitting the difference—arriving somewhere between $2.5 billion and $3.5 billion, say—might have made sense for everyone concerned.

Bad management by both Texaco and Pennzoil transformed an awkward dispute into a disaster of historic proportions. Managers hoping to avoid making epic messes of their own are finding this miserable saga a rich source of lessons.

Lesson Number 1 is that even the most learned and famous lawyers and investment bankers that money can buy may give imperfect advice.

Lesson Number 2: Before you agree to indemnify people, ask yourself why they need indemnity in the first place. Marty Lipton's request that Texaco indemnify the Getty interests could have alerted Texaco's McKinley to the considerable risk he faced.

Lesson Number 3: Never engage in a jury trial if you can avoid it. If you can't avoid it, treat even the silliest-seeming jury trial with life-and-death seriousness. No one knows what a jury will do.

Lesson Number 4: Corporate shareholders do not require their fiduciaries to fight for matters of principle, but they get very testy when their financial interest is threatened. It is often wiser to settle, even if you are right.

Lesson Number 5: If you're going to negotiate at all, you must be prepared to respect your opponent's position. As of mid-April, that was a lesson that Hugh Liedtke and James Kinnear apparently still had not learned.

PART 3

The Sale Process

CHAPTER 10

Structuring Your Transaction

The following are the most common sale structures:

- sale of assets
- sale of stock
- mergers (direct, reverse, triangular, and forward)
- consolidations
- management agreements, licenses, leases, joint ventures, etc.

You should avoid management agreements, licenses, leases, and joint ventures with the potential buyer if you really want to sell your business.

Management agreements with the buyer, with no guarantee that a sale will ultimately occur, are particular "no-nos," unless you are desperate. A management agreement permits the buyer one long look at the seller's business in which the buyer will inevitably find warts to help drive down the ultimate selling price.

ASSETS SALES VS. STOCK SALES

A sale of your assets is one of the most common forms of structuring. Buyers prefer this structure since they can pick and choose what assets they want to acquire. A buyer may decide not to purchase your cash or accounts receivable and thereby reduce the buyer's financing requirements. Even more importantly, buyers can assume only certain disclosed liabilities of the seller and not assume any other liabilities.

This contrasts with a sale of stock in which the buyer in effect acquires, indirectly through stock ownership, all of your assets (both desired and undesired) and all of your liabilities (both known and unknown). Although it is possible to escrow a portion of the sale consideration to protect the buyer from unknown liabilities, many buyers are concerned that the escrow may not be sufficient to cover the potential unknown liabilities. There may also be tax advantages to a buyer of an asset sale over a stock sale, which are discussed in Chapter 11.

A stock sale is the preferable structuring from a seller's viewpoint. The seller can (with minor exceptions) obtain long-term capital gains treatment on the gain resulting from the sale of stock. The sale is less expensive to effectuate since there is no requirement to transfer individual assets and there is no potential sales tax (as is the case in some states on asset sales). All that is required is to assign the stock certificates to the buyer.

From the seller's viewpoint, an asset sale is probably the least desirable structure (assuming that the seller is not remaining in business). After the selling entity (the "target") receives cash or other consideration for its assets, the selling entity must pay (or make provision to pay) all remaining unassumed liabilities (including taxes resulting from the sale) prior to any distribution to shareholders.

If the board of directors of the selling entity distributes the sale consideration and any remaining unpurchased assets to its shareholders without paying (or making provision to pay) unassumed liabilities, the directors may have personal liability to these unpaid creditors.

The distribution of the full sale consideration from an asset sale could be held up for many years until litigation against the selling entity is settled and other contingent liabilities are resolved.

Under most state laws, if the selling corporation is formally dissolved, the unpaid creditors only have a short period of time (typically two years after formal dissolution) to assert their claims. Therefore, it is best to dissolve the selling corporation as soon as possible to start this statute of limitations on creditors.

Upon liquidation or dissolution, the sale consideration and any remaining unpurchased assets would be distributed to a liquidating trust of which you could be the trustee. The liquidating trust would pay all claims once they were resolved and distribute its remaining assets to shareholders.

TRAP WARNING If the selling corporation fails to formally dissolve, there is, depending upon state law, no short time limit on the assertion of claims by unpaid creditors against directors and shareholders. Therefore, after an asset sale (assuming you are not remaining in business), dissolution should occur as quickly as possible to commence the running of the statute of limitations.

There may be other disadvantages of an asset sale as opposed to a stock sale. As noted, in some states (such as California) an asset sale can trigger sales tax. However, many buyers insist upon this structure because of its advantages from their viewpoint.

A stock sale is generally preferred by buyers only when there are nontransferable assets in the selling entity, such as a nontransferable lease or license that does not contain a change-in-control clause. Buyers may also desire to purchase your stock when you have tax loss carryover (see Chapter 11).

MERGERS AND CONSOLIDATIONS

In a merger, all of the assets and liabilities of one corporation are transferred to the other corporation (the survivor
of the merger) by operation of law. The consideration
payable to the shareholders of each of the merging corporations is specified in an agreement or plan of merger. The
transfer of assets and liabilities automatically occurs when
the plan or agreement of merger is filed with the Secretary
of State or the Corporation Bureau of the state or states in
which the two corporations are incorporated. The plan or
agreement of merger may specify an effective merger date
that is later than the filing date if state law so permits. An
example of a plan of merger is contained in Appendix 7.

In contrast to an asset sale, which requires specific
bills of sale and assignments to transfer title to your assets,
the transfer of title occurs automatically by operation of
law on the effective date of the merger. No bills of sale or
assignments are normally necessary to transfer title. State
law specifically provides that the transfer occurs automatically on the merger effective date.

The problem with a merger is that it transfers to the survivor all of the assets (known or unknown) of the disappearing corporation and all of its liabilities (known or unknown).
The buyer may not wish to acquire all of your assets. More
importantly, the buyer does not want to assume unknown
liabilities you may have. Therefore, many buyers avoid
mergers and prefer to purchase only specific assets and to
assume only specified liabilities.

The following are different kinds of mergers that can
be effectuated:

- forward direct merger: buyer survives merger with target
- forward triangular merger: buyer's subsidiary survives
  merger with target
- reverse direct merger: target survives merger with buyer
- reverse triangular merger: target survives merger with
  buyer's subsidiary

The accompanying chart gives a pictorial description of a triangular merger.

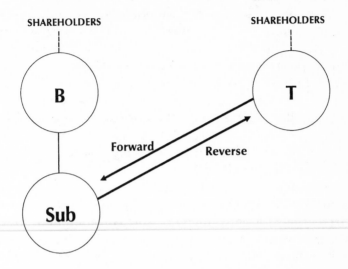

Consolidations are identical to mergers except that a newly formed third corporation survives the merger between the target and the buyer or between the target and the buyer's subsidiary.

Under most state laws, all of the shareholders of each party to the merger or consolidation can be forced, by a majority vote, to exchange their shares for the consideration specified in the agreement or plan of merger or consolidation. This includes any of the following:

- cash
- stock or other equity securities of the surviving entity or of a parent corporation of the surviving entity
- notes of the surviving entity or of a parent of the surviving entity
- an earnout payable in cash, stock, or notes
- any combination of the foregoing

Any objecting minority shareholders are usually given dissenters' rights of appraisal in these transactions. Dissenters' rights of appraisal entitle the dissenting minority shareholders to receive cash equal to the fair value of their stock in one of the parties to the merger or consolidation. This is true even though the plan or agreement of merger specifies that the shareholders of the same corporation are to receive stock or notes.

The fair value of the stock of the dissenter is determined by the court under a statutory procedure specified by state law, if the parties cannot otherwise agree.

An agreement and plan of merger is contained in Appendix 7. It specifies the consideration to be received by the shareholders of the target (the disappearing corporation), which is merged into a subsidiary of the buyer in a triangular forward merger. The consideration to be received by the target's shareholders is either common stock of the parent corporation (the buyer) of the survivor to the merger or cash as elected by each shareholder, subject to limits set forth in the agreement and plan of merger.

SUMMARY

The following summarizes the major advantages and disadvantages of each of the most common sale structures. Target refers to the entity that operates your business.

Sale of Assets

Primary advantages:
Step up in tax basis for buyer; no hidden liabilities acquired by buyer (but may have some carryover liabilities)

Primary disadvantages:
Nonassignable assets; potential sales tax; target's shareholder may pay double taxes and/or taxes at ordinary income rates (see Chapter 11); greater expense; target must be dissolved

Sale of Stock

Primary advantages:
Long-term capital gains to target's shareholders; mechanically simpler and less expensive; avoids problems of nonassignable assets (provided there is no "change-of-control" clause); avoids potential sales tax; retains target's unemployment tax rate (if favorable)

Primary disadvantages:
Hidden liabilities acquired by buyer, including tax, tort, and contract liabilities; retain target's unemployment tax rate (if unfavorable)

Mergers and Consolidations

Advantages:
All assets and liabilities transferred to survivor by operation of law; minority shareholder can be forced to sell by vote of majority shareholder (in contrast to a stock sale)

Disadvantages:
Unknown and contingent liabilities transferred; unwanted assets transferred (like a stock sale)

USING STRUCTURING TO SOLVE PROBLEMS

The following are four different problems that are common in sale transactions and how each can be solved by the structuring of the transaction.

Problem Number 1
Target has below market rate on leased property, and lease prohibits direct assignment by operation of the law.

Solution
Reverse direct merger or reverse triangular merger (provided there is no "change of control" clause in lease).

Problem Number 2
Target has minority shareholders who are opposed to sale.

Solution
Merger or consolidation or asset sale.

Problem Number 3
Target has large contingent liability.

Solution
Asset sale (does not work if specific assets sold are environmentally contaminated or if deemed fraudulent transfer).

Problem Number 4
Target has large federal income tax loss carryover that buyer wishes to preserve.

Solution
Purchase target's stock or reverse merger (direct or triangular), but normally limited yearly use of carryover postclosing to long-term federal interest rate multiplied by target's value at closing. (See Chapter 11.)

CHAPTER 11

Think After Taxes: Cash Flow to You

The combination of federal and state income taxes can take 43 percent or more of taxable income resulting from the sale of your business. Therefore, you should give careful consideration to methods of minimizing these taxes.

You must learn to think in terms of after-tax cash flow to yourself. To illustrate: suppose you had a $10 million cash offer and a $9 million cash offer for your business. Which should you take?

If you automatically answered the $10 million cash offer, you are wrong. You are thinking in *pretax dollars* instead of *after-tax cash flow*. The correct answer requires you to determine the after-tax cash flow to you of each offer.

A $9 million offer for your stock is better than a $10 million cash offer of which $3 million is for stock and $7 million is for a noncompete covenant and consulting agreement.

To prove that the $9 million offer is better, make the following assumptions:

- Assume a 30% combined federal and state tax rate on long-term capital gains
- Assume a 43% combined federal and state tax rate on ordinary income.

The following computation demonstrates that the $9 million cash offer creates after-tax cash flow to you of $6.3 million, compared with after-tax cash flow of only $6.09 million (ignoring the additional cost of self-employment taxes) from the $10 million cash offer.

Computation	
$9.0 million	**$10.0 million**
Less 30%, or $2.7 million	Less 30% of $3 million, or $0.900 million
	Less 43% of $7 million, or $3.010 million
Net $6.3 million	**Net $6.09 million**

C CORPORATIONS VS. S CORPORATIONS

Most businesses to be sold are conducted through corporations. Your after-tax cash flow from the sale of your business depends in part on whether your corporation is a so-called C corporation or a so-called Subchapter S corporation.

If your business is conducted as a sole proprietorship, general or limited partnership, limited liability company, or other tax flow-through entity, skip this section.

C Corporations

If you are unlucky enough to have a C corporation, you have two levels of tax that you will have to pay if you sell the assets of the corporation. The first is a tax at the corporate level on the gain the corporation has on the sale of the business assets. The second is a tax at the shareholder level on the net assets of the corporation received by the shareholders.

Assuming that all of the corporation's assets were sold and all of its liabilities assumed by the buyer, the assets distributed to shareholders would equal the gross sale proceeds to the corporation, less federal and state income taxes paid by the corporation. Combined federal and state income tax at the corporate level can be as high as 40 percent or more on the gain to the corporation.

To illustrate: assuming that the gross sale proceeds for the corporation assets are $1,000, and that the gain on the assets sold is taxable at ordinary income rates, the corporation will be left with $600 (assuming a 40 percent tax rate). When the $600 is then distributed to the shareholders, and again assuming the receipt of the $600 by the shareholders is all taxable as long-term capital gain at a 30 percent rate, the shareholders are left with $420.

Effectively, between the tax at the corporate level and the tax at the shareholder level, 58 percent of the $1,000 gain on the sale is paid in income taxes.

Your first reaction may be to say, "Well, why should I sell corporation assets? Let me just sell the stock of my C corporation and only pay a 28 percent federal long-term capital gains tax on the gain."

That is fine if you can get the buyer to agree. However, the buyer may not wish to acquire the stock of your corporation and be subjected to its hidden liabilities. Moreover, the buyer does not get a step up on the tax basis of depreciable assets of your C corporation if they buy your stock. If the buyer purchases your stock and then elects to step up the tax basis of your assets to equal the purchase price for your stock plus the corporation's liabilities, the buyer will have to pay the tax on the gain resulting from the step-up.

The net result is that buyers either will not purchase stock of C corporations or will reduce the purchase price for the stock to equal the loss of tax benefits. Either way it comes out of the seller's pocket.

To avoid a double tax, sellers of C corporations are increasingly asking that a significant portion of the consideration be paid to them in the form of consulting fees or an employment contract. This reduces the amount of the

consideration actually paid for the assets of the C corporation and effectively reduces the large income tax bite
resulting from two levels of tax. However, consulting fees
and salary are still subject to ordinary income tax rates as
well as employment taxes.

Any allocation of the purchase price to a covenant
not to compete, as opposed to a consulting fee or an
employment contract, may cause the buyer to reduce the
purchase price, since the buyer cannot obtain a current tax
deduction for a covenant not to compete. These payments
are treated as goodwill and are amortizable by the buyer
over a fifteen-year period.

Fifty Percent Exclusion

If you sell stock of your C corporation and your stock was
"qualified small-business stock" issued after August 10,
1993, and held for five years, 50 percent of your long-term
capital gain is not normally taxable (Section 1202 of Internal
Revenue Code). In effect, your top federal tax bracket is 14
percent (50 percent of 28 percent). The limit on the exclusion
is the greater of $10 million or 10 times the aggregate
adjusted basis for all "qualified small-business stock" issued
by the corporation and disposed of by you during a tax year.

"Qualified small-business stock" refers generally to a
corporation engaged in manufacture, wholesale, or retail
whose aggregate gross assets do not exceed $50 million
(subject to qualification and exceptions). The corporation
must meet active business requirements during substantially all of the period you held the stock.

The first qualified sales under this provision cannot be
made until August 10, 1998, since the stock must be initially
issued to you *after August 10, 1993 and held for five years.*

S Corporations

The major advantage of the S corporation is that it is not
subject for federal income tax purposes to a double tax

upon sale of its assets. There is typically no income tax at the corporate level (subject to certain exceptions) when the S corporation sells its assets. The only federal income tax is at the shareholder level on the gain realized by the corporation, which is then allocated to the shareholders in accordance with their proportionate shareholder interests.

Some states do not recognize S corporations, and in those states a double tax will apply for state income tax purposes upon the sale of your assets.

The nature of the gain allocable to the shareholders on the sale of the S corporation's assets depends upon the character of the assets that are sold. Capital assets held for more than one year will produce long-term capital gain, whereas items such as inventory and accounts receivable will produce ordinary income.

Allocating the Purchase Price to Lower Seller's Taxes

Let us assume that the buyer wants to purchase your corporation's assets and is not interested in purchasing your corporation's stock. The proper allocation of the purchase price to these assets can significantly reduce your income tax resulting from the sale. Therefore, it is important to understand the differing tax interests of you and the buyer.

It is in the buyer's interest to allocate the purchase price consideration to those assets that produce the most immediate tax benefit to the buyer. Accordingly, the buyer will want to allocate as much as possible to your inventory and to your accounts receivable, since these allocations reduce the buyer's taxable income and hence taxes at the earliest point in time.

For example, assume that you have on your books inventory that has a book value and a tax basis of $1.1 million, but that inventory has a retail market value of $2 million. It is in the buyer's interest to allocate as much as possible of the purchase price to your inventory, since when the inventory is sold for $2 million (presumably within the next year), this allocation will reduce the buyer's taxable income and taxes.

Although the buyer may desire to allocate $2 million of the purchase price to the inventory, the buyer's tax advisor will probably tell the buyer that the IRS would challenge such a high allocation, since it is unusual to pay retail for a bulk purchase of inventory. However, the buyer may well place a figure as high as $1.8 million on the inventory purchase, so that when the inventory is sold for $2 million the buyer will have only $200,000 in taxable income.

If the buyer allocated only the seller's book value of $1.1 million to the inventory and the buyer resold the inventory within one year, the buyer would have $900,000 of taxable income on the inventory resale.

A public company buyer might allocate only $1.1 million to the inventory in order to show higher accounting earnings. However, most buyers are interested in reducing income taxes and would use the higher allocation.

The following chart illustrates the discounted present value to the buyer of the allocation of $1 of purchase price consideration to different assets you may sell.

Discounted Present Value*
of Each $1 Tax Cash Flow to Buyer

Allocation to inventory and receivables (1-year return) = $.91

Allocation to goodwill (average 8-year return) = .47

Commercial real estate (average 20-year return) = .15

*Assuming 10 percent per annum compounded annually

It is in the seller's interest to allocate as much of the consideration as possible that is in excess of the tax basis to items that produce long-term capital gain to the seller. Under law, the long-term capital gain is taxed generally at a maximum combined federal and state rate of approximately 30 percent. In contrast, the top combined federal and state rate on ordinary income can be 43 percent or more.

The following are some of the capital assets of the corporation that normally produce long-term capital gain when sold and are not subject to so-called recapture of depreciation deductions at ordinary income rates:

- land
- buildings not depreciated by use of accelerated depreciation
- patent rights
- copyrights
- trademarks
- goodwill

Assume that the above assets do not have an aggregate fair market value that is sufficient to absorb the full purchase price (including any liabilities assumed by the buyer). The seller should next be interested in allocating the remaining purchase price consideration (including any liabilities assumed by the buyer) to the following group of depreciable assets even though a portion of the allocation over your tax basis may be ordinary income to the extent of depreciation deductions previously taken:

- buildings depreciated by use of accelerated depreciation rates
- machinery and equipment
- furniture and fixtures

Stock is a capital asset. Therefore, if the seller is able to persuade the buyer to purchase the stock of his corporation, all of the gain would be generally taxed at long-term capital gain rates.

As noted previously, the buyer may not want to purchase stock of the corporation because the buyer is thereby assuming hidden liabilities of the corporation. Even an escrow by the buyer of a portion of the purchase price may not be sufficient to protect the buyer from such hidden liabilities, which could exceed the amount of the escrow and might even exceed the full purchase price.

Occasionally, buyers must purchase the stock of a corporation (or use a reverse merger) because of nontransferable assets in the corporation, such as a long-term lease or other nontransferable contracts on very favorable terms (provided such leases or other contracts do not contain a change-of-control clause). However, in these situations, buyers typically seek to lower the purchase price to compensate themselves for the smaller tax benefits they receive and to reflect the higher tax benefits received by the seller.

If the buyer is successful in the negotiations in allocating the purchase price (including assumed liabilities) to assets that produce immediate tax benefits to the buyer, such a concession by the seller should add to the value of the business to the buyer. This is true because the buyer's after-tax future cash flow will be increased as a result of the seller's concession. Therefore, the seller should negotiate additional consideration to compensate the seller for this concession. This is particularly true if the allocation favoring the buyer increases the seller's taxes.

A typical allocation clause is contained in section I(D) of the agreement of sale contained in Appendix 6, involving the sale of the assets of a physical therapy center.

TAX-FREE EXCHANGES

A seller cannot have a tax-free exchange with the buyer unless the seller is willing to accept stock of the buyer for at least 50 percent of the total consideration. Although tax-free treatment is possible when less than 50 percent of the total consideration constitutes stock, the IRS, for ruling purposes, will not give you a favorable ruling unless the 50 percent test is satisfied. Unless you would like to litigate with the IRS, you should avoid transactions that are intended to be tax free unless at least 50 percent of the consideration is in stock.

If you receive cash or other forms of consideration other than stock of the buyer above the 50 percent threshold, the portion above 50 percent is taxable. To be 100 percent tax free, you will need 100 percent of the consideration in the form of stock of the buyer.

An example of a partial tax-free exchange is contained in Appendix 7. See Chapter 12 for tax-free exchanges with a public company.

VALUING TAX LOSS CARRYOVERS

Businesses that have an operating tax loss carryover should consider this carryover as an asset of the business. Under the Internal Revenue Code of 1986 (as amended), the buyer cannot acquire your tax loss carryover if the transaction is structured as a sale of assets or is deemed to be a sale of assets (e.g., a forward merger). The buyer must structure the transaction as sale of stock or a reverse merger (see Chapter 10).

Even if the transaction is structured to obtain the tax loss carryover, the buyer's ability to use the seller's loss carryover is subject to significant limitations if the buyer acquires more than 50 percent of your stock. Under these circumstances, the buyer is limited to using such portion of the tax loss carryover that equals (1) the long-term tax-exempt rate multiplied by (2) the value of your business on the date of closing.

The "long-term tax-exempt rate" is the highest of the adjusted federal long-term rates and is based on the average market yield on outstanding marketable U.S. debt instruments with remaining periods to maturity exceeding nine years. This rate is determined monthly by the Internal Revenue Service.

For example, assume that your business is being purchased for $10 million, that you have a $30 million loss carryover, and that the federal long-term interest rate is 5 percent per annum. The buyer is limited to using $500,000 of your tax loss carryover (5 percent times $10 million) in each year to offset the buyer's taxable income. This results in the spreading out of the buyer's ability to utilize the loss and significantly decreases its current discounted value to the buyer.

In addition, tax loss carryovers cannot extend for more than fifteen years after the date that they were incurred. Thus, the fifteen years may run out before the tax loss carryover is fully absorbed by the buyer. In the above example, the buyer would in fifteen years utilize a maximum of $7.5 million (15 times $500,000 per year) of the $30 million carryover.

The 50 percent test is subject to a three-year look-back period. Thus, you cannot avoid the 50 percent test if the buyer acquires 50 percent of your stock in one year and the balance of your stock the next year.

Likewise, giving the buyer options to purchase your stock or securities convertible into your stock does not prevent the tripping of the 50 percent test, since the IRS may treat these options and conversion rights as if they were exercised for purposes of applying the 50 percent test.

The only practical method of avoiding the tripping of the 50 percent test is for the buyer to acquire 50 percent or less of the stock and value of your business and to wait for more than three years to buy the rest of the stock. Few buyers are willing to structure their purchase in this manner.

Some major accounting firms have suggested having the buyer acquire 50 percent or less of the target's (seller's) stock and giving the target a loan for the balance of the purchase price that is due three years and one day after the closing. The theory is that the target would not have the funds to pay the loan and the buyer can receive the balance of the target's stock in payment of the loan. Again, it takes a very aggressive buyer to engage in this type of transaction.

CHAPTER 11 BANKRUPTCY

The 50 percent test does not apply in a Chapter 11 bankruptcy proceeding provided the shareholders of the old loss corporation and qualified creditors own 51 percent of the voting power and value of the stock of the new loss corporation. *Qualified creditors* refers to persons to whom the corporation was indebted provided either (1) the indebtedness was held by the creditor at least eighteen months before the Chapter 11 filing or (2) the indebtedness is held in the ordinary course of the trade or business of the old loss corporation and is held at all times by the same person.

If your company is in Chapter 11, the potential buyer can acquire the debt from your creditors who held their indebtedness for more than eighteen months before your filing and can then receive your stock in exchange for that debt in a Chapter 11 plan of reorganization, all without tripping the 50 percent test.

This area is very complex, and there can be some minor loss of tax attributes (including loss carryovers). However, Chapter 11 does provide an interesting vehicle to permit the preservation of tax loss carryovers. Only sophisticated buyers will consider this type of transaction.

CHAPTER 12

Selling to a Public Company

Public companies are ideal buyers. This is particularly true of companies that have just had a public offering and need a home for their cash.

Unlike private companies, public companies are under pressure from securities analysts and from the public market to increase their current earnings. Consequently, they will make decisions that will maximize their future reported accounting earnings even though this may cost them additional income taxes.

Because tax benefits are of lesser significance than accounting earnings to a public company, it is easier for the seller to negotiate a more favorable after-tax cash flow from the purchase price. For example, it is not unusual for public companies to suggest larger allocations of the purchase price to capital assets with a long useful life. Capital assets that can be depreciated by the buyer over long periods of time produce very low depreciation charges to reduce the buyer's reported income.

Obviously, the seller prefers these allocations since the seller obtains the benefit of long-term capital gain for all or a portion of the allocation.

ACCEPTING PUBLIC COMPANY STOCK

If you accept the public company's stock for all or a portion of the sale price, you have made a major investment decision. Since a large percentage of your wealth will likely be tied up in the buyer's stock, you will not want to accept stock consideration unless it has the following characteristics:

- The buyer must be a publicly held company that is sufficiently well capitalized and has sufficient growth prospects so that you will not be taking major economic risks in accepting the buyer's stock.
- There must be a liquid market for the stock, i.e., the stock is publicly traded in a recognized marketplace and is freely tradable.

TRAP WARNING There are many stocks traded on Small Cap NASDAQ, the NASDAQ National Stock Market, and other exchanges that have inadequate trading activity. The market for these stocks is so thin that any significant sell order reduces the market price. Avoid these stocks and so-called pink sheet stocks and bulletin board stocks.

Even if the buyer is a large New York Stock Exchange company, you may wish to consider whether it is wise having so much of your wealth in one specific stock. The principle of diversification would suggest that it is not.

Even if the buyer looks like it is going to do well in the future, no one can tell. Likewise, if the industry of which the buyer is a part or the stock market as a whole does poorly, that can have disastrous results on your personal wealth.

Many public companies use their stock to make acquisitions because of its high price-to-earnings multiplier. For example, if the public company's stock is selling for 25 times their trailing twelve-months' earnings, and they can purchase with stock your company for 10 times its earnings, their stock price would presumably be increased by the fact that your earnings are now multiplied by 25, whereas they only paid you a multiplier of 10. This is particularly true if they use pooling accounting for the acquisition, as discussed below.

TRAP WARNING A favorite negotiating ploy of public companies is to value your business at a high price and then give you their stock, which is overly inflated in value, as the sale consideration. If their stock price subsequently drops before you can sell it, you may have severely undervalued your business.

If you become a large shareholder of the buyer, you may be required to hold a substantial portion of the buyer's stock for an extended period in order to preserve the tax-free status of the exchange.

If you decide on a tax-free exchange, make certain that the buyer's stock is fully registered and freely tradable at all times after the closing of the sale.

If the stock is not freely tradable at all times (see the next section, on pooling accounting), the stock is not worth its current price. Indeed, any valuation expert would require a significant discount from the current trading price in computing the market value of restricted stock. Depending upon the nature of the restriction, this discount can be as much as 33⅓ percent to 50 percent of the trading price and even more than 50 percent if the stock is very volatile.

Unless you receive fully registered stock at the closing of the sale or you can demand registration of your stock, you will generally have to wait two years before selling the stock under Rule 144 of the Securities Act of 1933. Even after two years, your ability to sell under Rule 144 is restricted by the availability of current information about the buyer, and there will be limitations on the amount you sell and the manner in which you sell.

After three years from the closing, and provided you have not become a director of the buyer or assumed any other control relationship with the buyer, you may sell even unregistered stock without restriction.

Under Rule 144, you may every three months sell the greater of 1 percent of the outstanding buyer's stock or one week's average trading volume, during the preceding four weeks.

TRAP WARNING Sellers who take 100 percent of the purchase price in buyer's stock and who do not have freely tradable stock are taking a huge risk with their personal wealth. Avoid these transactions like the plague. The only possible exception is if you receive a "market floor" clause (not possible with pooling accounting), which gives you more stock if the trading price falls. Receiving more of the buyer's stock under a "market floor" clause does not adequately protect you from buyer's bankruptcy or from dramatic trading price drops during the period the stock is not fully tradable.

INTRODUCTION TO POOLING ACCOUNTING

Many public companies also engage in acquisitions that can be accounted for by the pooling method of accounting. Pooling accounting permits the public company buyer to reflect the seller's preclosing earnings as if they belonged to the buyer and permits the buyer to avoid stepping up its depreciation and amortization charges. This permits the buyer to show higher reported earnings.

This method of accounting is discussed in more detail below. If you are considering selling to a public company, the following is suggested reading. The pooling rules dictate the structure of its transaction. By fully understanding pooling accounting, you can better negotiate terms with a public company buyer.

POOLINGS VS. PURCHASES

There are two methods of accounting for acquisitions by one corporation of another:

- purchase accounting
- pooling accounting

All acquisitions that do not satisfy the strict requirements for pooling accounting are accounted for by the use of purchase accounting. Pooling accounting requires, among other things, that the acquisition consideration consist solely of the voting stock of the buyer. Therefore, any acquisition in which the purchase price consideration involves cash or notes, whether or not it also involves voting stock, is accounted for by the purchase method of accounting.

In applying purchase or pooling accounting, the form of the acquisition is ignored. Thus, purchase or pooling accounting will apply whether or not the purchase is in the form of the purchase of stock or assets, or in the form of a merger, consolidation, or otherwise. Accountants view each of these acquisitions as involving the purchase of assets of the selling corporation for accounting purposes.

Under purchase accounting, the acquisition consideration plus any assumed liabilities are allocated to the assets of the acquired corporation in accordance with the fair market value of these assets. To the extent that the acquisition consideration plus any assumed liabilities exceed the fair market value of the acquired assets, the excess is treated as goodwill. For purposes of the buyer's income statement, under purchase accounting the assets are deemed acquired on the date of closing, and income earned by the buyer prior to the date of closing is not considered part of the buyer's income.

The theory of pooling accounting is that both entities are treated as if they were historically one business. Pursuant to this theory, the buyer can reflect the income of the acquired entity accruing *before* the acquisition date as if such income belonged to the buyer as long as the closing is held on or before the last day of the buyer's fiscal year. Likewise, the book value of the assets of the acquired entity is carried over to the acquiring entity.

Thus, under pooling accounting, the buyer need not increase the book value of the assets acquired to reflect their fair market value. The fair market value is likely to be much higher than the book value of the assets on the seller's books. *This permits the buyer to show higher future income under pooling accounting, since depreciation and amortization expense is not increased to reflect the fair market value of depreciable assets and there is no need to reduce the buyer's future income by goodwill charges (i.e., the excess of the consideration paid over the fair market value of the assets acquired).*

The ability to use pooling accounting permits management of the buyer significant control over accounting results. For example, pooling accounting permits a buyer with poor income for a fiscal year to dramatically increase its own reported income by effectuating an acquisition of a very profitable company before the end of its fiscal year. The buyer can reflect the past income of the acquiree as if the income were earned by the buyer.

Example

The net assets of T Corp. (the seller) are acquired by B Corp. for $1 million on December 31, 1996, the last day of B Corp.'s fiscal year. The net income of T Corp. for the full year was $100,000.

T Corp. Net Assets
December 31, 1996

Assets[A]	$1,000,000
Liabilities	400,000
Net worth	$600,000
Composed of:	
Capital stock	$200,000
Retained earnings	400,000
	$600,000

A. Includes fixed assets (10-year remaining life) with a book value of $100,000 and a fair market value of $400,000.

Balance Sheets
December 31, 1996 (000s omitted)

	T Corp.	B Corp.	Pooling of Interests	Purchase[1]
Assets				
Current assets	$900	$2,000	$2,900	$2,900
Fixed assets—net	100	1,000	1,100	1,400
Other assets		100	100	100
Goodwill				100
Total assets	$1,000	$3,100	$4,100	$4,500
Liabilities				
Current liabilities	$400	$1,200	$1,600	$1,600
Shareholder equity				
Capital stock	200	300	500	500
Paid in capital				800
Retained earnings	400	1,600	2,000	1,600
	600	1,900	2,500	2,900
Total liabilities and shareholder equity	$1,000	$3,100	$4,100	$4,500

1. Reflects the allocation of total consideration of $1 million in stock plus $400,000 in assumed liabilities to the T Corp. assets, which are then combined with B Corp.'s assets

Statement of Income

for the Year Ended December 31, 1996

(000s omitted)

	T Corp.	B Corp.	Pooling of Interests	Purchase[1]
Sales	$2,000	$5,000	$7,000	$5,000
Cost of sales	1,400	3,500	4,900	3,500
Gross profit	600	1,500	2,100	1,500
Selling, general and administrative expense	450	900	1,350	900
Income before taxes	150	600	750	900
Income taxes	50	300	350	300
Net income	$100	$300	$400	$300

1. Reflects the allocation of total consideration of $1 million in stock plus $400,000 in assumed liabilities to the T Corp. assets, which are then combined with B Corp.'s assets

The acquisition is effected by the issuance of 200,000 shares of $1 par value per share of common stock, with a total market value of $5 per share. Prior to the acquisition, B Corp. had 300,000 shares outstanding, with a par value of $1 per share.

In this example, although the consideration paid was the same, purchase accounting increased the net worth of B Corp. by $1 million, whereas under the pooling method the net worth increased $600,000. In addition, the purchase transaction recorded goodwill of $100,000 and an additional $300,000 of fixed assets.

The effect on income for 1996 is also significant. B Corp. reports $100,000 of T Corp.'s income in 1996 in the pooling transaction. In the purchase transaction none of T Corp.'s earnings are reported as income because the acquisition took place on the last day of the year. Furthermore, the reported income for subsequent years will be lower for the transaction recorded as a purchase. Under the purchase transaction, B Corp. will record higher depreciation expense for the next ten years, and for up to forty years it will record the additional expense resulting from the amortization of goodwill.

CRITERIA FOR A POOLING OF INTERESTS

The twelve specific criteria that, if met, require pooling accounting are the following:

(1) A corporation offers and issues only common stock with rights identical to those of the majority of its outstanding voting common stock in exchange for substantially all of the voting common stock of another corporation at the date the combination is consummated.

"Substantially all" is defined as meaning at least 90 percent of the outstanding voting common stock. Specific requirements are provided for the treatment of intercorporate investments of the combining corporations. These conditions are designed to prevent abuses of the 90 percent test. One of the situations they are designed to prevent is one in which either corporation buys shares of the other's stock prior to the initiation or consummation of the merger, thereby reducing the number of shares that would be issued—effectively using cash to account for a larger portion of the combination.

The 90 percent requirement permits up to 10 percent of the shares to be bought for cash or other consideration. This allows the corporation to purchase fractional shares or buy out dissident stockholders. However, no pro rata distribution is allowed.

The combination can also be effected through a transfer of net assets rather than the acquisition of the capital stock. There are specific tests to ensure that the substance of the 90 percent criterion is met.

(2) Each of the combining corporations is autonomous and has not been a subsidiary or division of another corporation within two years before the plan of combination is initiated.

The two-year rule does not apply to a new corporation incorporated within the preceding two years unless the new corporation was a successor to a part of a corporation.

A plan is initiated when the major terms of the plan, including the ratio of exchange of stock, have been agreed to and the stockholders of any of the combining corporations have been informed of the terms.

The substance of this condition is that, generally, a division or a subsidiary of another company cannot be a party to a pooling of interests. Two exceptions are the following:

(a) Divestiture of a business to comply with an order of a governmental agency.

(b) A wholly owned subsidiary that distributes voting stock of its parent to effect the combination. Thus, the buyer can form a wholly owned subsidiary to effectuate the purchase without violating the pooling rules.

Under this criterion, a company that is spun off from a corporation could not be included in a pooling of interests for two years.

(3) The combination must be resolved when a plan is consummated and no provision of the plan relating to the issue of securities is pending.

This precludes a combination that has a contingent purchase price based on a market price guarantee (a "market floor" clause) or an "earnout" contingency from being recorded as a pooling.

Shares placed in escrow at the closing for such purpose are considered the same as shares contingently issued after this closing.

Contingency agreements are permitted for "general management representations" or to adjust the number of shares issued for the later settlement of a contingency at an amount different from that recorded by the acquired corporation. The maximum period permitted for "general management representations" generally runs to the time of the issuance of the first audit report of the acquired corporation. The requirement effectively eliminates the liability of the seller for breaches of general warranties or representations discovered by the buyer after the first audit report.

In pooling transactions, escrows are usually limited to 10 percent of the purchase price, whereas in purchase transactions there is no limit on amount of escrows.

(4) None of the combining corporations changes the equity interest of the voting common stock in contemplation of effecting the combination either within two years before the plan of combination is initiated or between the dates the combination is initiated and consummated.

This condition would, among other things, prevent a corporation from redeeming shares of a shareholder or recapitalizing the corporation in order to create a new class of stock. A corporation is permitted to pay normal dividends to shareholders. The normality of the dividends is determined in relation to earnings and to the previous dividend policy.

(5) Treasury stock acquired within a two-year period generally cannot be used in a pooling of interests. An exception is allowed if the amount is not material in relation to the total number of shares issued to effect the combination. Treasury shares are not material if they are within the 10 percent margin, which is available in all poolings to accommodate cash purchases and minority interests that remain outstanding.

In the absence of persuasive evidence to the contrary, there is a presumption that all acquisition of treasury stock during the two years preceding the date of the plan of combination is initiated and between initiation and consummation was made in contemplation of effecting a business combination to be accounted for as a pooling.

Under certain circumstances, there are specific purposes for which treasury shares may be reacquired during this period. Lacking the specific purposes, the combination would be accounted for by the purchase method of accounting, regardless of whether treasury stock or unissued shares or both are issued in the combination. The specific purposes include, among others, shares acquired for stock options and compensation plans, convertible debentures, and convertible stock.

(6) The ratio of the interest of an individual common shareholder to those of other common shareholders in a combining corporation remains the same as a result of the exchange of stock.

The relative interests of individual shareholders in each of the combining corporations must not be realigned by the exchange of securities.

(7) The voting rights to which the common stock ownership interests in the resulting combined corporation are entitled and exercisable only by the shareholders.

There cannot be any voting trusts created as a condition of the acquiring corporation that would prevent a shareholder from voting his shares of stock.

(8) Each of the combining corporations is independent of the other combining corporations.

A combining corporation is not independent if it holds investments in any of the combining corporations of more than 10 percent of the outstanding voting common stock of any combining corporation.

This is another condition provided to prevent the possibility of assets being used to reduce the shares outstanding of either corporation, thereby requiring that less common stock be issued to effect the combination.

(9) The combination is effected in a single transaction or is completed in accordance with a specific plan within one year after the plan is initiated. This condition prevents prolonged step transactions in which stock can be acquired under different terms over a period of time.

The last three conditions relate to the absence of the planned transactions.

(10) The combined corporation does not agree directly or indirectly to retire or reacquire all or part of the common stock issued to effect the combination.

This condition should not apply to the usual type of shareholders' agreement that some closely held corporations have, whereby the corporation may be obligated to acquire shares of stock of a shareholder under certain conditions and circumstances. In that instance, the acquiring corporation should be able to reacquire the shares based on the shareholders' agreement without barring pooling treatment.

(11) The combined corporation does not enter into other financial arrangements for the benefit of the former shareholders of the acquired corporation—e.g., guarantee of loans secured by the stock issued.

(12) The combined corporation does not intend or plan to dispose of a significant part of the assets of the combining corporations within two years after the combination, other than disposals in the ordinary course of business of the formerly separate corporations and to eliminate duplicate facilities or excess capacity.

Criteria 10 and 11 are designed to prevent the corporation from using its own funds to pay for part or all of the acquisitions, and criterion 12 is intended to provide for continuity of the business.

SEC RULES ON POOLINGS

The Securities and Exchange Commission (SEC) has announced in Accounting Series Release number 130 that pooling-of-interest accounting requires that no affiliate of either company in the business combination "sells or in any other way reduces his risk relative to any common shares received in the business combination until such time as financial results covering at least 30 days of post merger combined operations have been published." (See also Accounting Series Release number 135.) The term *affiliate* refers to persons in a control relationship with the buyer or seller such as a director, officer, or significant shareholder.

De minimis exceptions are permitted by SEC Staff Accounting Bulletin number 76. To be viewed as "de minimis," (1) the sales by an affiliate must not be greater than 10 percent of the affiliate's precombination (or equivalent postcombination) shares, and (2) the aggregate sales by all affiliates of a combination company must not exceed the equivalent of 1 percent of that company's precombination outstanding shares. Furthermore, the staff will generally not raise a question as the result of charitable contributions or bona fide gifts; however, the recipients of such gifts would have to hold the shares for the above-referenced thirty-day period.

For example, if the buyer is a calendar year public company, and the closing of the pooling transaction occurs June 1, 1996, the buyer would not be publishing thirty days of combined operation until the publication of the nine-month financial report for the period ending September 30, 1996. This is because the six-month financial report for the period ending June 30, 1996, would contain only twenty-nine days of combined operations, i.e., June 2, 1996, through June 30, 1996.

TRAP WARNING The timing of the closing of a pooling transaction is crucial to the length of the risk sharing by the seller, as noted in the above example. The closing date should be carefully negotiated by the seller's shareholders so as to minimize the period of the pooling restriction.

If the pooling transaction were to have closed on May 31, 1996, the seller's shareholders (i.e., T Corp.'s shareholders) could sell as soon as the six-month report had been published, because the six-month report would have contained thirty days of combined operations. This assumes, of course, either that the shares given to T Corp.'s shareholders are registered under the Securities Act of 1933 or that the sale is exempt from such registration.

CHAPTER 13

Selling a Publicly Held Company or a Control Block

If your company is already publicly held, there are special problems applicable to its future sale.

These special problems are as follows:

- Any leak of your sales decision to the trading markets will usually result in a run-up of your market price. This is because speculators will be anticipating the receipt of a control premium over the normal trading price as a result of the potential future sale. If the leak is attributable to the company or its directors, officers, or employees, you will be forced to issue a press release to inform the trading markets of your sale decision—even though you would prefer not to announce it.
- Any run-up in the market price of your stock as a result of a leak may discourage potential buyers who are not willing to pay a price that equals the overall market value of your company. However, some of these discouraged buyers might otherwise be preferable buyers from your company's cultural or other perspective.
- Once a sale decision is made, some states, such as Delaware, require the directors to act as "auctioneers" to maximize the price, especially if there are competing

bidders. This "auctioneer duty" may not be in your interest if you would prefer for cultural or other reasons a particular buyer who does not offer the highest price. One solution is to reincorporate your company well in advance of the sale target date in a state that does not impose an auctioneer duty (e.g., Pennsylvania).

- Delaware, where many public companies are incorporated, imposes a duty of "candor" on the directors. The full parameters of this duty of candor are unclear in a sale situation; however, this duty may force directors to make disclosure of the sale decision and major events in the negotiations prematurely, thereby interfering with the sale process. A possible solution is to reincorporate outside of Delaware well in advance of the sale target date.

- Any decision to withhold information from the trading markets of the negotiation of a potential sale can create Rule 10b-5 liability for the directors under the so-called probability/magnitude test adopted by the U.S. Supreme Court. This test requires the directors to weigh the magnitude of the event against the probability of its occurrence in making disclosure decisions. In view of the vagueness of this test, it is wise to maintain a substantial amount of director and officer liability insurance coverage before commencing the sale process.

CONTROL PREMIUMS

The law in most states generally permits the holder of a control block to receive a premium for the block over and above the price paid to all other shareholders. This is true whether the company is public or private.

The American Law Institute has articulated this rule and its exceptions in the following statement contained in section 5.16 of the 1994 version of the American Law Institute's *Principles of Corporate Governance: Analysis and Recommendations:*

A controlling shareholder . . . has the same right to dispose of voting equity securities . . . as any other shareholder, including the right to dispose of those securities for a price that is not made proportionally available to other shareholders, but the controlling shareholder does not satisfy the duty of fair dealing to the other shareholders if:

(a) The controlling shareholder does not make disclosure concerning the transaction . . . to other shareholders with whom the controlling shareholder deals in connection with the transaction; or

(b) It is apparent from the circumstances that the purchaser is likely to violate the duty of fair dealing . . . in such a way as to obtain a significant financial benefit from the purchaser or an associate.

It is clear that 51 percent of the outstanding stock is a control block. It is not clear how much less than 51 percent of the outstanding stock will constitute a control block for purposes of permitting you to receive a control premium. Nor is it clear that you can receive a control premium if you own 30 percent and your spouse owns 21 percent. Therefore, it would be in your interest to be certain that you have 51 percent of the outstanding stock registered either in your name alone or in your name and your spouse's name as tenants by the entireties.

The SEC's so-called "all holders rule" requires that a buyer making a tender offer for the stock of a publicly held company (i.e., a company whose stock is registered under section 12 of the Securities Exchange Act of 1934) offer the same price to each shareholder. However, the all holders rule does not prevent the buyer from privately negotiating with you for a price that includes a control premium and then launching a tender offer at a lower price.

Any control premium that is received in public company acquisition is usually subjected to litigation. Therefore, great care should be exercised in structuring this type of transaction.

CHAPTER 14

Selling to Your Own Employees or to an ESOP

It is not unusual during the sale process to receive an expression of interest from a group of key employees. Indeed, you may, through feelings of loyalty and camaraderie, prefer your key employees to be the buyer, even though they are not necessarily the highest bidder.

The primary difficulty in selling to key employees is that they usually lack the capital and require you to finance them. Moreover, once your key employees become active bidders, they will not necessarily be as cooperative with other potential buyers who are willing to pay a higher price and do not need you to finance them.

MBO AND LBO

If your business has the cash flow or assets to support a leveraged recapitalization (see Chapter 19), your key employees can probably find institutional financing for a management buyout (MBO) or a leveraged buyout (LBO). The only practical difference between the two is that in an MBO the management receives much more equity and generally leads the transaction. Even in an LBO it is not unusual for management to obtain at least 5 percent to 10 percent of the equity. An equity position of 30 percent or more is not unheard of in an MBO.

For your employees to locate institutional financing for an MBO or LBO, your business must be large enough to attract institutional lenders and investors. Typically, these institutional lenders and investors will not want to structure a transaction involving less than $5 million to $10 million in senior debt. Senior debt is unsubordinated debt which may or may not be collateralized.

Federal income tax law changes adopted in 1991 have made MBOs and LBOs that require annual interest payments of more than $5 million (subject to reduction) less attractive by denying interest deductions for these excess interest payments. These MBOs and LBOs typically involve $40 million to $50 million or more in order to create an annual interest payment of approximately $5 million.

As discussed more fully in Chapter 19, the senior institutional lenders will typically lend on an asset or cash flow basis to your company to permit the repurchase of your stock with the proceeds of the loan. If your company has excellent growth prospects but does not have the assets or cash flow to satisfy senior institutional lenders, mezzanine lenders (typically unsecured lenders and subordinated lenders) or investors and possibly equity funds might be interested in financing the MBO or LBO.

Great care must be taken to be certain that your company has enough cash after the repurchase of your stock to pay its debts in the ordinary course of business and that it is adequately capitalized. If not, in the event of a subsequent bankruptcy, the trustee in bankruptcy or trade creditors will challenge the transaction as a fraudulent transfer.

If your key employees are able to obtain institutional financing for an MBO or LBO, this probably means you could obtain institutional financing for a leveraged recapitalization. In a leveraged recapitalization, which is discussed in Chapter 19, you retain control of your company and receive some cash for some of your stock from the money supplied by the institutional lenders and investors. Of course, thereafter you must work in a highly leveraged environment and with significant restrictions on your operations.

If you are not willing to work under these conditions, an MBO or LBO with your key employees would be a reasonable choice, since, unlike in a leveraged recapitalization, you could receive cash for 100 percent of your stock.

On some MBOs and LBOs, the senior lenders and investors may require you to accept a portion of the purchase price for your stock in deferred payments, with the balance paid in cash at the closing. Typically, these deferred payments are evidenced by a note that is specifically subordinated to the senior lender's debt. Consequently, in the event of a default on the senior debt, you may never be paid your note.

The usual reason for requiring you to accept a subordinated note for a portion of the purchase price is that otherwise there will not be enough cash flow to satisfy the senior lender cash flow coverage ratios (see Chapter 19).

To protect yourself under these circumstances, you may try to negotiate the following:

- a right to resume control of the company in the event of a default until any defaults are cured
- a right of first refusal on any sale of the company by the senior lenders
- a lien on all assets and stock subordinate only to the senior lender

ESOP FINANCING

If you have a large annual payroll, an employee stock ownership plan (ESOP) might be used to purchase your stock. An ESOP is a type of qualified retirement plan that invests primarily in your company's stock.

From your viewpoint, the primary advantage of an ESOP is that a qualifying sale is free of any federal income tax and you can roll the cash you receive into a diversified portfolio of investments. Here is how is works.

- You sell anywhere from 30% to 100% of all outstanding stock to the ESOP.
- Your company must not be publicly traded.
- If you held your stock for three or more years prior to the sale, there is no federal income tax on your gain if you use the cash to purchase securities of most U.S. corporations.

For example, you can use the cash from the ESOP sale to purchase a diversified portfolio of blue-chip corporate debt securities, preferred stock, or common stock. Thus, you can acquire debt securities of the baby-bells (for example, Bell Atlantic), preferred stock of Exxon, and common stock of Microsoft—all without paying any federal income tax on the sale and rollover into the diversified portfolio.

The only limitation on your portfolio is that all of the investments must be in U.S. corporations that derive not more than 25 percent of their gross receipts from passive investment income (e.g., a mutual fund) and that use more than 50 percent of their assets in the active conduct of a trade or business. Most of the blue-chip companies will qualify under this standard.

A qualified cash sale to an ESOP is thus far more advantageous to you than a cash sale for the same price to an unaffiliated buyer or even a tax-free merger. For example, in a tax-free merger you receive stock of only one company—all of your eggs are in that one basket. In order to diversify yourself, you must sell that stock and pay a tax and then reinvest the after-tax money into a diversified portfolio.

In contrast, the qualified ESOP sale permits you to achieve a diversified portfolio without ever paying any federal income tax.

An ESOP has other advantages as well. An ESOP can usually borrow from a bank more cheaply than your company if the ESOP holds more than 50 percent of your stock. This is because the bank can exclude from its taxable income 50 percent of the interest the bank receives on the ESOP loan. This typically results in banks being willing to lend to an ESOP at below the prime rate of interest.

In general, the company's contribution to an ESOP is deductible for federal income taxes, but the deduction is limited to 25 percent of your annual payroll (including other qualified plans) plus interest on the ESOP loan. Thus, if your company's annual payroll is $10 million and your company has no other qualified plans, your company can contribute $2.5 million a year to the ESOP (plus any interest on ESOP loans).

This means that the principal amortization on the bank loan to the ESOP loan can equal as much as $2.5 million per year. If the ESOP repurchased your stock for $12.5 million, the ESOP could finance the purchase with a five-year level principal amortizing loan requiring principal paydown of $2.5 million per year. This assumes, of course, that your business has the cash flow to make contributions to the ESOP sufficient to permit the ESOP to pay principal debt service of $2.5 million per year plus interest. Since the contributions to the ESOP are deductible by the company for federal income tax purposes, including the amount used to pay the principal of the ESOP loan, the cash flow of the company is increased by the benefit of these tax deductions.

The only limit on the duration of the ESOP loan is what lenders are willing to provide (assuming stock collateral is released from the loan in proportion to principal and interest payments). If you could obtain a ten-year level principal amortizing loan in the above example, the ESOP could repurchase your stock for $25 million, provided it was worth that much.

If you pay dividends on your stock, the dividend paid to the ESOP on the stock it holds may be tax deductible for federal income tax purposes if certain conditions are met.

From your viewpoint, an ESOP sale is ideal if the following are true:

- You sell 100% of your stock.
- The sale is all cash.
- The ESOP sale price is the same price that an unaffiliated buyer would pay.

If any of the above is untrue, the advantages of selling to the ESOP must be balanced against the disadvantages.

For example, if you only sell 30 percent of your stock to the ESOP, rather than 100 percent, you may wind up some day with minority shareholders. Generally, when your employees retire they have the absolute right to receive their portion of the ESOP's stock ownership in your company. They also will have a right to "put" the stock to your company or the ESOP, thereby forcing the company or the ESOP to repurchase it for cash. Your company or the ESOP might not be able to afford the repurchase, particularly if a large group of employees retire at the same time and "put" all of their stock.

Most employees who retire will not want to keep your stock. Those who do keep the stock can be prevented from selling the stock to outsiders without giving your company a right of first refusal. You can also adopt a bylaw preventing nonemployees from holding stock.

If you do not receive all cash from the ESOP upon the sale of your stock and instead take a note, you are still at the risk of the business. The ESOP funding to pay the note depends upon the cash flow of the company. Moreover, unlike a note which you receive from an unaffiliated buyer, you will probably not be able to obtain a guarantee of repayment from anyone other than your own company.

The stock you sold to the ESOP can also serve as collateral for the note.

An ESOP can also be costly to maintain because of the bookkeeping and the necessity for yearly, or at least frequent, appraisals. Typically, an ESOP appraisal can be obtained for $5,000 a year if you are not too picky about the appraiser. The bookkeeping costs can easily run another $5,000 to $7,500 per year.

Even if you do not sell 100 percent of your stock to the ESOP, the ESOP can still be used by an unaffiliated buyer to sweeten your after-tax cash flow. For example, an unaffiliated buyer might purchase 70 percent of your stock and have you sell the remaining 30 percent to an ESOP with a tax-free rollover.

INTERNAL CASH FLOW ACQUISITIONS

If you want to sell to key employees and they cannot obtain outside financing, you may structure a sale that permits them to use internally generated cash flow to pay the purchase price.

You could sell your stock to your company in exchange for deferred installments of the purchase price. Your employees would be given the right to purchase small amounts of stock, with their own funds, through payroll deductions, or both. You have to protect yourself against default through liens on the stock you sold and on the assets of your business.

If your company is an S corporation and has never been a C corporation, you can sell your stock back to your company slowly until your key employees' stock constitutes a majority of the outstanding stock. The price paid to you would be treated as long-term capital gains (assuming that you held the stock for more than one year).

However, if your company is or was previously a C corporation, a slow sale of your stock may produce ordinary income to you equal to the earnings and profits of the C corporation. To avoid this result and to obtain long-term capital gain, you may have to sell all of your stock at once back to your company or at least create a "substantially disproportionate redemption."

To create a substantially disproportionate redemption, you must after the redemption own less than 50 percent of the combined voting power of all classes of stock entitled to vote, and the ratio of your voting stock to all voting stock after the redemption must be less than 80 percent of the same ratio before the redemption. Thus, if before the redemption you owned 100 percent of all voting stock, you must own not more than 49 percent after the redemption. If you own 60 percent before the redemption, you must own less than 48 percent after the redemption. In computing these percentages, you are deemed to constructively own the stock of other related persons and entities, including your spouse and children.

Selling to your key employees who use internally generated cash flow to pay the purchase price is a dangerous method of selling your business. You are still at the risk of the business to receive your full purchase price. Such a sale should only be attempted if you have no ability to sell to outsiders or you feel such loyalty to your key employees that you are willing to assume these risks

PART 4

Sale Terms

CHAPTER 15

Deferred Purchase Price Payments: How to Become the Buyer's Banker

Although you would prefer to have the full purchase price paid at closing in cash, it is not unusual for the buyer to insist upon deferred payments of a portion of the purchase price. In effect, you are lending your money to the buyer. If this occurs, you must think like a banker.

Bankers do not lend money without obtaining all of the collateral and guarantees that they can possibly obtain. That should also be your attitude as a seller lending your money to the buyer.

When the buyer asks you for a deferred payout, ask the buyer why he cannot borrow the money from a bank. The buyer's answers may give you some insight into the risks of the buyer's business.

Bankers want to make certain that the borrower has a significant equity stake in the business, which will be lost if there is a default. Therefore, you should insist upon a substantial down payment by the buyer. If you finance 100 percent of the purchase price, the buyer has little to lose if there is a default. Moreover, as discussed subsequently, if there is a default, you may have to pay more in income taxes to reacquire your corporation than you received in cash from the buyer.

COLLATERAL

If you cannot avoid accepting deferred payment terms, ask initially for an irrevocable bank letter of credit to secure the payout. Retreat from this position only reluctantly.

At a minimum, you will want a lien and security interest on whatever assets you sold to the buyer. If you sold stock, you will want a lien and security interest on the stock as well as all of the assets of the entity whose stock you sold. You may have to subordinate your lien to the lien of the buyer's bank, but it is still worthwhile to obtain the lien.

Likewise, you would want to have a guarantee by the buyer and, if the buyer is an individual, his or her spouse. It would also be helpful to obtain a lien on the buyer's assets.

PRINCIPAL AND INTEREST

Payments of principal and interest under any note should be made frequently, at least monthly or quarterly. Avoid notes that balloon at the end of a long period of time. Frequent payments permit you an early warning of the buyer's financial problems. Preferably, the interest rate should equal the buyer's cost of borrowing from banks under comparable terms. If the interest rate is less than this figure, the buyer has no incentive to prepay the note. The interest rate should at least compensate you for your loss of use of the money.

If any payment of principal or interest is missed, the note should provide for the acceleration of all future payments of principal and interest.

NOTES

Like a bank, you should request a note to evidence the deferred payments. The notes should, if possible, not be subject to be set off by amounts you owe the buyer and should be negotiable by you.

Negotiation permits you to transfer the note to a holder in due course (such as by pledging the note to your bank for a bank loan to you). Such a transfer has the legal effect of cutting off most of the buyer's legal defenses to payment under the note. The pledging of large installment notes, generally over $5 million in principal amount, can produce advance tax consequences (see "Tax Issues").

WHO IS LIABLE UNDER THE NOTE?

Many buyers form special-purpose subsidiaries to acquire new businesses. These special-purpose subsidiaries typically have minimal capital.

Consequently, you will want this note not only to be signed by the special-purchase subsidiary but also to be guaranteed by the parent corporation buyer and, in appropriate cases, the principal shareholders of the buyer and their spouses.

If the maker of the note and the other guarantors do not have adequate net worth to pay the note (other than the assets you sold them), you have entered into what is in effect a nonrecourse sale. You are permitting the buyer to acquire your business, and your only effective recourse is against the assets you just sold.

In some circumstances, this is the best deal you can get. This situation tends to happen if you are selling to an employee or group of employees. In any situation in which your only real recourse is to the assets you just sold, you should negotiate an additional premium over the selling price to compensate you for the risk you are assuming.

AFFIRMATIVE AND NEGATIVE COVENANTS

You should also request affirmative and negative covenants from the buyer similar to what a bank would demand of the buyer. If the covenants are violated, you should have the right to accelerate and collect the deferred payments.

Examples of affirmative covenants include the following:

- requiring the buyer to maintain a minimum amount of insurance on its business
- requiring the buyer to conduct its business in a lawful manner and consistent with past practices
- requiring the buyer to pay all taxes due

If you have the bargaining power, you should request negative covenants pursuant to which the buyer will not permit certain things to happen to itself or to subsidiaries.

Examples of negative covenants include the following:

- requiring the buyer not to permit its working capital amount to fall below a certain figure or a certain ratio
- requiring the buyer not to permit its debt-to-equity ratio to exceed a certain figure
- placing restrictions on the buyer's capital spending
- placing restrictions on insider transactions and distributions, including dividends, salaries, leases, purchases, and sales

DEFAULTS

If there is a default by the buyer on other debt, you will want this event also to be a default on your note. This will enable you to accelerate the deferred payments and immediately foreclose.

If you have an employment or consulting agreement with the buyer, or a real estate lease, a default under these agreements by the buyer should also constitute a default on your note.

You will also want the buyer to be required to pay all of your attorney's fees and costs in any collection effort.

FORECLOSURES

If the buyer defaults, your misery will be compounded by the difficulties of reacquiring your business and by the adverse tax consequences.

If the buyer defaults, you can foreclose on the stock or other collateral you received. However, you must go to the expense of holding a public foreclosure sale to permit yourself to become a bidder in it. In a private foreclosure sale, you cannot be a bidder.

You can avoid a foreclosure sale and just take back the stock or other collateral for your note only if the buyer does not object and you give up any rights against the buyer for a deficiency judgment (i.e., a judgment for the excess of your note over what the returned collateral is worth).

At a foreclosure sale, you can use your unpaid note to bid for the stock or other collateral.

If you are the successful bidder in a foreclosure, the value of the stock or other collateral you acquire is deemed to be taxable to you as if you received cash in an equal amount. The same is true if you just take back your collateral without objection from the buyer and give up your rights to a deficiency judgment.

The effect of being subjected to federal income taxes on your collateral recovery is that you must use some of the cash you previously received from the buyer (less the tax you already paid) to pay the tax on your collateral recovery. This adds insult to injury.

If the buyer voluntarily agrees to a purchase price "adjustment" in lieu of a foreclosure, which reduces the purchase price to the amount you actually received, you may be able to avoid these adverse tax consequences. However, this requires the cooperation of the defaulting buyer, and you will have to pay a price for such cooperation.

TRAP WARNING If you finance 100 percent or close to 100 percent of the purchase price and the buyer defaults, you may be taxed on foreclosure or other recovery of your collateral for the entire value of your business on the date you recover it. You may not have received enough cash from the buyer to pay for your federal income taxes and consequently will be required to pay the taxes out of your own pocket.

Therefore, never sell a business on a deferred payout of 100 percent or close to 100 percent of the purchase price. Always insist on receiving in cash at least the amount of taxes you will have to pay on a subsequent foreclosure.

In general, if you sell stock, insist on receiving 30 percent of the purchase price (less your tax basis) in cash. If you sell ordinary income assets, insist on receiving 43 percent of the purchase price (less your tax basis) in cash.

TAX ISSUES

A selling shareholder who receives part or all of the purchase price in notes or deferred payment obligations and who recognizes gain on the sale will generally be taxed on the installment method of reporting for federal income tax purposes. This means that you will report a proportionate part of your total gain on the sale each time you collect a part of the note or deferred purchase price.

You must be certain that your note or deferred payment obligation qualifies for installment reporting. If not, your gain is all taxed at closing even though you have not received all of the cash.

There are a number of technical requirements for installment reporting that must be satisfied. For example, if you receive a note from a person other than the purchaser or the note is payable on demand or is issued by a corporation and readily tradable, you will lose installment reporting.

A 1988 amendment to the Internal Revenue Code limited the benefits of the installment method for larger sales to stock. An annual interest charge on the seller's tax liability deferred by the installment method is imposed for certain sales of property to the extent that the aggregate amount of installment receivables that arose from such sales during the year and that are outstanding at the end of the year exceeds $5 million. In addition, there are antipledging rules that provide that any pledge of these large installment notes triggers taxable gain to the extent of the net proceeds from the pledge.

Therefore, carefully review with your tax consultant your entitlement to the full benefit of installment reporting prior to signing any sale agreement.

There is only one significant advantage of a note over cash. If the purchase price was entirely cash, you would only be able to invest the after-tax portion of the purchase price. To the extent that the note allows you to defer taxes because of installment reporting, the buyer will be paying you interest on these deferred taxes.

CHAPTER 16

Earnouts: Another Litigation Recipe

An earnout is a method of paying the seller for her or his business based upon the performance of the business after the date of closing. An earnout is a useful method of reconciling the buyer's and seller's conflicting valuations of the business.

The buyer may say to the seller that if the seller's projections of future income come true, the seller should be paid the seller's asking price. The seller should, of course, counter that if the seller's projections become true, the seller should receive an even higher amount than originally asked to compensate the seller for the risk being assumed in the earnout. Ultimately, a formula is worked out by the parties through negotiations.

Sellers should generally avoid 100 percent earnouts. They should insist that a high percentage of the purchase price consideration be fixed.

When the seller does not have the bargaining power to negotiate a high fixed consideration, consideration should be given to not selling the business. In effect, the seller is giving up ultimate control of the business to the buyer without being assured of any control premium.

CONTROL

Earnouts do not work very well unless the seller continues to control the business. If the buyer controls the business, the buyer can make certain decisions that effectively undermine the earnout.

For example, if the buyer controls the business, the buyer may decide to step up marketing or research and development (R&D) in the years in which the earnout is measured. The buyer will get the benefit of the additional marketing or R&D in the years after the earnout is over. However, that does not help the seller.

LEGAL PROTECTIONS

Even if the seller maintains managerial control, the buyer will almost never give up potential legal control of the business. Therefore, the seller needs legal protection to permit the maximization of the earnout. Some of these protections are summarized below.

The seller must protect him- or herself from being forced to hire new employees during the earnout period. New employees increase costs and decrease earnout payments.

The seller also needs protection from having unwanted marketing or R&D costs imposed upon the business.

Sometimes the issue of unwanted marketing costs, R&D, and employees is reconciled by permitting the buyer to force the seller to incur these costs but eliminating these costs from the seller's income for the purpose of computing the earnouts. Even if the buyer accepts this solution, care must be taken to be certain that the cash necessary for these buyer-imposed costs is paid by the buyer and does not reduce the cash available to operate the business. Otherwise, the earnout will be reduced by interest costs on loans that must be incurred to fund these buyer-imposed costs.

Any purchases, sales, or other transactions between the earnout business and the buyer or its affiliates must be at arm's-lengths prices and terms. If you do not obtain this legal protection, you may find yourself selling to the buyer without profit or at a loss.

The buyer must also be obligated to supply the cash needs of the business during the earnout period. A cash-starved business cannot grow in a manner to maximize the earnout.

Care must be taken to prevent the buyer's general and administrative (G&A) and overhead from being charged against the business. A large buyer will typically have much higher G&A and overhead costs than the seller. If these costs can be charged to the business during the earnout period, the earnout will be substantially reduced, if not eliminated.

Likewise, the methods of accounting practiced by the seller prior to the closing should be continued during the earnout period. For example, if the seller was taking straight-line depreciation on equipment prior to the date of closing, you do not want the buyer to impose an accelerated depreciation after the closing, thereby artificially decreasing accounting income for earnout purposes.

Earnouts require a very careful negotiation of the terms. Your lawyer and accountant are very valuable during this negotiation.

NEGOTIATING EARNOUT AMOUNT

Earnout negotiations typically revolve around determining what is a home run with the bases loaded and what is a single. Earning levels that will make the buyer smile should give the seller the maximum earnout earnings; levels that are barely passable should give the seller the minimum earnout.

If the seller understands the buyer's valuation formula, it should not be too hard to figure out what constitutes a home run with the bases loaded. For example, suppose your business sells between 4 and 8 times EBITDA. The buyer offers you 4, and you counter with 8. The buyer says that she will not go beyond 5 EBITDA unless it is in the form of an earnout.

In this example, the earnout should, at a minimum, give the seller the opportunity to earn back the 3 times EBITDA that was lost in the negotiations. The buyer may be willing to accede to that demand if during the earnout period the higher EBITDA when multiplied by 5 equals the earnout figure demanded by the seller.

NEGOTIATING MEASUREMENT PERIOD FOR AN EARNOUT

After negotiating the amount of the earnout, the buyer and seller then negotiate the measurement period for the earnout. The measurement period should be long enough to permit the seller to maximize the earnout amount. Sellers must determine in what future years their earnings will likely be maximized and then provide some room for slippage.

For example, if the earnout goal is likely to be achieved in year 2, the seller should negotiate to permit the goal to be achieved in year 3 and still maximize the earnout.

If the earnout is measured by setting specified goals for years 1, 2, and 3, the earnout should permit the seller to miss the goal for year 1 and be able to make up for it in a subsequent year. Likewise, if year 1 is a super year, but year 3 is poor, the seller seeks the right to apply excess earnings from year 1 to year 3.

In effect, the seller should retain the right to "sprinkle" earnings throughout the measurement period in a manner that will maximize the earnout amount.

PROTECTING PAYMENT OF THE EARNOUT

Since an earnout is really a method of deferring some of the purchase price payments, you need to have the same protections as if you accepted a note for a portion of the price. If all of the earnout payments are due in five years, this is no different from a balloon note due in five years, which should be avoided.

In general, earnouts have less risk of nonpayment than notes because they are payable only if there are earnings. Nevertheless, you should take care to protect your ability to collect earnout payments by using the following:

- early payments of earnout amounts
- prohibiting distributions or loans to the parent buyer corporation until all earnout payments have been satisfied
- escrowing of excess cash for the benefit of earnout recipients

EARNOUT LITIGATION

Since earnouts are a form of deferred payments, the seller who accepts an earnout needs the same protections as the seller who accepts a buyer's note.

Earnouts breed litigation because of their complexity. It is common to have serious disputes as to the amount of the earnout that has actually become earned by the seller. Therefore, you should exercise great caution before agreeing to an earnout.

Consideration should be given to negotiating a clause in an earnout requiring the buyer to pay the seller's attorney's fees if there is a dispute concerning the earnout and the seller is successful in the litigation. A typical negotiating response to this request is that the buyer would like a similar clause if the seller sues on the earnout and loses.

Although this reciprocal clause is not desirable from the seller's viewpoint, in general the seller is better off with a "winner-take-all" attorney's fees clause, especially when dealing with a large, wealthy buyer. These buyers typically have more financial resources than the seller can afford. They can engage in "scorched-earth" litigation tactics that the seller may not be able to afford and may thereby force the seller to settle cheaply.

If there is a winner-take-all litigation clause, the seller may be able to engage an attorney to represent the seller in the earnout litigation who will work on a partial or whole contingent fee basis. This permits the seller to level the playing field in any litigation with a wealthy buyer.

IMPUTED INTEREST

A portion of each of your earnout payments (whether payable in cash or stock) will be deemed to be imputed interest taxable to you at ordinary income rates. This is true even though you sold stock to the buyer, which normally produces capital gain. The only way to avoid this result is to require the buyer to pay interest to you on the earnout payment at least equal to the minimum rate necessary to avoid imputed interest.

If you cannot negotiate such a minimum interest payment from the buyer, you should attempt to negotiate an increase in the amount of each earnout payment to compensate you for the fact that it is not all taxed to you as long-term capital gain.

For example, a very significant portion of the earnout payment due in the fifth year of a five-year earnout will be imputed interest taxable to you as ordinary income and not as long-term capital gains, even though you sold stock to the buyer. Assuming that the fifth-year earnout payment was $10 million and the imputed interest rate was 7 percent per year, approximately $3,287,900 ($10 million discounted at an 8 percent per annum rate, compounded monthly) would be taxed at ordinary income tax rates as imputed interest, and the remaining $6,712,100 (less tax basis) would be taxed as long-term capital gain.

Earnout payments in the form of stock are also subject to the imputed interest rules. Imputed interest income is deemed to be realized when you receive the earnout stock and, in some cases, even earlier. This is true even though you are not taxed on the receipt of the earnout stock because of a tax-free reorganization.

If you receive a stock earnout, you will need to have the cash necessary to pay the income tax on the imputed interest income portion of the stock earnout payment. As noted in the previous example of a $10 million fifth-year earnout payment, this could be a substantial sum. Therefore, you should, if possible, negotiate for the buyer to pay a minimum interest rate on the stock earnout payment or be prepared to pay the tax out of your own pocket.

CHAPTER 17

Negotiating Employment and Consulting Agreements

The buyer may wish to retain your services after the sale and want you to execute an employment or consulting agreement. Likewise, you may wish an employment or consulting agreement for either of the following reasons:

- A significant part of the consideration for your business is being paid to you pursuant to an employment or consulting agreement.
- You have an earnout and need assurance that you will be in control after closing.

The legal protections provided to the seller by employment or consulting agreements are often misunderstood. For example, if the seller has a five-year employment contract at $200,000 per year, is the seller assured of receiving $1 million?

The answer is "not necessarily."

First, the payments under the employment or consulting agreement are just another form of deferred payment. The seller needs all of the same protections as if the seller were given a note for $1 million, including protections from buyer's bankruptcy, etc. The seller also needs collateral, acceleration rights, and other protections afforded to a seller who is taking back a note from the buyer.

Of course, if the seller can easily get another job for $200,000 a year, the seller does not need these protections. However, even if the seller's prospects are bright for such a job on the closing, will they be equally bright three years later? Since few sellers can be certain of the answer, caution would dictate that most sellers should obtain some security from the buyer that the payments be made under the employment or consulting agreement.

Second, under most employment or consulting agreements, if the buyer breaches the agreement and fires the seller, the seller is obligated to "mitigate damages." This means that the seller must look for a new job and the buyer is only liable for the difference between what the new job pays and the $200,000 per year. If the seller immediately finds another job that pays $200,000 or more, the seller has no remedy against the buyer for the breach.

The only method of protecting against this result is to insert into the employment or consulting agreement a "no-mitigation" clause. Such a clause says that if the buyer breaches the agreement, the seller has no duty to mitigate damages, and any income the seller earns from another job will not offset the damages owed by the buyer to the seller.

If your employment or consulting agreement is silent on this issue, the law requires you to mitigate. Therefore, be certain to insist on a no-mitigation clause in your contract.

There are a number of other traps in employment and consulting agreements, described in the following sections.

Problem Number 1

If the contract is silent, the buyer can move the business across the country and require you to change work locations.

Solution

Protect yourself from having to move more than twenty miles from your existing home by a specific clause in the contract.

Problem Number 2

The buyer may retain a very broad right in the contract to terminate you "for cause" and cut off your salary and benefits.

Solution

Limit for cause terminations by narrowing the language as to what constitutes cause (e.g., criminal convictions). Also require the seller in the contract to give prior written notice of any event that can trigger a for cause termination together with an opportunity to cure that event (if a cure is possible).

Problem Number 3

The contract is not specific about your fringe benefits or contains language that permits the buyer to change your fringe benefits.

Solution

Spell out specifically what fringe benefits you require and eliminate the right of the buyer to change them unless the change gives you equivalent value.

Problem Number 4

The agreement of sale or the employment or consulting agreement forbids you to compete with the buyer even if your employment is terminated during the employment period under your employment agreement.

Solution

Condition the noncompete provision on the requirement that you continue to receive your salary and fringe benefits under the employment contract or consulting agreement.

TRAP WARNING The buyer may resist this solution because it raises a tax issue for the buyer, i.e., whether any part of the consideration paid under the employment or consulting agreement is really not for services (and therefore is not currently tax deductible by buyer) but is part of the sale price (and therefore must be allocated to the assets or stock purchased or to the noncompete agreement). If the buyer is unwilling to take this risk, the noncompete provision should be modified or deleted.

NONCOMPETITION AGREEMENTS

It is not unusual for the buyer to request you to sign a non-competition agreement. The noncompetition agreement may be inserted into the employment or consulting agreement or may be inserted into the definitive agreement of sale, or both.

Although noncompetition agreements are not always enforceable in a pure employment setting, the courts are generally more willing to enforce noncompetition agreements that are negotiated in connection with the sale of a business. Therefore, you should assume that a noncompetition agreement will be enforced against you by the courts.

The attorneys for buyers typically overdraft the noncompetition agreements so that they extend well beyond what the buyer needs to protect itself. It is the function of your attorney to narrow these noncompetition agreements so that they provide no more protection than the buyer absolutely needs.

Particular care should be taken with clauses that restrict your working for a large company that has one division that competes with the buyer, even though you are working in an entirely different division that does not compete with the buyer. Likewise, you should not be restricted from purchasing minor amounts of publicly traded stock of a company that may compete with the buyer.

The noncompetition agreement should require the buyer to notify you in writing of any alleged breach and give you an opportunity to cure the alleged breach before the buyer takes legal action.

The buyer may verbally assure you that you will be released from the noncompetition agreement when it makes sense to do so and that the buyer will not be unreasonable. *Do not accept such assurances.*

Your bargaining power to obtain exceptions from the noncompetition agreement is highest just prior to the signing of the final sale documents. This is the honeymoon period. After closing the sale of your business, your bargaining power is severely diminished. *Therefore, get the exceptions in writing before signing.*

If you are receiving deferred payments of the purchase price, the noncompete provision should immediately terminate if there is a default by the buyer on the deferred payments.

CHAPTER 18

Avoiding Traps in the Agreement of Sale

The final agreement of sale typically consists of the following major provisions:

- business terms
- warranties and representations of buyer and seller
- closing date provisions
- covenants (i.e., agreements) imposed on the seller prior to and after closing
- conditions precedent to the buyer's obligation to close
- conditions precedent to the seller's obligation to close
- indemnification clauses
- miscellaneous provisions

A sample agreement of sale involving the sale of the assets of a physical therapy center to a large public company buyer is contained in Appendix 6.

If you have a good bargaining position, it is a good idea to have your attorney, rather than the buyer's attorney, prepare the first draft of the agreement of sale.

WARRANTIES AND REPRESENTATIONS

The warranties and representations are intended to require the seller to describe the company and serve to allocate risk between parties. These warranties and representations include the following subjects:

- organization and good standing
- authority; no conflict
- capitalization
- financial statements
- books and records
- title to properties, encumbrances
- condition and sufficiency of assets
- accounts receivable
- inventory
- existence of undisclosed liabilities
- legal proceedings, orders, judgments
- absence of certain changes and events
- contracts; no defaults
- insurance
- environmental matters
- employees, labor relations, compliance
- intellectual property
- certain payments
- full disclosure
- transactions with related persons
- brokers and finders

Section II of the agreement of sale contained in Appendix 6 contains the seller's warranties and representations.

Each of the numerous warranties and representations must be separately true and correct, even if they cover overlapping areas. For example, the agreement of sale will typically contain a warranty and representation that you have no pending or threatened litigation and a separate warranty and representation that you have no contingent liabilities. A threatened lawsuit is also a contingent liability. Therefore, if you qualify your "no litigation" warranty by reference to a specific lawsuit, you must also qualify your "no contingent liability" warranty by reference to the same lawsuit.

Typically, at the end of the document there is a schedule of exceptions that permits the seller to indicate where the warranties and representations are incorrect. For example, if there is a warranty and representation that the seller has no lawsuits or environmental liabilities, this is usually preceded by the words "except as provided in this schedule." If the seller has lawsuits or environmental liabilities, they must be described in these schedules.

TRAP WARNING The agreement of sale should make it clear that whatever information is contained in the schedule of exceptions modifies all warranties, representations, and covenants contained in the agreement and cannot be the basis for an indemnification claim against the seller except as specifically provided for in the agreement. If you fail to do this, you may find that you are liable to the buyer even if you made full disclosure in the schedule of exceptions but failed to make reference in the schedule to all of the overlapping warranties, representations, and covenants.

If these schedules are not correct and complete, the buyer has the right to sue the seller (and its shareholders if they signed the agreement) for breach of the warranty and representation. The buyer also has the right to refuse to close the sale.

If the seller breaches any warranty and representation, the buyer typically has the following options:

- Refuse to close the agreement of sale.
- Close the agreement of sale and seek damages from the seller.
- If the buyer first discovers the breach after closing, rescind the transaction if the breach is material.

It is extremely important to be truthful and careful in making warranties and representations. Even innocent mistakes can result in your having to return a portion of the sale price.

A seller can seek to have all of his or her warranties and representations terminate at the closing in order to avoid post-closing breach claims. However, unless the seller has an excellent bargaining position, most buyers will refuse this request.

RULE 10b-5 WARRANTY AND REPRESENTATION

The following warranty and representation contained in the agreement of sale set forth in Appendix 6 deserves special note:

No representation or warranty made under any Section hereof and none of the information set forth herein, in the exhibits hereto or in any document delivered by any of the Companies or any of the Shareholders to the Purchaser, or any authorized representative of the Purchaser, pursuant to the express terms of this Agreement contains any untrue statement of a material fact by the Companies or the Shareholders or omits to state a material fact by the Companies or the Shareholders necessary to make the statements herein or therein not misleading.

(See Section II[C] of the agreement of sale contained in Appendix 6.)

This warranty and representation requires the seller to disclose any other material facts (particularly adverse facts) about the seller's business that the buyer ought to know. This disclosure is required whether or not the buyer has requested the information in the agreement of sale. In effect, the burden is placed on the seller to disclose other adverse facts about the business that the buyer neglected to have warranted and represented.

This warranty and representation is sometimes called the Rule 10b-5 warranty, since a portion of the language is based on Rule 10b-5 under the Securities Exchange Act of 1934.

However, this warranty differs markedly from Rule 10b-5. Under Rule 10b-5, a seller is not liable in making material misstatements or material omissions unless the seller did so intentionally or with reckless disregard for the truth. In contrast, this warranty does not require the buyer to prove that the seller intentionally or recklessly deceived the buyer. All the buyer needs to prove is that the seller in fact failed to provide such material information. The fact that the seller's error was in good faith is irrelevant and is not a legal defense against the buyer's lawsuit.

ACCOUNTS RECEIVABLE

The following accounts receivable warranty and representation appears in the agreement of sale contained in Appendix 6:

The accounts receivable of each of the Companies that are part of the Assets are in their entirety valid accounts receivable, arising in the ordinary course of business. On or before 180 days from the date of the Closing, the Purchaser shall collect at least $160,000 of such accounts receivable.

(See Section II[K] of the agreement of sale contained in Appendix 6.)

This warranty and representation requires the seller to guarantee the collection of $160,000 of accounts receivable within 180 days after the closing. This warranty is in addition to representing that all of the acquired accounts receivable are valid and arose "in the ordinary course of business."

There are a number of variables in the accounts receivable warranty. The buyer can have you warrant any or all of the following:

Version 1: The accounts receivable reflected on your financial statements represent amounts due for products or services you sold in the ordinary course of business in accordance with generally accepted accounting principles.

Version 2: The accounts receivable are all collectible.

Version 3: The accounts receivable will in fact be collected.

The seller should have no difficulty with version 1. Version 2 (the accounts receivable are collectible) is ambiguous, since it is not clear whether this warranty means that you are guaranteeing collection. Version 3 (the accounts receivable will be collected) is clear but also the least favorable from the seller's viewpoint.

CLOSING DATE

From the seller's point of view, it would be preferable to sign the agreement and have the closing the same day. This is true because the agreement of sale in many cases effectively converts the sale into an option given to the buyer to close the transaction.

For example, in many cases there is a so-called due diligence out in the conditions precedent that permits the buyer to terminate the agreement if upon completion of due diligence the buyer is not satisfied. Likewise, if the buyer discovers even an inadvertent breach by the seller of any material warranties and representations or the buyer cannot get exactly the legal opinion required from his attorney, the buyer is not obligated to close.

There are cases in which it may be necessary to have time between signing the agreement of sale and the actual closing. This may occur because the buyer does not want to expend the funds necessary to do a complete due diligence investigation until the seller has signed an agreement of sale. It may also occur because certain consents of third parties are needed to complete the sale or there are required government filings, such as Hart-Scott-Rodino filings, which generally apply to certain transactions involving more than $15 million.

When there is time between the signing and closing, the seller should attempt to eliminate as many of the buyer's "outs" as possible at the earliest possible time. For example, if there is a due diligence out, the buyer should lose this "out" after a certain period of time, such as ten or twenty days after the date of signing, even though the closing may not occur for sixty days after the signing because of the necessity of a third-party consent or some other factor.

If the buyer obtains a due diligence out that extends until the moment of closing, the buyer is really receiving an option to buy the seller without ever paying for that option. In addition, during this period of time, your company is removed from the market for other potential buyers.

TRAP WARNING Make certain that the agreement of sale terminates on a specific date if a closing has not occurred by that date. Otherwise, the buyer can indefinitely delay the closing, thereby preventing you from selling to others. If the closing does not occur by the specified date because of your fault or breach, limit the buyer's remedy to damages, so that you can sell to someone else.

CONDITIONS PRECEDENT

Conditions precedent are extremely important. If the conditions precedent to the buyer's obligation are not satisfied, the buyer does not have to complete the sale. The same is true as to conditions precedent to the seller's obligation. However, a breach of a condition precedent (in contrast to a breach of a warranty, representation, or covenant) may not necessarily allow the innocent party to sue for damages. Rather, the innocent party's only remedy is typically limited to walking away from the transaction, i.e., refusing to close the sale.

Buyer's Obligations

The typical conditions precedent to the buyer's obligation to close are the following:

- The seller's warranties and representations must be true and correct as of the date of closing, and all of its covenants must have been complied with.
- Satisfactory legal opinions have been issued to the buyer.
- The buyer's due diligence has been completed satisfactorily.
- All necessary third-party consents have been obtained, including any necessary clearance under the Hart-Scott-Rodino Antitrust Improvements Act of 1976 (generally applicable to nonexempt sales involving more than $15 million in sale consideration).
- There must be no lawsuits seeking to prevent the consummation of the transaction.
- If applicable, approval by the buyer's and/or seller's shareholders must have been obtained.

The seller should negotiate the wording of the conditions precedent to the buyer's obligation so as to minimize the buyer's ability to change his mind at the last minute.

For example, if there are legal opinions that must be given to the buyer to require the buyer to close, have such opinions given by your attorney and not the buyer's attorneys. Likewise, the form and substance of the legal opinion should be negotiated before executing the agreement of sale so that the buyer cannot impose new legal opinion requirements at the last minute.

As noted, any due diligence out for the buyer should have a short time frame so the agreement of sale does not turn into an option.

If the seller has a good bargaining position, the seller may wish to negotiate limitations on the buyer's right to walk from the deal once the agreement of sale is signed. For example, if the seller can negotiate a so-called hell or high water clause, there is no bringdown of the warranties and representations to the closing date and the buyer's walk-away rights are extremely limited. In addition, if a seller warranty or representation is untrue on signing but is true at closing, the buyer should not be able to refuse to close.

The seller should also seek to negotiate a provision requiring the buyer to give the seller prompt written notice of the buyer's discovery of a breach by the seller of one of the seller's warranties, representations, or covenants. The written notice should be accompanied by the buyer's election either to waive the breach and proceed with the closing or to terminate the agreement. In the absence of such a provision, the buyer could discover a breach by the seller and then wait until the last minute to spring this on the seller. In addition, if the buyer discovers a breach by the seller before the closing, the buyer should not be permitted to close the sale and then sue the seller after the closing under the indemnification clause.

If you are to receive an employment or consulting agreement, this should be added to the conditions precedent to the seller's obligations.

TRAP WARNING Be careful that the agreement contains all of the conditions precedent to the seller's obligations.
If your employment or consulting agreement is listed as a condition precedent to the buyer's obligations but not the seller's obligation to close, you are required to close whether or not the buyer executes the employment or consulting agreement. The buyer can merely waive the condition precedent to its obligation to close and force you to close.

Seller's Obligations

The conditions precedent to the seller's obligations to close typically include the following:

- The buyer's warranties and representations must be true and correct as of the date of closing, and all of its covenants must have been complied with.
- Satisfactory legal opinions have been issued to the seller.
- The seller's shareholders have been released from personal liabilities for corporate obligations.
- All necessary third-party consents shall have been obtained, including any necessary clearance under the Hart-Scott-Rodino Antitrust Improvements Act of 1976.
- There must be no lawsuits seeking to prevent the consummation of the transaction.
- If applicable, approval by the buyer's and/or seller's shareholders must have been obtained.

Care should be taken that the conditions precedent to the seller's obligation to close generally parallel the conditions precedent to the buyer's obligation to close.

RELEASE OF PERSONAL GUARANTIES

It is important that you obtain a release from your personal guaranties, corporate bank loans, leases, licenses, and similar obligations and debts of your business to the extent they are assumed by the buyer.

The buyer may offer indemnification against these personal guaranties to the extent that they cannot be released at the closing. Indemnification is a poor substitute for a release. Indeed, a postclosing deterioration in the buyer's financial condition may cause such indemnification to be illusory.

Moreover, if the third party (such as the bank whose loan you personally guaranteed) will not release you even if the buyer substitutes its guaranty, this probably means that the buyer is not sufficiently creditworthy. Accordingly, you would be foolish to rely on the buyer's indemnification.

In situations where you do close without obtaining a release of your personal guaranty, you are, in effect, providing a credit enhancement for the buyer. You should request compensation from the buyer for the credit enhancement. The compensation can take the form of an increased purchase price, equity in the buyer, or other forms of compensation.

INDEMNIFICATION CLAUSE

The indemnification clause typically requires the seller and its shareholders to indemnify the buyer not only for breaches of warranties, representations, and covenants but also for other kinds of claims (such as tax liabilities or environmental liabilities) that may occur after closing that were not agreed to be assumed by the buyer.

The indemnification clause typically creates liability to the buyer after the date of closing even for matters that the seller had no knowledge of before the closing. For example, a typical indemnification clause may require the seller to indemnify the buyer from any postclosing claim resulting from a preclosing "act, omission or event." This indemnification obligation applies even if the seller did not know about the preclosing "act, omission or event."

Unless the indemnification clause is properly limited, this clause serves as an excellent vehicle for the buyer to readjust the sale price after the closing. The indemnification clause creates liability to the buyer after the date of closing.

Even if there is no indemnification clause as such, a breach of any of the warranties or representations or covenants contained in an agreement to sell assets or stock will also create such liability unless the agreement specifically provides that no lawsuit can be brought after the date of closing.

In a merger or consolidation, in which your entity disappears into the buyer or its subsidiary, the seller's shareholders have no indemnification liability after the closing unless they specifically agree to assume such liability.

It is important to limit claims under the indemnification clause so that they may be bought within only a short period of time or they are barred. Typically a seller can negotiate for short periods of time for certain kinds of liabilities that the buyer should discover very shortly after the closing. Other kinds of indemnification claims, such as tax liabilities, may require a longer claim period. See Section XIIIB of the agreement of sale contained in Appendix 6.

If the buyer received a tax benefit from the loss that the buyer is asking you to pay under the indemnification clause, it should be made clear that the buyer's tax benefit reduces your indemnification obligation. Similarly, if the buyer recovers money from his insurance company or from a third party, this should reduce your liability.

Likewise, you should preclude the buyer from any right to undo (or rescind) the transaction after closing because of a material loss subject to indemnification. The buyer's legal remedy should be limited to a price adjustment under the indemnification clause. Likewise, the buyer should agree not to seek punitive damages from you.

If the buyer discovers a breach by the seller before the closing and nevertheless chooses to close, the seller should be able to treat such closing as a waiver of the seller's breach. If there were no such wavier, the buyer could choose to close the purchase with full knowledge of the breach and then seek indemnification. The buyer's right of indemnification thus effectively lowers the selling price after the seller has already sold his business.

If the buyer has a claim asserted against it by a third party for which you are responsible under the indemnification clause, you will also be liable for their attorney's fees. The buyer's attorneys typically have no incentive to limit their fees, since you, not their client, are paying for the litigation.

Consequently, it is important that you have the right to appoint the attorneys for the buyer, since you thereby will have more leverage to control their fees. You should also give yourself the right to control the defense of the claim.

This will be agreeable to the buyer only if you choose from a list of law firms acceptable to the buyer and there is no doubt as to your ability to pay any adverse judgment. If there is doubt as to your ability to pay an adverse judgment, the buyer will probably require an attorney of its choosing to participate in the litigation and will not give you control of the defense.

Section X of the agreement of sale contained in Appendix 6 of this book contains examples of the clauses suggested in this section.

TRAP WARNING Be certain that there is a ceiling on your liability under the agreement of sale. The ceiling should apply not only to the indemnification clause but also to your liability for breach of any provision of the agreement of sale. The ceiling figure should, at a maximum, not exceed the purchase price to the extent paid in cash.

It is also customary to negotiate a so-called basket clause, which limits your liability for smaller claims. For example, the basket clause may provide that you are not liable for the first $50,000 of claims and are liable only for amounts in excess of $50,000. The theory of the basket clause is that the buyer should have recourse only for more significant claims against the seller and that the buyer probably would have consummated the agreement of sale if the buyer had to pay an additional immaterial amount.

Obviously, what is immaterial depends on the size of the transaction. In general, a basket clause equal to 1 per-

(continues)

cent of the consideration is usually not objectionable to most buyers. However, in appropriate circumstances, you may be able to negotiate a much higher percentage of the purchase price in the basket clause. Some basket clauses provide that if the total claims exceed the basket clause figure, the entire amount of the claims is collectable by the buyer, not just the amount in excess of the basket clause amount. Thus, in the preceding example, if the total claims were $51,000, the seller would be liable for the entire $51,000, rather than just $1,000.

INDEMNIFICATION OF SELLER

The seller and its directors, officers, and shareholders need indemnification protection as well as the buyer. For example, if the buyer after closing sells a defective product or service and the seller or its directors, officers, or shareholders are sued along with the buyer, they should also be entitled to indemnification.

Therefore, the seller and its directors and officers should receive indemnification from the buyer's conduct of the business after the closing. For an example of this clause, see Section X(B) of the agreement of sale contained in Appendix 6.

The seller also needs indemnification from any claims by former employees who were hired by the buyer. It is not unusual for such former employees to join the seller in any lawsuit that they bring against the buyer for wrongful termination after the closing or for other kinds of claims.

In general, the seller should be indemnified from any claims resulting from liabilities that the buyer agreed to assume in the agreement of sale. For example, if the buyer agreed to assume any pension liabilities due to the seller's employees, the seller must be indemnified by the buyer from any claims brought by a former employee resulting from disputes as to the amount of such pension. The same is true as to environmental liabilities, accounts payable, or other liabilities that are specifically assumed by the buyer in the agreement of sale.

INSURANCE

It is important to have the buyer maintain insurance after closing that protects you against third-party claims, particularly accident claims.

For example, if you sell a defective product or service before closing, that defective product or service could give rise to a claim after closing. You must be insured for that claim, preferably at the buyer's expense.

However, regardless of who maintains or pays for the insurance, you still need protection from such claims. You may have to continue your own insurance for some time after closing to protect yourself. This is particularly true if you sell assets, since the buyer typically will not agree to pay for unasserted claims due to defective products or services that you sold.

Even if the buyer maintains the insurance, you will need an insurance certification from the buyer's insurer, together with their agreement to notify you of any amendments or deletions of coverage or any terminations of the buyer's policies.

As noted, you also need protection from any claims resulting from defective products or services sold by the buyer after the closing. At a minimum, you will want indemnification from the buyer for these claims and to be named as an additional insured on the buyer's liability policies.

WHO IS LIABLE UNDER AGREEMENT OF SALE?

In general, anyone who signs the agreement of sale has liability under the agreement unless the agreement specifically provides otherwise.

If the agreement of sale provides for the sale of your stock in your corporation to the buyer, you are, of course, liable under the agreement.

Resist any attempt to secure your spouse's signature on the agreement of sale unless your spouse is also a shareholder of the shares or the shares are owned jointly or by the entireties. It is acceptable to permit your spouse to consent to the sale as long as your spouse has no liability under the agreement of sale.

By removing your spouse from liability, you can, in many states, insulate personal assets from the buyer if you own such personal assets as tenants by the entireties with your spouse.

If your corporation enters into an agreement of sale to sell assets to the buyer, it is customary for the buyer to require the shareholders of the selling corporation to sign the agreement of sale as guarantors. The same is true if the transaction is structured as a merger or consolidation.

TRAP WARNING If there are minority shareholders of your corporation, try to limit your personal liability to your proportionate share of the stock. If you fail to negotiate this limitation, you can be liable for 100 percent of the loss unless you have some kind of contribution agreement with your minority shareholders.

You can be personally liable under the agreement of sale even if you did not sign it. For example, securities laws may make you personally liable as a control person, if your corporation is otherwise liable under these laws.

You may also incur personal liability if you give a certification to the buyer as a corporate officer pursuant to the agreement of sale and the certification is wrong. You may avoid this liability by making it clear in the certification that you are only acting as a corporate officer and not in a personal capacity.

GENERAL

These legal clauses are really part of the overall business negotiation. For example, the buyer may be willing to trade a small price reduction for the elimination of warranties and representations or other protective clauses to the buyer.

Therefore, you must work closely with your attorney to create package proposals in which concessions you are giving to the buyer on business terms are linked with concessions your attorneys wants from the buyer's attorney on legal terms.

PLANNING FOR THE CLOSING

At closing you will receive your check or wire transfer and any promissory notes and stock that were part of the purchase price. In return, you must transfer the stock or assets of your business or effectuate any mergers or consolidations.

If the closing involves a plant closing or a mass layoff, there are various federal, state, and local laws that require prior notice, usually sixty days. For example, the U.S. Worker Adjustment and Retraining Notification Act requires employers of 100 or more employees (subject to exceptions) to give employees and local governments sixty calendar days of advance written notice of plant closings and mass layoffs. You will not want to provide such notice until you have signed an agreement of sale and any due diligence outs have been waived; therefore, your closing may be delayed until the required waiting period has been satisfied.

Similarly, if your transaction is subject to the Hart-Scott-Rodino Antitrust Improvements Act of 1976 (certain transactions generally involving over $15 million sale consideration), a prior notice and thirty-day waiting period are required.

There are three planning items for the closing:

- Insist that your attorneys do a preclosing, or dress rehearsal, well before the actual closing date so that the closing is not held up by last-minute issues.
- You should always request a wire transfer of immediately available funds to your account. Your right to a wire transfer must be contained in the agreement of sale. Absent a wire transfer, request a bank check or a certified check.
- Plan in advance of the closing as to exactly how you will invest the funds you receive at closing.

The last two planning items can best be illustrated by the actual case history of a businessman who had received a $25 million check at closing and then stupidly mailed it to himself. The check was lost in the mail and, in fact, was not replaced for thirty days. The loss of interest on the check at an 8 percent per annum interest rate was over $164,000.

Prior to the closing, you should know exactly how and where your funds will be invested so that these transactions can be effectuated on the closing date without loss of interest.

PART 5

Alternatives to Selling Your Business

CHAPTER 19

Leveraged Recapitalization

Before you decide to sell your business, you should explore the alternatives of a leveraged recapitalization or going public. Although going public is a familiar concept, leveraged recapitalization is not.

A leveraged recapitalization typically involves having your company borrow money from institutional lenders or investors, who receive a senior debt security together with warrants to purchase your company's stock. Your company then uses the money to recapitalize your company, and you receive cash in the recapitalization for a portion of your stock. You wind up with a significant stock position in your company (usually a majority), plus the cash.

If your motive for selling your business is that you are tired of working, skip this chapter. Leveraged recapitalizations require you to work harder—not retire.

Likewise, if your motivation for selling is that your business is going downhill quickly, skip this chapter. You are not going to be able to take a declining business public. Likewise, institutional lenders and investors will not be interested in a leveraged recapitalization.

Many companies cannot qualify for a leveraged recapitalization. They do not have either the assets or the cash flow to support a leveraged recapitalization or the growth prospects necessary to attract mezzanine lenders, an equity fund, or an underwriter of a public offering. These companies really have little choice but to sell to an outsider or to their own employees (including an ESOP) (see Chapter 14).

Leveraged recapitalizations work only if your company can attract an asset-based lender or a cash flow lender or has such a high growth potential that you can attract a mezzanine or equity investor.

To attract an asset-based lender, you will need substantial asset values, particularly liquidation values. The following are the normal requirements for asset-based lenders:

- accounts receivable: 70% to 85%
- inventory: 40% to 65%
- machinery and equipment: 75% to 80% of orderly liquidation value
- real estate: the lesser of 50% of fair market value or 75% of quick auction value
- senior term debt (fixed or adjusted rate; three-to-seven-year term)
- working capital revolver (floating rate; one-to-three-year term)

To attract a cash flow lender, your company needs cash flow sufficient to cover 2.5 times the debt service on senior debt and at least 2.0 times all debt service. If your business does not have this kind of cash flow, a leveraged recapitalization will not work.

The following are the normal requirements for a cash flow lender:

- based on cash flow coverages (cash flow divided by total interest cost)
- 2.0 times total coverage typical (2.5 times senior interest coverage)

- senior revolving credit facility (floating rate; one-to-three-year term)
- senior term debt (fixed or floating rate; three-to-seven-year term)
- mezzanine debt (fixed rate; five-to-ten-year term; "equity kicker")

Leveraged recapitalizations do not require any personal guarantee by you for the institutional debt.

A leveraged recapitalization does not require significant growth prospects. Your company must have only sufficient assets to attract an asset-based lender or sufficient cash flow to cover the senior debt service and other debt service until their maturity.

If you cannot qualify for a senior debt recapitalization but have significant growth prospects, and you are not ready to go public, you may still be able to effect a leveraged recapitalization.

There are providers of so-called mezzanine debt who will lend your company money in exchange for debt plus an equity kicker if they can project a return of least 22 percent to 28 percent per annum. This does not mean that you have to pay 22 percent to 28 percent interest per year. It means that the potential growth in value of the equity kicker, plus the interest, must equal at least 22 percent to 28 percent per year.

Assume that your business has explosive growth potential, but you are not ready to go public and your current cash flow cannot support much more debt service than you already have. You should consider a private equity fund as an investor. They typically are interested only if they can expect a return of 35 percent to 45 percent per year.

The problem with any leveraged recapitalization is that you will have to provide an exit for your lenders/investors. The exit for the senior and mezzanine debt is obviously the maturity date of that debt. However, the exit for the equity must usually occur in five to seven years through any of the following:

- going public
- selling the business
- repurchasing the lender/investor equity

The primary advantages of the leveraged recapitalization are the following:

- You receive some cash from the company, thereby achieving a degree of liquidity.
- You retain control of the company, subject to the restriction imposed by the lender or institutional investors.

The primary disadvantages are the following:

- Your company is highly leveraged, and you must operate in that environment.
- The institutional lenders/investors have some equity in your business, so you have minority shareholders to contend with.
- The institutional lenders/investors will impose restrictions on the operation of your company until they exit.

If you engage in a leveraged recapitalization, consider making family gifts of stock immediately thereafter, since your stock valuation will be depressed.

A leveraged recapitalization could be followed by a public offering after an appropriate growth period.

CHAPTER 20

Going Public

To go public you typically need a company with significant growth prospects, at least in the short term. Going public with your company requires hard work.

The primary advantage of an initial public offering versus a sale is that you will either initially or ultimately receive cash and still control your company. In contrast, in a sale you lose control.

If you have an S corporation, many underwriters will permit you to withdraw your previously taxed undistributed earnings at the time of initial public offering (IPO). Thus, even if you do not sell a single share of stock in the IPO, you may still wind up with substantial dollars in your pocket after the IPO.

The following are the advantages and disadvantages of an IPO as taken from my book *Going Public* (Prima Publishing, 1994).

THE ADVANTAGES

The major advantages of being public are as follows:

(1) *Lower cost of capital.* A public company has more alternatives for raising capital than a private company. A

private company, once it has exhausted its bank lines, generally raises additional equity and subordinated debt capital from institutional investors. These institutional investors, such as venture capital funds, insurance companies, and others, usually require very stiff terms including significant operational restrictions.

In contrast, a public company has the additional alternative of going to the public marketplace. The public marketplace typically does not demand the same stiff terms. This results in less dilution to the existing shareholders and fewer operational restrictions.

Investors will value two identical companies, one private and the other public, quite differently. Investors in the private company will discount the value of its equity securities by reason of their "illiquidity," that is, the inability to readily sell them for cash.

The availability of the public capital alternative also permits the public company greater leverage in its negotiations with institutional investors. Many institutional investors prefer investing in public companies since they have a built-in exit, that is, they can sell their stock in the public market.

(2) *Personal wealth.* A public offering can enhance your personal net worth. Stories abound of the many millionaires and multimillionaires created through public offerings. Even if you don't realize immediate profits by selling a portion of your existing stock during the initial offering, you can use publicly traded stock as collateral to secure loans.

For approximately six months after the IPO, the underwriter will restrict you from selling your personal stock. Thereafter, you can sell stock under Rule 144. Rule 144 permits you to personally sell up to 1 percent of the total outstanding stock of the company every three months, or if higher, one week's trading volume. The sales have to be in unsolicited brokerage transactions or transactions with brokerage firms that make a market in your stock. You also will have to publicly report these sales. Thus, it may not be desirable for you to utilize Rule 144 too frequently for fear of giving the investment community the impression that you are "bailing out."

Approximately one or two years after your IPO, you may have another registered public offering in which you sell a greater amount of your holdings than in the IPO. You generally can only do so if your company's earnings have grown since your IPO.

(3) *Competitive position.* Many businesses use the capital from the IPO to enhance their competitive position. The additional capital resources permit greater market penetration.

Some businesses have only a short window of opportunity. For example, a technology-based company can use the IPO proceeds to achieve a dominant position in the marketplace well before its underfinanced competitors.

Customers like to deal with well-financed businesses. A strong balance sheet is a good marketing tool.

(4) *Prestige.* You and your cofounders gain an enormous amount of personal prestige from being associated with a company that goes public. Such prestige can be very helpful in recruiting key employees and in marketing your products and services.

(5) *Ability to take advantage of market price fluctuations.* The market price of public company stock can fluctuate greatly. These fluctuations may relate to overall stock market trends and have nothing to do with your company's performance. The stock market from time to time tends to unreasonably overprice your stock or severely underprice it.

During the period that the market severely underprices your stock, your company has the ability to repurchase the stock in the stock market at these depressed prices. Likewise, during the period that the market unreasonably overprices your stock, your company can sell stock on very favorable terms. None of these opportunities are available to a private company.

(6) *Enhanced ability to grow through acquisitions.* Underwriters prefer companies that can use the IPO proceeds to grow the business. You can use the cash proceeds from the

IPO to effectuate acquisitions, which can help your company grow faster. A publicly traded company may also grow by using its own stock to make acquisitions. This option is generally not available to a private company, which is forced to use cash or notes for acquisitions. Private company stock is not attractive to a seller because it lacks liquidity.

The ability to grow through stock acquisitions may permit your company to use pooling-of-interest accounting for acquisitions. An acquiring company using pooling-of-interest accounting can reflect, as part of its own reported income, the income the acquired company earned even before the date of the acquisition. Pooling accounting also avoids the reduction of your company's future income caused by goodwill amortization resulting from the acquisition and the extra depreciation resulting from writing fixed assets of the acquired company up to their current values. If pooling accounting is available, no goodwill is created and no write-up of fixed assets is required.

Spectacular increases can occur in your company's reported earnings per share as a result of pooling accounting for acquisitions. This could occur, for example, where your company's stock is valued at 20 times earnings and you can use your stock to effectuate mergers based on paying 10 times the acquired company's earnings. After the merger, your stock price will presumably reflect the acquired company's earnings multiplied by 20.

Since your company's stock will trade for a multiple of your reported earnings per share, significant increases in your reported earnings per share can, in turn, result in dramatic increases in your company's stock price.

(7) *Enhanced ability to borrow; no personal guarantees.* When your company sells stock, it increases its net worth and improves its debt-to-equity ratio. This should allow your company to borrow money on more favorable terms in the future.

Banks often require the principals of private companies to personally guarantee bank loans made to their companies.

Once your company is public, banks and other financial institutions are less likely to require any personal guarantees.

(8) *Enhanced ability to raise equity.* If your company continues to grow, you will eventually need additional permanent financing. If your stock performs well in the stock market, you will be able to sell additional stock on favorable terms.

(9) *Attracting and retaining key employees.* Stock options offered by emerging public companies have much appeal and can help you to recruit or retain well-qualified executives and to motivate your employee-shareholders.

(10) *Liquidity and valuation.* Once your company goes public, your stock will have a market and you will have an effective way of valuing that stock. Subject to Rule 144, you can sell whenever the need arises.

You can easily follow your stock prices. The market will quote prices daily, and the newspapers may even print them.

(11) *Estate planning.* Many private companies have to be sold upon the death of their founder in order to pay death taxes. This may prevent you from passing the ownership of your private company to your family or to key employees.

Founders of private companies sometimes fund death taxes by maintaining large life insurance policies on their lives. However, the premiums paid on these life insurance policies can be a significant drain on the business. These premiums are not deductible for federal income tax purposes.

If you publicly trade your company's stock, your estate will have a liquid asset with which to pay death taxes.

THE DISADVANTAGES

The major disadvantages of going public are as follows:

(1) *Expense.* The cost of going public is substantial, both initially and on an ongoing basis. As for the initial costs, the underwriters' discount or commission can run as high as 10 percent or more of the total offering. Additionally,

you can incur out-of-pocket expenses, which typically range from $150,000 to $500,000 for even a small offering of $10 million of your securities. If your IPO is cancelled at the last minute because of adverse market conditions or other reasons, you will be liable for substantial costs.

On an ongoing basis, regulatory reporting requirements, stockholders' meetings, investor relations, and other expenses of being public can run from $25,000 to $100,000 or more annually. This is in addition to your management time, which can be considerable. For example, the cost of printing and distributing your annual and quarterly reports, proxy statements, and stock certificates can be extremely expensive.

In addition, you may need to hire additional financial and accounting personnel to help prepare your company's financial disclosures. Likewise, you may need to hire a shareholder relations employee and to upgrade the quality of existing financial and accounting employees. These are all additional hidden costs of going public.

A number of smaller public companies have developed methods of minimizing their ongoing costs of being public. These methods include the judicious use of outside professionals, sending bare-bone annual and quarterly reports to shareholders, using inexpensive techniques to reproduce and mail these shareholder reports (e.g., third class mail), avoiding expensive shareholders' meetings, and so on. Minimization of such expenses can reduce your ongoing costs to just $20,000 per year.

(2) *Pressure to maintain growth pattern.* After going public, there will be considerable pressure to maintain the growth rate you have established. If your sales or earnings deviate from an upward trend, investors may become apprehensive and sell their stock, driving down its price. You may not have the capital with which to buy back the stock at these depressed prices. As a result, you will have unhappy stockholders.

Additionally, you will have to begin reporting operating results quarterly. People will evaluate the company on a quarterly, rather than annual, basis. This will intensify the pressure and shorten your planning and operating horizons significantly. The pressure may tempt you to make short-term decisions that could have a harmful long-term impact on the company.

(3) *Disclosure of information.* Your company's operations and financial situation are open to public scrutiny. Information concerning the company, officers, directors, and certain shareholders—information not ordinarily disclosed by privately held companies—will now be available to competitors, customers, employees, and others. You legally must disclose such information as your company's sales, profits, your competitive edge, material contracts with major customers, and the salaries and perquisites of the chief executive officer and certain highly paid executive officers. You must disclose it not only when you initially go public but also on a continuing basis thereafter.

The SEC (Securities and Exchange Commission) staff has a procedure to authorize confidential treatment for documents you file. However, you must apply to the SEC early in the IPO registration process to avoid holding up the IPO. Very sensitive information can typically be excluded from public scrutiny.

The SEC mandated disclosures should not be a major concern to most businesses. Your competitors may already possess a lot more information about you than you realize. Customers, suppliers, and ex-employees may have already revealed this information to them. Many companies already provide some financial information to business credit agencies, such as Dun & Bradstreet. Although public companies disclose much more financial information than private companies, the additional information is not necessarily a competitive disadvantage.

In general, the SEC requires public companies to disclose information that is material to investors. You do not have to disclose information about specific customers for your products unless the customer's purchases are such a high percentage of your total sales as to be material to investors. Likewise, you do not normally have to disclose the exact profitability of specific products, provided that the product lines do not constitute a separate industry segment for financial reporting purposes. The SEC gives management reasonable discretion in determining whether its business includes separately reportable industry segments. Accordingly, it is usually possible to avoid disclosure of the exact profitability of separate product lines.

(4) *Loss of control.* If a sufficiently large proportion of your shares is sold to the public, you may lose control of the company. Once your company is publicly held, the potential exists for further dilution of your control through subsequent public offerings and acquisitions. Likewise, you may be subject to a hostile tender offer.

You can alleviate this disadvantage by the careful insertion of antitakeover provisions in your charter or by creating two classes of stock with disproportionate voting rights. Although there are few, if any, antitakeover defenses that are completely, legally foolproof, some defenses can in practice be very effective against raiders. Defenses that deprive the raiders of voting power or that otherwise penalize the raiders are particularly effective.

Many underwriters will object to unusual antitakeover defenses in the charter of IPO companies. Such defenses may make it more difficult to attract certain institutional investors. Underwriters who do not seek institutional investors will usually be more relaxed about these clauses.

What is a "normal" antitakeover defense and what is "unusual" is typically a matter of negotiation with the underwriter. For example, some underwriters will object to the staggering of the terms of the members of the board of directors so that all directors are not elected each year. Others will not. In general, antitakeover provisions, which are part of state law and require special shareholder action to opt out of, will usually be accepted by underwriters.

Even if antitakeover defenses cannot be inserted into your charter prior to your IPO, you can usually amend your charter after your IPO to insert these defenses. You should accomplish this before your personal stock ownership falls below 50 percent of the outstanding stock.

(5) *Shareholder lawsuits.* Public companies, and their directors, officers, and control persons, can be sued by their shareholders.

Shareholder class action lawsuits typically follow a significant drop in the market price of your company's stock caused by adverse news about your company. The theory of these lawsuits is that your company knew or should have known of the adverse news and had a duty to publicize it at an earlier date than the date the news actually became public. The lawsuit will allege that failure to publicize the information earlier constitutes "fraud on the market."

Overly optimistic or exaggerated statements contained in your company's reports to shareholders, or in press releases, are usually cited in these lawsuits to support their allegations. These statements are typically the result of a misguided attempt to generate interest in your company.

Public companies can prevent such lawsuits, or at least win them if brought, only by a careful program of promptly disclosing adverse news to the trading markets and by avoiding overly optimistic or exaggerated comments in shareholder and press releases. This requires that you be sensitive to the need for such disclosures.

Since everyone makes a mistake occasionally, it is a good idea to obtain liability insurance for directors and officers. Such insurance can cost anywhere from $15,000 to $100,000 per year or more in addition to the out-of-pocket expenses described earlier. However, some private companies maintain this insurance, but usually at lower cost.

Thus, only consider the extra insurance premium costs of being public a disadvantage of an IPO.

(6) *Estate tax disadvantage.* One of the advantages of an IPO is to create sufficient liquidity to pay death taxes. However, there is a concomitant disadvantage. It is more difficult to obtain a low estate tax valuation for a publicly traded stock than for the stock of a private company. This is true because the public market tends to value stocks on a multiple of earnings basis, rather than a book value basis.

APPENDIX 1

Selected Recent Sales of Businesses with Sale Prices from $10 Million to $1 Billion

INTRODUCTION

This appendix contains valuation information on selected businesses whose sale prices are between $10 million and $1 billion. The appendix is not intended to be exhaustive, but merely to provide the reader with a few examples of valuation methodology. The appendix is arranged in the order of the total fixed sale price, with businesses having the highest sale price first.

The appendix was compiled from submissions by three investment bankers and contains only a few examples of recent sale transactions handled by such investment bankers. Since valuation information, particularly valuation methodology, is usually not readily available in private sales, this appendix provides a unique glimpse into the valuations obtained in the presented transactions.

The names of the three investment bankers are as follows:

The Chicago Corporation
208 South LaSalle
Chicago, Illinois 60604

(312-855-5204)
Attn: Michael Walker
    Robert C. Douglas

Legg Mason Corporate Finance
Legg Mason Wood Walker, Inc.
1735 Market Street
Suite 1100
Philadelphia, PA 19103
(215-496-8300)
Attn: Seth Lehr

Parker/Hunter Incorporated
1735 Market Street
Suite 4301
Philadelphia, PA 19103
(215-557-0130)
Attn: Susan H. Wolford

The references to DCF in the appendix refer to discounted cash flow.

SALE TRANSACTION

1. Year of Closing: 1995

2. Industry: Financial Services

3. Product or Service: Asset-Based Financing,
                                 Asset Management

4. SIC Code (if available):   6153

5. Gross Revenue During
   Last Full Fiscal Year: $110.4 million

6. EBITDA During Last
   Full Fiscal Year: $N/A

7. Total Fixed Sale Price: $523,250,000

8. Portion Paid After Closing: $523,250,000

9. Total Maximum Earnout
   (if applicable): $N/A

10. Primary Basis for valuation (please check and fill in):

    Total EBITDA   Specify the Multiplier
    Valuation $N/A   N/A x

    Discounted   Specify the Discount
    Cash Flow $240–456 million Rate   14.3%

    Other (specify)_____

11. Structure (check appropriate blank):

    Sale of Assets _____   Merger___X_____
    Sale of Stock _____   Consolidation _____
    Other (specify) _____

12. Discuss Valuation Theory and Special Valuation Factors (attach
    additional pages, if necessary).

    DCF valuation was supported by various analyses, including
    public market and merger and acquisition comparables analy-
    ses for each of the companies' income streams.

SALE TRANSACTION

1. Year of Closing: 1995

2. Industry: Power Protection

3. Product or Service: Uninterruptable Power Supply Products

4. SIC Code (if available):   3577 Computer Peripherals

5. Gross Revenue During Last Full Fiscal Year: $149.4 million

6. EBITDA During Last Full Fiscal Year: $20.2

7. Total Fixed Sale Price: $196.0 million cash

8. Portion Paid After Closing: $0

9. Total Maximum Earnout (if applicable): $0

10. Primary Basis for Valuation (please check and fill in):

     Total EBITDA Valuation $198 million   Specify the Multiplier   9.8 x

     Discounted Cash Flow $N/A   Specify the Discount Rate   N/A%

     Other (specify) _____

11. Structure (check appropriate blank):

     Sale of Assets _____   Merger __X____

     Sale of Stock _____   Consolidation _____

     Other (specify) _____

SALE TRANSACTION

1. Year of Closing: _____1995_____

2. Industry: _____Soft drink_____

3. Product or Service: _____Root beer_____

4. SIC Code (if available): _____2087 2086_____

5. Gross Revenue During Last Full Fiscal Year: _____$28.8 million_____

6. EBITDA During Last Full Fiscal Year: _____$8.3 million_____

7. Total Fixed Sale Price: _____$90 million_____

8. Portion Paid After Closing: _____$0_____

9. Total Maximum Earnout (if applicable): _____$0_____

10. Primary Basis for Valuation (please check and fill in):

    Total EBITDA Valuation _____$80–110 million_____ Specify the Multiplier _____9.6 x 13.2 x_____

    Discounted Cash Flow _____$83.3 million_____ Specify the Discount Rate _____10%_____

    Other (specify)_____

11. Structure (check appropriate blank):

    Sale of Assets __X_____   Merger_____
    Sale of Stock _____   Consolidation _____
    Other (specify)_____

12. Discuss Valuation Theory and Special Valuation Factors (attach additional pages, if necessary).

    Our client was a privately owned, highly successful niche player in the beverage market. Several of its competitors had recently undergone M&A transactions that established "strategic" valuations.

However, our client had only one logical buyer, who also was a competitive threat. Therefore, we performed an extensive valuation that looked at comparable companies to establish a public stock market valuation and comparable M&A transactions that established a high and "strategic" value. We supported these with a discounted cash flow analysis. We also analyzed an LBO buyout valuation to establish a minimum value for the company that a financial buyer could pay through leveraging the company.

SALE TRANSACTION

1. Year of Closing: 1995–Pending (Sept. 29)

2. Industry: Computer Components

3. Product or Service: LAN

4. SIC Code (if available):   3677

5. Gross Revenue During
   Last Full Fiscal Year: $65 million

6. EBITDA During Last
   Full Fiscal Year: $Negative

7. Total Fixed Sale Price: $53 million

8. Portion Paid After Closing: $0

9. Total Maximum Earnout
   (if applicable): $0

10. Primary Basis for Valuation (please check and fill in):

    Total EBITDA   Specify the Multiplier
    Valuation $N/A   8.8 x

    Discounted   Specify the Discount
    Cash Flow $55 million   Rate   10.36%

    Other (specify) Represented the buyer who analyzes all
                     investments on a DCF basis. Furthermore, the
                     target had lost money on an EBITDA basis;
                     therefore DCF became more important.

11. Structure (check appropriate blank):

    Sale of Assets _____   Merger   X
    Sale of Stock _____   Consolidation _____
    Other (specify) Our client was a "white knight" in a hostile
                     takeover situation.

12. Discuss Valuation Theory and Special Valuation Factors (attach additional pages, if necessary).

Our valuation theory was based on discounted cash flow (DCF) because our buyer analyzes all investments on a DCF basis and target had lost money at the operating level. The DCF also became more relevant as our client performed extensive due diligence over a six-month period, which allowed it to identify specific synergies and cost savings. Furthermore, the operating performance of the target had suffered for specific identifiable reasons. Therefore, applying a multiple to historical earnings was meaningless. We developed conservative projections and applied a discount rate. The discount rate was based on a weighted average cost of capital. We supplemented the DCF by applying comparable public company multiples to the projected operating performance. We also supplemented the DCF valuation by analyzing projected operating performance of the two companies on a combined basis relative to the projected operating performance of our client on a stand-alone basis. This allowed us to determine whether the merger, on a projected basis, would improve or worsen the projected EPS of our client on a standalone basis. The pro forma analysis also allowed us to analyze various consideration packages.

SALE TRANSACTION

1. Year of Closing   1995

2. Industry: Distribution

3. Product or Service: Automotive Parts Aftermarket

4. SIC Code (if available):   5013

5. Gross Revenue During Last Full Fiscal Year: $40 million

6. EBITDA During Last Full Fiscal Year: $6.7 million

7. Total Fixed Sale Price: $42.8 million

8. Portion Paid After Closing: $0

9. Total Maximum Earnout (if applicable): $0

10. Primary Basis for Valuation (please check and fill in):

Total EBITDA Valuation $33–42 million	Specify the Multiplier 4.9 x 6.3 x	
Discounted Cash Flow $N/A	Specify the Discount Rate N/A%	

Other (specify) This was a competitive process between several industry buyers, including a competitor. Orchestrated a successful auction that drove the price up.

11. Structure (check appropriate blank):

Sale of Assets X   Merger _____

Sale of Stock _____   Consolidation _____

Other (specify) _____

12. Discuss Valuation Theory and Special Valuation Factors (attach additional pages, if necessary).

Our valuation was one of many in analyzing up to eighteen divestitures for our client, which was a publicly traded holding company. Therefore, we focused on a comparable public company valuation analysis to determine the independent market value of each of eighteen different entities, and we then determined whether the sale of a division would generate value in excess of the value the division's earnings received as part of the holding company. Ultimately the value received was a function of a strategic buyer winning a well-orchestrated auction process. It also reflected potential synergies and cost savings the strategic buyer could achieve.

SALE TRANSACTION

1. Year of Closing: 1994

2. Industry: Manufacturing

3. Product or Service: Safety Products

4. SIC Code (if available): _____

5. Gross Revenue During
   Last Full Fiscal Year: $60 million

6. EBITDA During Last
   Full Fiscal Year: $5.5 million

7. Total Fixed Sale Price: $35.0 million

8. Portion Paid After Closing: $None

9. Total Maximum Earnout
   (if applicable): $None

10. Primary Basis for Valuation (please check and fill in):

    Total EBITDA   Specify the Multiplier
    Valuation $N/A   6.4 x

    Discounted   Specify the Discount
    Cash Flow _____ Rate _____

    Other (specify)_____

11. Structure (check appropriate blank):

    Sale of Assets _____   Merger X_____
    Sale of Stock _____   Consolidation _____
    Other (specify) _____

12. Discuss Valuation Theory and Special Valuation Factors
    (attach additional pages, if necessary).

    The sale of this company generated significant interest among
    financial buyers, due to the beliefs that the company was
    selling at the bottom of an industry cycle and that financial per-
    formance understated potential cash-generating ability. A rela-
    tively high multiplier was applied to this company, which had
    exhibited no growth in sales or earnings for the five years prior
    to the sale.

SALE TRANSACTION

1. Year of Closing: _1994_

2. Industry: _Distribution_

3. Product or Service: _Electrical products and components_

4. SIC Code (if available): _5085_

5. Gross Revenue During Last Full Fiscal Year: _$110 million_

6. EBITDA During Last Full Fiscal Year: _$4.6 million_

7. Total Fixed Sale Price: _$30.2 million_

8. Portion Paid After Closing: _$0_

9. Total Maximum Earnout (if applicable): _$0_

10. Primary Basis for Valuation (please check and fill in):

    Total EBITDA Valuation _$22–28 million_   Specify the Multiplier _4.6 x 5.9 x_

    Discounted Cash Flow _$N/A_   Specify the Discount Rate _N/A%_

    Other (specify) _This was a successful auction process in which several industry bidders competed for the company. As a result, valuation was a function of competition and buyers' synergies._

11. Structure (check appropriate blank):

    Sale of Assets _X_   Merger _____
    Sale of Stock _____   Consolidation _____
    Other (specify) _____

12. Discuss Valuation Theory and Special Valuation Factors (attach additional pages, if necessary).

SALE TRANSACTION

1. Year of Closing: 1994

2. Industry: Manufacturing

3. Product or Service: Steel Fittings

4. SIC Code (if available):   3494 (Valves and Pipe Fittings)

5. Gross Revenue During
   Last Full Fiscal Year: $42.2 million

6. EBITDA During Last
   Full Fiscal Year: $6.1 million

7. Total Fixed Sale Price: $30.0 million

8. Portion Paid After Closing: 40% to be repaid through
   seller notes

9. Total Maximum Earnout
   (if applicable): $None

10. Primary Basis for Valuation (please check and fill in)

Total EBITDA Valuation $N/A	Specify the Multiplier 6.63 x
Discounted Cash Flow	Specify the Discount Rate

    Other (specify) Repurchase of 30% of private investor shares.

11. Structure (check appropriate blank):

Sale of Assets	Merger X
Sale of Stock X	Consolidation
Other (specify)	

12. Discuss Valuation Theory and Special Valuation Factors
    (attach additional pages, if necessary).

    The valuation included an examination of comparable publicly
    traded companies, discounted cash flow analysis, and an analy-
    sis of acquisition premiums paid for publicly traded companies.

The company was valued as a whole, assuming it was sold as a going concern. Valuation issues included accounting for the value of ownership in a foreign company and deducting for total debt obligations of $10.1 million. Other issues included accounting for foreign exchange risk to the future cost of imported inventory, the predictability of ongoing performance, adjustments for temporary excess inventory, outstanding litigation between the company and outside shareholders, and non-recurring expenses and income. Public company valuation multiples were adjusted downward to reflect the greater risks associated with the company.

A P P E N D I X   2

Selected Recent Sales of Businesses with Sale Prices from $500,000 to $10 Million

SIC	=	Small-Business Industry Classification Number
BUS TYPE	=	Best Description of Subject Business
ASK PR	=	Asking Price (000's) (IN THIS STUDY INVENTORY IS INCLUDED IN ASKING PRICE)
ANN GR	=	Annual Gross Sales (Normally Net of Sales Tax)
SDCF	=	Seller's Discretionary Cash Flow (Net Profit Before Taxes and ANY COMPENSATION TO OWNER plus Amortization, Depreciation, Other Non-Cash Expense and Non-Business-Related Expense (Normally to One Working Owner)
SALE DATE	=	Actual Date of Sale
SALE PR	=	Actual Sale Price (in 000's) (IN THIS STUDY INVENTORY IS INCLUDED IN SALE PRICE)
% DOWN	=	Down Payment as a Percent of Sale Price
TERMS	=	Terms of New or Assumed Encumbrance
SALE/GR	=	Sale Price Divided by Gross Sales
SALE/SDCF	=	Sale Price Divided by Seller's Cash Flow
INV	=	Inventory at the Time of Sale (in 000's) (IS INCLUDED IN BOTH ASKING AND SALE PRICE)
FF&E	=	Estimate of Value of Furniture, Fixtures, and Equipment
RENT/SALES	=	Rent as a Percent of Sales
AREA	=	Region of Geographical Location of Business

SIC #	BUS TYPE	ASKING PR (000) W/INV	ANN SALES (000)	SDCF (000)	SALE DATE	SALE PR (000) W/INV	% DOWN	TERMS	SALE/ SALES	SALE/ SDCF	INV AMT	FF&E (000)	RENT/ SALES	AREA
3079	Mfg-Injection Molding	3,500	7,000	950	01/31/95	3,000	33%	5 Yrs @ 8%	0.43	3.2	1,800	N/A	1.3%	Los Angeles, CA
3079	Mfg-Plastic Prod	895	1,345	446	09/30/94	850	70%	10 Yrs @ 7.5%	0.63	1.9	22	300	3%	Rocky Mountain
3079	Mfg-Irrigation Prod	5,420	10,000	1,550	06/30/94	5,020	78%	5 Yrs @ 7%	0.50	3.2	1,900	N/A	3%	Riverside, CA
5147	Distr-Meat & Food Products	1,800	5,294	608	06/30/94	1,800	100%	N/A	0.34	3.0	150	450	N/A	Central Florida
2899	Remfg-Wood Prod	6,600	18,000	1,250	04/30/94	6,300	100%	N/A	0.35	5.0	1,300	2.3M	1.2%	East Washington
3671	Mfg-Security Systems	1,200	1,500	300	09/30/93	1,300	38%	5 Yrs @ 7%	0.87	4.3	200	139	5%	Austin, TX
5047	Distr-Medical Equip	775	1,118	206	09/30/93	685	47%	7 Yrs @ 10%	0.61	3.3	50	260	3%	Carlsbad, CA
2521	Mfg-Office Furniture	1,320	3,000	350	06/30/93	1,072	83%	7 Yrs @ 8%	0.36	3.1	180	800	2%	Central Florida
3471	Metal Plating Company	750	1,060	298	06/30/93	700	29%	15 Yrs @ 10%	0.66	2.3	0	250	4.5%	Dallas, TX
3499	Mfg-Gears	550	500	N/A	03/31/93	550	100%	N/A	1.10	#ERRC	100	550	N/A	Dallas, TX
2599	Mfg-Chairs	600	2,134	262	03/31/93	550	51%	7 Yrs @ 8%	0.26	2.1	75	63	5%	Southeast Florida
5031	Distr-Doors & Windows	1,130	3,100	400	02/28/93	830	20%	10 Yrs @ 10%	0.27	2.1	70	39	N/A	New England
5161	Distr-Sealants	830	1,500	190	02/28/93	630	38%	7 Yrs @ 8%	0.42	3.3	170	13	N/A	New England
3544	Mfg-Machine Shop	673	696	115	03/31/93	615	31%	9 Yrs @ 8%	0.88	5.3	127	483	5.1%	Central NC
2752	Litho Printing Shop	4,500	6,900	1,087	02/28/93	4,500	30%	7 Yrs @ Pr+1	0.65	4.1	100	1.8M	1.5%	Dallas, TX
7372	Computer Software	505	1,000	300	10/31/92	505	36%	5 Yrs @ 9%	0.46	1.7	5	100	3%	Phoenix, AZ
5085	Distr-Indust Suppl	530	975	262	08/31/92	505	33%	10 Yrs @ 9.5%	0.52	1.9	55	47	1%	Oceanside, CA
3544	Mfg-Tool & Die	635	882	247	06/30/92	590	26%	7 Yrs @ 9%	0.67	2.4	1	490	2.4%	North Carolina
3551	Mfg-Modular Homes	720	3,400	282	06/30/92	620	40%	10 Yrs @ 8%	0.18	2.2	115	182	6%	Western PA
3544	Mfg-Tool & Die	1,400	3,512	397	05/31/92	900	70%	7 Yrs @ 10%	0.26	2.3	400	500	N/A	Northeast IN
5044	Distr-Office Equipment	2,200	3,600	650	04/30/92	1,450	40%	7 Yrs @ 7.5%	0.40	2.2	200	150	1%	Boise, ID

(continues)

SIC #	BUS TYPE	ASKING PR (000) W/INV	ANN SALES (000)	SDCF (000)	SALE DATE	SALE PR (000) W/INV	% DOWN	TERMS	SALE/SALES	SALE/SDCF	INV AMT	FF&E (000)	RENT/SALES	AREA
7342	Pest Control	650	2,000	150	01/01/92	630	30%	5 Yrs @ 10%	0.31	4.2	5	200	0.5%	Midwest
3600	Mfg-Small Parts	795	5,000	525	01/01/92	690	100%	N/A	0.14	1.3	195	150	N/A	LaVergne, TN
2752	Printing Shop	2,900	3,800	725	01/01/92	2,900	50%	10 Yrs @ 10%	0.76	4.0	0	N/A	2.5%	Cincinnati, OH
2741	Specialty Publication	650	610	52	05/31/95	515	79%	5 Yrs @ 9%	0.84	9.9	0	23	4.6%	Central Florida
3544	Mfg-Tool & Die	1,000	3,512	397	05/31/92	500	70%	7 Yrs @ 10%	0.14	1.3	400	500	N/A	Northeast IN
3545	Mfg-Fastening Tools	2,000	3,275	830	06/30/95	1,800	92%	7 Yrs @ 9%	0.55	2.2	600	380	2.7%	Central Florida
5035	Distr-Steel	830	1,832	278	08/31/95	651	69%	4 Yrs @ 10%	0.36	2.3	400	50	N/A	South Florida
5211	Sales/Install Vinyl Siding	610	1,200	196	10/30/94	540	52%	7 Yrs @ 8%	0.45	2.8	80	76	2%	Central NC
5812.02	Restr-Dinnerhouse	891	2,200	234	10/31/92	741	20%	10 Yrs @ 9%	0.34	3.2	9	196	14%	Westchester, NY
5812.02	Restr-Dinnerhouse	892	2,000	289	10/31/92	742	20%	10 Yrs @ 9%	0.37	2.6	8	200	11%	Westchester, NY
5812.06	Restr-Seafood	785	1,400	163	05/31/93	610	100%	N/A	0.44	3.7	15	325	7.5%	Southwest FL
6361	Title Insurance	550	1,300	268	09/30/92	550	60%	3 Yrs @ 8%	0.42	2.1	0	50	N/A	Tampa Bay, FL
7364	Photo Lab-5 Loc	659	1,050	127	10/30/93	519	36%	5 Yrs @ 7%	0.49	4.1	31	747	11.9%	Central NC
7538	Auto Repair W/Gas	525	1,250	273	08/31/95	525	26%	15 Yrs @ 8.25%	0.42	1.9	70	184	N/A	Central Virginia
7542	Car Wash-Full Service	1,330	1,300	310	03/31/94	1,330	40%	10 Yrs @ 8%	1.02	4.3	20	220	7.7%	Palm Beach, FL
7542	Car Wash	1,350	1,256	300	03/31/94	1,350	41%	10 Yrs @ 8%	1.02	4.3	20	220	7.7%	Palm Beach, FL

APPENDIX 3

Selected Recent Sales of Businesses with Sale Prices from $100,000 to $500,000

DATABASE REPORT KEY

SIC	=	Small-Business Industry Classification Number
BUS TYPE	=	Best Description of Subject Business
ASK PR	=	Asking Price (000's) (IN THIS STUDY INVENTORY IS INCLUDED IN ASKING PRICE)
ANN GR	=	Annual Gross Sales (Normally Net of Sales Tax)
SDCF	=	Seller's Discretionary Cash Flow (Net Profit Before Taxes and ANY COMPENSATION TO OWNER plus Amortization, Depreciation, Other Non-Cash Expense and Non-Business-Related Expense.) (Normally to One Working Owner)
SALE DATE	=	Actual Date of Sale
SALE PR	=	Actual Sale Price (in 000's) (IN THIS STUDY INVENTORY IS INCLUDED IN SALE PRICE)
% DOWN	=	Down Payment As a Percent of Sale Price
TERMS	=	Terms of New or Assumed Encumbrance
SALE/GR	=	Sale Price Divided by Gross Sales
SALE/SDCF	=	Sale Price Divided by Seller's Cash Flow
INV	=	Inventory at the Time of Sale (in 000's) (IS INCLUDED IN BOTH ASKING AND SALE PRICE)
FF&E	=	Estimate of Value of Furniture, Fixtures, and Equipment
RENT/SALES	=	Rent As a Percent of Sales
AREA	=	Region of Geographical Location of Business

SIC #	BUS TYPE	ASKING PR (000) W/INV	ANN SALES (000)	SDCF (000)	SALE DATE	SALE PR (000) W/INV	% DOWN	TERMS	SALE/ SALES	SALE/ SDCF	INV AMT	FF&E (000)	RENT/ SALES	AREA
0782	Plant Rental	155	192	62	12/31/94	115	60%	3 Yrs	0.60	1.9	30	25	10%	Southwest Florida
0782	Contr-Comm Landscape	248	525	97	03/31/93	215	44%	5 Yrs @ 9%	0.41	2.2	2	95	1.5%	Southwest Florida
1731	Contr-Electrical	200	N/A	25	05/31/94	115	35%	6 Yrs @ 6%	#ERRC	4.6	0	75	4%	Southwest Florida
1793	Design-Inst Baths &	128	978	115	12/31/93	113	44%	N/A	0.12	1.0	112	45	N/A	Southeast US
1799	Parking Lot Maintenance	126	344	66	03/31/92	126	46%	4 Yrs @ 9%	0.37	1.9	4	56	2%	Central Florida
2047	Distr-Dog Food	530	1,580	167	07/05/94	410	80%	7 Yrs @ 8%	0.26	2.5	70	50	1.9%	Central Florida
2096	Mfg-Popcorn Products	147	137	64	06/30/94	118	25%	8 Yrs @ 8%	0.86	1.8	2	42	3.7%	South Florida
2396	Silk Screen Printing	136	346	83	06/30/94	126	39%	5 Yrs @ 9%	0.36	1.5	23	31	2.6%	Central Florida
2431	Mfg-Wood Windows/ Grills	217	521	79	07/31/94	222	62%	7 Yrs @ 8%	0.43	2.8	43	113	3.7%	Central NC
2499	Mfg-Wood Serving Boards	400	1,600	204	06/30/95	400	31%	10 Yrs @ 11%	0.25	2.0	400	325	2.7%	Vermont
2511	Mfg-Lawn Furniture	245	767	(60)	01/01/92	210	25%	5 Yrs @ 10%	0.27	-3.5	70	70	7%	Central Florida
2521	Mfg-Custom Furniture	127	250	35	06/30/93	102	83%	5 Yrs @ 8%	0.41	2.9	23	56	5.6%	Central Florida
2599	Mfg-Chairs	525	2,134	262	04/30/93	475	51%	7 Yrs @ 8%	0.22	1.8	75	63	5%	Southeast Florida
2679	Mfg-Paper Boxes	170	392	85	05/31/92	130	29%	5 Yrs @ 9%	0.33	1.5	79	75	3%	Rhode Island
2752	Printing Shop	120	266	(7)	05/31/94	120	0%	10 Yrs @ Pr+	0.45	-17.1	5	72	10.4%	Central VA
2752	Printing Shop	231	332	83	07/31/95	171	86%	1 Yr @ 9%	0.52	2.1	4	80	3.5%	Southwest Florida
2752	Printer-Commercial	121	249	47	12/31/93	102	92%	6 Mos @ 0%	0.41	2.2	4	50	3.4%	Cincinnati, OH
2752	Printer-Commercial	223	205	53	02/28/93	205	22%	7 Yrs @ 10%	1.00	3.9	2	68	N/A	New England
2752	Printing Shop	220	350	90	01/31/93	215	23%	10 Yrs @ 10.5%	0.61	2.4	0	75	6.2%	Southwest Florida
2752	Printing Shop	294	232	93	10/31/92	249	33%	5 Yrs @ 10%	1.07	2.7	0	100	4%	Indian Harbor Beach
2752	Printing Shop	155	233	65	03/31/92	130	37%	10 Yrs @ 9%	0.56	2.0	5	50	5%	Southwest Florida
2752	Printer-Commercial	385	240	93	04/30/95	165	94%	1 Yr @ 8%	0.69	1.8	5	25	5.5%	Maine
2841	Mfg-Windshield Solvent	269	900	210	02/28/93	258	29%	N/A	0.29	1.2	65	25	N/A	Southeast US
2841	Dist-Cleaning Supplies	130	530	101	01/01/92	130	56%	5 Yrs @ 10%	0.25	1.3	100	25	3.2%	North Atlanta, GA

(continues)

SIC #	BUS TYPE	ASKING PR (000) W/INV	ANN SALES (000)	SDCF (000)	SALE DATE	SALE PR (000) W/INV	% DOWN	TERMS	SALE/ SALES	SALE/ SDCF	INV AMT	FF&E (000)	RENT/ SALES	AREA
2851	Mfg-Paint	220	500	110	08/15/94	160	77%	N/A	0.32	1.5	40	110	2.6%	Central Florida
3079	Mfg-Molds for Plastics	570	610	220	12/31/92	480	25%	10 Yrs @ 7%	0.79	2.2	20	275	4%	Melbourne, FL
3315	Mfg-Staples	144	291	74	10/30/94	157	52%	5 Yrs @ 9%	0.54	2.1	54	42	6%	Central NC
3544	Mfg-Tool & Die	1,000	3,512	397	05/31/92	500	70%	7 Yrs @ 10%	0.14	1.3	400	500	N/A	Northeast Indiana
3552	Mfg-Indust. Blowers	264	1,154	246	06/08/94	253	28.5%	N/A	0.22	1.0	26	72	N/A	Southeast US
3599	Mfg-CNC Machining	125	250	80	12/31/93	125	100%	N/A	0.50	1.6	25	95	1.6%	Cincinnati, OH
3599	Mfg-Sheet Metal	350	347	65	01/31/93	205	59%	5 Yrs @ 8%	0.59	3.2	0	175	11.5%	Central Florida
3600	Mfg-Small Parts	600	5,000	525	01/01/92	495	100%	N/A	0.10	0.9	195	150	N/A	La Vergne, TN
3711	Mfg-Custom Truck Tops	455	291	113	02/29/92	305	20%	5 Yrs @ 7.5%	1.05	2.7	20	30	N/A	N. Central Indiana
3721	Mfg-Utility Trailers	160	550	90	12/31/92	160	100%	N/A	0.29	1.8	15	80	4.4%	Central Florida
3993	Sign Manufacturer	117	292	62	08/31/93	117	40%	10 Yrs @ 10%	0.40	1.9	8	50	3.4%	Southwest Florida
4724	Travel Agency	150	2,414	11	08/31/92	150	33%	5 Yrs @ 8%	0.06	—	N/A	15	12%	Rhode Island
4724	Travel Agency	230	1,800	85	06/30/92	230	30%	5 Yrs @ 10%	0.13	2.7	2	72	1.8%	St. Petersburg, FL
4724	Travel Agency	180	2,000	25	04/30/92	130	30%	8 Yrs @ 8%	0.06	5.2	20	20	0.6%	Southwest Florida
4724	Travel Agency	180	2,000	62	03/31/92	130	30%	8 Yrs @ 8%	0.06	2.1	0	15	7.5%	Southwest Florida
5013	Distr-Truck Parts	204	1,200	156	08/31/92	149	90%	5 Yrs @ 10.2%	0.12	0.9	0	100	4.2%	Central Florida
5085	Distr-Pipes Valves Fittings	147	1,100	175	12/31/92	151	23%	N/A	0.14	0.9	346	38	N/A	Southeast US
5086	Distr-Lawn & Garden	194	1,200	77	11/30/92	175	75%	7 Yrs @ 8.5%	0.15	2.3	81	100	3%	Cincinnati, OH
5086	Distr-Lawn & Garden	194	1,200	95	11/30/92	175	75%	7 Yrs @ 6.5%	0.15	1.8	81	100	4%	Cincinnati, OH
5147	Distr-Meat & Food	530	1,580	167	07/05/92	410	80%	7 Yrs @ 8%	0.26	2.5	70	50	1.9%	Central Florida
5148	Distr-Produce	165	1,082	150	02/17/94	145	89%	2 Yrs @ 9%	0.13	1.0	20	20	0.3%	Central Florida
5148	Produce Delivery	175	1,250	60	12/02/92	175	50%	5 Yrs @ 8%	0.14	2.9	25	40	5%	Southwest Florida
5149	Mfg/Dist-Candy	170	116	33	06/30/92	149	34%	8 Yrs @ 8%	1.28	4.5	14	48	20%	North Atlanta, GA
5211	Distr-Building Supplies	120	696	41	04/30/94	105	44%	6 Yrs @ 8%	0.15	2.6	55	123	2.6%	Cincinnati, OH

(continues)

SIC #	BUS TYPE	ASKING PR (000) W/INV	ANN SALES (000)	SDCF (000)	SALE DATE	SALE PR (000) W/INV	% DOWN	TERMS	SALE/SALES	SALE/SDCF	INV AMT	FF&E (000)	RENT/SALES	AREA
5231	Retail-Wallpaper	165	757	101	09/30/94	110	100%	N/A	0.15	1.1	30	32	8.3%	Atlanta, GA
5231	Retail-Window Glass	142	452	104	02/28/94	112	58%	3 Yrs @ 9%	0.25	1.1	8	38	4.2%	Lee County, FL
5231	Retail-Home Decorating	162	636	89	04/30/93	122	93%	6 Mos @ 0%	0.19	1.4	29	117	6%	North Atlanta, GA
5251	Retail-Hardware	150	1,214	92	02/28/93	106	23%	10 Yrs @ 10%	0.09	1.2	500	66	N/A	New England
5251	Hdwe & Rental Equipment	214	850	130	08/31/92	108	62%	5 Yrs @ 8%	0.13	0.8	336	66	4%	Carolinas
5411	Retail Market W/Cafe	165	675	117	08/31/95	148	17%	SBA	0.22	1.3	30	71	5.3%	Massachusetts
5411	Retail-General Store	150	950	126	08/31/95	150	40%	20 yrs @ 9%	0.16	1.2	150	150	N/A	Vermont
5411	Retail-General Store	175	1,700	119	05/31/95	150	25%	7 Yrs @ 11%	0.09	1.3	75	45	1%	Maine
5411	Retail-General Store	392	1,200	158	03/31/95	274	16%	15 Yrs @ 8%	0.23	1.7	94	80	N/A	Maine
5411	Convenience Store	250	1,500	200	10/31/92	200	89%	3 Yrs @ 9%	0.13	1.0	200	100	4.4%	Central Florida
5461	Bakery-Custom Cakes	135	177	78	03/31/95	113	59%	5 Yrs @ 10%	0.64	1.4	15	30	7.3%	Central Florida
5461	Whsle Bakery-Bagels	140	275	50	08/31/94	130	20%	5 Yrs @ 8%	0.47	2.6	10	45	8%	Southwest Florida
5461	Bakery-Bagel Shop	148	280	45	07/31/94	138	25%	10 Yrs @ 9%	0.49	3.1	2	90	N/A	Southwest Florida
5461	Whsle & Retail Bakery	273	740	89	02/28/94	273	58%	7 Yrs @ 8%	0.37	3.1	12	150	3.3%	Cincinnati, OH
5461	Donut Shop	165	300	75	01/01/92	130	37%	5 Yrs @ 9%	0.43	1.7	1.7	65	N/A	Central Florida
5499	Retail-Natural Foods	130	800	115	08/31/95	130	30%	10 Yrs @ 9%	0.16	1.1	64	30	4.7%	Vermont
5541	Mini-Mart W/Gas	195	1,106	70	08/31/95	160	21%	20 Yrs Prime +	10.14	2.3	30	N/A	2%	Massachusetts
5541	Mini-Mart W/Gas	545	2,659	117	05/31/95	350	66%	N/A	0.13	3.0	30	105	3.8%	Central Florida
5541	Service Station	135	1,217	69	02/28/94	105	100%	N/A	0.09	1.5	15	30	2.3%	Central Florida
5541	Service Station	180	1,692	103	09/30/92	145	100%	N/A	0.09	1.4	15	50	1%	Central Florida
5541	Mini Mart W/Gas	140	1,315	65	02/01/92	124	48%	5 Yrs @ 10%	0.09	1.9	10	37	3.2%	Central Florida
5571	Motorcycle Dealer	700	2,601	267	07/31/92	443	29%	10 Yrs @ 10%	0.17	1.7	407	90	1.2%	North Carolina
5571	Retail-Motorcycles	197	1,208	41	06/30/94	135	29%	10 Yrs @ 7%	0.11	3.3	128	70	4.2%	Central VA
5699	Uniform Sales	275	750	125	08/31/92	250	30%	7 Yrs @ 9%	0.33	2.0	75	70	10%	Southwest Florida
5712	Retail-Furniture & H/H	185	1,260	161	07/31/95	160	88%	1 Yr @ 0%	0.13	1.0	25	50	1.9%	Central Florida
5713	Retail-Carpets	135	644	63	09/30/94	115	100%	N/A	0.18	1.8	0	82	5.3%	Central Florida

(continues)

SIC #	BUS TYPE	ASKING PR (000) W/INV	ANN SALES (000)	SDCF (000)	SALE DATE	SALE PR (000) W/INV	% DOWN	TERMS	SALE/ SALES	SALE/ SDCF	INV AMT	FF&E (000)	RENT/ SALES	AREA
5713	Retail-Carpets	165	607	77	05/31/94	135	70%	1 Yr @ 8%	0.22	1.8	0	69	4%	Central Florida
5734	Computer Sales &	125	275	100	05/31/95	120	97%	N/A	0.44	1.2	25	15	4%	Central Florida
5734	Retail-Computers	185	900	90	11/30/93	185	35%	N/A	0.21	2.1	55	10	N/A	Southeast US
5734	Computer Sales &	645	1,083	207	01/31/93	470	18%	10 Yrs @ 8%	0.43	2.3	30	164	1.9%	North Carolina
5812.01	Restr-Sports Bar	130	300	100	06/30/93	113	87%	5 Yrs @ 8%	0.38	1.1	5	78	8%	Central Florida
5812.01	Restr-Dinner W/ Cocktails	342	1,491	87	01/31/93	117	100%	N/A	0.08	1.3	8	107	5%	North Carolina
5812.02	Restr-Dinnerhouse	225	775	75	08/31/93	100	10%	10 Yrs @ 10%	0.13	1.3	8	100	6%	Middleton, MA
5812.02	Restr-Dinnerhouse	240	600	50	06/30/93	225	44%	5 Yrs @ 8%	0.38	4.5	5	180	5%	Putnam County, NY
5812.02	Restr-Beach Casual	147	230	30	06/30/93	147	13%	7 Yrs @ 9%	0.64	4.9	3	60	11.5%	Southwest Florida
5812.02	Restr-Dinnerhouse	300	750	45	03/31/93	225	50%	2 Yrs @ 10%	0.30	5.0	7	120	6%	Brookline, MA
5812.02	Restr-Dinnerhouse	294	900	N/A	12/31/92	274	33%	10 Yrs @ 7%	0.30	#ERRC	6	175	9%	Westchester Cty, NY
5812.02	Restr-Dinnerhouse	250	1,000	120	11/30/92	250	40%	10 Yrs @ 8%	0.25	2.1	16	175	8%	Westchester Cty, NY
5812.02	Restr-Dinnerhouse	150	700	24	10/31/92	140	100%	N/A	0.20	5.8	8	110	12%	Boston, MA
5812.02	Restr-Dinnerhouse	188	672	72	07/31/92	158	32%	7 Yrs @ 8%	0.24	2.2	12	125	7.5%	Southwest Florida
5812.02	Restr-Dinnerhouse	440	1,480	112	05/31/92	140	100%	N/A	0.09	1.2	10	150	N/A	Kittery, ME
5812.03	Restr-Family	300	604	99	05/31/93	275	49%	10 Yrs @ 9%	0.46	2.8	5	70	5.3%	Southwest Florida
5812.03	Restr-Family Style	150	569	45	05/31/93	145	100%	N/A	0.25	3.2	5	100	11%	Boston, MA
5812.03	Restr-Family	319	780	123	04/30/92	289	33%	10 Yrs @ 8%	0.37	2.3	6	97	8.5%	Westchester Cty, NY
5812.03	Restr & Lunch Only	160	421	88	05/31/95	155	19%	SBA	0.37	1.8	5	40	4.4%	Vermont
5812.04	Restr-Breakfast &	125	225	50	05/31/95	108	32%	5 Yrs @ 8%	0.48	2.2	1	45	6%	Southwest Florida
5812.04	Restr-Breakfast & Lunch	211	328	94	04/27/94	195	93%	5 Yrs @ 8%	0.59	2.1	5	20	4.3%	Central Florida
5812.07	Restr-Chinese	150	320	104	11/30/94	249	96%	6 Mos @ 10%	0.78	2.4	0	120	15.6%	Central Florida
5812.07	Restr-Thai Food	175	479	42	07/31/93	145	100%	N/A	0.30	3.5	5	75	10%	Marblehead, MA
5812.09	Restr-Italian	150	700	70	08/31/93	130	100%	N/A	0.19	1.9	5	120	5%	Marblehead, MA
5812.09	Restr-Italian	345	480	130	03/31/93	245	100%	N/A	0.51	1.9	5	150	N/A	Westchester Cty, NY
5812.09	Restr-Italian	395	430	85	06/30/92	245	50%	4 Yrs @ 10%	0.57	2.9	5	100	6%	Coastal S. Carolina

(continues)

SIC #	BUS TYPE	ASKING PR (000) W/INV	ANN. SALES (000)	SDCF (000)	SALE DATE	SALE PR (000) W/INV.	% DOWN	TERMS	SALES/ SALES	SALES/ SDCF	INV. AMT	FF&E (000)	RENT/ SALES	AREA
5812.12	Fast Food-Hamburgers	225	832	90	10/31/94	200	89%	N/A	0.24	2.2	0	120	9.6%	Central Florida
5812.12	Restr-Beer & Burgers	300	604	100	05/31/93	275	49%	10 Yrs @ 9%	0.46	2.8	10	90	5.3%	Southwest Florida
5812.16	Retail-Ice Cream	147	179	50	04/30/93	147	37%	7 Yrs @ 10%	0.82	2.9	3	75	9.3%	Southwest Florida
5812.16	Retail-Ice Cream	150	185	52	02/28/93	141	43%	5 Yrs @ 10%	0.76	2.7	0	60	N/A	New England
5812.16	Retail-Ice Cream	148	157	59	01/01/92	128	55%	5 Yrs @ 9%	0.82	2.2	2	80	13%	Pittsburgh, PA
5812.17	Fast Food-Yogurt	167	250	50	04/30/95	123	74%	5 Yrs @ 9%	0.49	2.5	5	30	10%	Central Florida
5812.22	Deli-Sandwiches	150	345	91	03/31/95	140	100%	N/A	0.41	1.5	25	30	5%	Maine
5812.22	Deli-Sandwiches	247	346	100	02/28/95	147	60%	N/A	0.42	1.5	3	70	17.3%	Central Florida
5812.22	Deli-Retail	172	214	25	02/28/93	137	80%	7 Yrs @ 8%	0.64	5.5	3	137	23.4%	Central Florida
5812.22	Deli-Sandwiches	118	232	53	02/28/93	101	49%	5 Yrs @ 8%	0.44	1.9	2	10	7%	Central Florida
5812.22	Deli-Franchise	185	459	99	04/30/92	175	34%	3 Yrs @ 8%	0.38	1.8	2	73	4.5%	S. Cobb County, GA
5912.25	Retail-Bakery/Deli	165	425	69	08/31/93	125	100%	N/A	0.29	1.8	0	30	6.4%	Westfield, NJ
5912.25	Deli-Bakery	185	635	116	01/31/93	115	52%	2 Yrs @ 9%	0.18	1.0	10	75	6.8%	Lee County, FL
5812.31	Food Catering-Mobil	352	570	111	05/31/94	295	41%	7 Yrs @ 7%	0.52	2.7	8	128	1.9%	Central N. Carolina
5813	Cocktail Lounge	185	300	89	06/12/95	140	76%	5 Yrs @ 9%	0.47	1.6	5	70	14.7%	Central Florida
5813	Bar/Restr/Billiards	325	355	84	09/30/94	277	18%	Various	0.78	3.3	5	75	14%	Southwest Florida
5813	Cocktail Lounge	123	250	45	10/30/92	123	35%	5 Yrs @ 8%	0.49	2.7	2	50	10%	Southwest Florida
5921	Liquor Store	149	399	87	03/31/93	149	40%	5 Yrs @ 10%	0.37	1.7	61	25	15%	Clearwater, FL
5961	Mail Order Clothing	201	425	115	06/30/94	151	50%	5 Yrs @ 8%	0.36	1.3	49	20	1%	Pittsburgh, PA
5962	Vending Machine Route	115	145	65	05/31/94	104	55%	4 Yrs @ 6%	0.72	1.6	10	60	3%	Pittsburgh, PA
5992	Retail-Florist	152	411	66	03/31/95	122	22%	5 Yrs @ 8%	0.30	1.8	13	14	3%	Atlanta, GA
5999	Retail-Pets & Supplies	225	539	67	07/31/93	200	20%	7.5 Yrs @ 9%	0.37	3.0	100	53	11%	Central Florida
6361	Title Insurance	185	270	92	12/31/94	140	76%	5 Yrs @ 8%	0.52	1.5	0	10	4.4%	Central Florida
6361	Title Insurance	200	350	112	07/31/93	190	65%	5 Yrs @ 8%	0.54	1.7	0	15	N/A	Tampa Bay, FL
6361	Title Insurance	304	380	160	02/28/93	213	100%	N/A	0.56	1.3	0	35	N/A	Tampa Bay, FL
6361	Title Insurance	235	125	85	02/28/93	235	55%	5 Yrs @ 10%	1.88	2.8	0	0	N/A	Clearwater, FL
7216	Dry Clean W/ Laundry	171	205	65	07/31/95	130	30%	7 Yrs @ 10%	0.63	2.0	5	35	14%	Atlanta, GA

(continues)

SIC #	BUS TYPE	ASKING PR (000) W/INV	ANN SALES (000)	SDCF (000)	SALE DATE	SALE PR (000) W/INV	% DOWN	TERMS	SALE/ SALES	SALE/ SDCF	INV AMT	FF&E (000)	RENT/ SALES	AREA
7216	Dry Clean/Coin Laundry	145	345	106	11/30/94	145	100%	N/A	0.42	1.4	15	114	2.0%	Central Florida
7216	Dry Clean Plant	348	277	101	03/31/93	283	35%	10 Yrs @ 9%	1.02	2.8	2	223	8.8%	North Carolina
7216	Dry Clean W/Coin	195	192	75	02/28/93	155	79%	7 Yrs @ 8%	0.81	2.1	1	50	8.3%	Central Florida
7216	Dry Clean Plant	280	390	105	09/30/92	260	50%	6 Yrs @ 7%	0.67	2.5	10	137	3%	Pittsburgh, PA
7217	Carpet Cleaning	162	391	120	09/30/95	162	42%	2 Yrs @ 6%	0.41	1.4	2	53	2.5%	Palm Beach, Florida
7217	Carpet Cleaning	260	375	75	07/31/92	250	30%	7 Yrs @ 8%	0.67	3.3	15	60	7%	Southwest Florida
7231	Beauty Salon-2 Loc	100	409	106	06/30/93	105	43%	4 Yrs @ 8%	0.26	1.0	0	57	11%	NW Metro Atl., GA
7336	Computer Graphics	192	201	71	03/31/94	157	57%	5 Yrs @ 8%	0.78	2.2	18	212	3%	Central N. Carolina
7338	Word Processor	120	240	60	02/28/93	105	45%	5 Yrs @ 10%	0.44	1.8	1	34	N/A	New England
7338	Medi Record Transcribe	148	218	52	04/30/92	115	44%	10 Yrs @ 10%	0.53	2.2	0	2	None	Southwest Florida
7349	Lawn Care Maint	110	106	52	02/01/92	100	50%	5 Yrs @ 8%	0.94	1.9	2	50	3.7%	Cincinnati, OH
7349	Lawn Maintenance	110	106	52	02/01/92	100	50%	5 Yrs @ 8%	0.94	1.9	1	50	3.4%	Cincinnati, OH
7349	Pressure Cleaning	124	160	55	04/30/94	100	35%	5 Yrs @ 7%	0.62	1.8	1	35	7%	Southwest Florida
7349	Spray Clean/Mildew	125	160	52	03/31/94	110	45%	3 Yrs @ 8%	0.69	2.1	1	50	1%	Southwest Florida
7349	Comm Metal Roof Repair	130	210	75	06/30/93	118	30%	4 Yrs @ 7%	0.56	1.6	0	14	4%	NW Metro Atl., GA
7349	Lawn Care Maintenance	450	451	249	05/31/93	375	83%	7 Yrs @ 9%	0.83	1.5	0	285	6.2%	Central Florida
7349	Home Inspection Service	148	165	65	02/28/93	135	41%	5 Yrs @ 10%	0.82	2.1	1	0	N/A	New England
7349	Vehicle Cleaning	250	401	109	04/30/92	190	42%	5 Yrs @ 9%	0.47	1.7	N/A	10	0.1%	Central Florida
7349	Truck Cleaning	250	401	109	04/30/92	190	76%	5 Yrs @ 9%	0.47	1.7	0	10	2.5%	Central Florida
7361	Temporary Employment	550	3,212	248	11/30/93	300	N/A	N/A	0.09	1.2	0	75	N/A	Southeast US
7361	Home Health Care	300	140	22	01/01/92	180	44%	10 Yrs @ 10%	1.29	—	N/A	35	6.5%	North Carolina
7361	Nurses' Registry	300	538	89	01/01/92	125	60%	3 Yrs @ 8%	0.23	1.4	0	6	1.1%	Virginia
7384	One Hour Photo	195	392	104	03/31/94	195	45%	10 Yrs @ 8%	0.50	1.9	5	110	4.5%	Southwest Florida

(continues)

SIC #	BUS TYPE	ASKING PR (000) W/INV	ANN SALES (000)	SDCF (000)	SALE DATE	SALE PR (000) W/INV	% DOWN	TERMS	SALE/ SALES	SALE/ SDCF	INV AMT	FF&E (000)	RENT/ SALES	AREA
7385	Mfg Representative	244	210	135	09/30/92	164	43%	7 Yrs @ 8%	0.78	1.2	N/A	25	3.4%	Cincinnati, OH
7389	Telco Answering Service	175	325	101	01/31/95	139	100%	N/A	0.43	1.4	0	74	2.2%	South Florida
7532	Auto Body Repair	158	650	90	04/30/94	138	50%	5 Yrs @ 8%	0.21	1.5	12	60	6%	Southwest Florida
7539	Auto Electric Repair	185	405	70	07/31/94	120	100%	N/A	0.30	1.7	5	81	7.7%	Palm Beach, Florida
7629	Electronic Repair	135	600	65	02/28/95	115	55%	3 Yrs @ 8%	0.19	1.8	35	35	12%	Southwest Florida
7629	Elect Testing & Refurbish	510	1,250	250	08/31/93	460	40%	10 Yrs @ 8%	0.37	1.8	40	125	3%	Southwest Florida
7629	Elect Breakers Repair	430	1,200	150	07/31/93	380	40%	7 Yrs @ 8%	0.32	2.5	120	110	2%	Southwest Florida
7699	Mower & Tractor Service	115	750	50	09/30/92	115	19%	6 Mos @ 10%	0.15	2.3	45	38	4%	NE Metro Atl., GA
8051	Nursing Home	310	482	131	05/31/92	150	20%	N/A	0.31	1.1	N/A	25	N/A	Rhode Island
8249	Vocational School	182	279	164	05/31/94	182	45%	5 Yrs @ 10%	0.65	1.1	0	30	11.9%	Lee County, FL
8249	Vocational School	165	444	233	03/31/94	165	39%	5 Yrs @ 9%	0.37	0.7	1	29	6.5%	Lee County, FL
8249	Vocational School	175	198	81	01/01/92	150	37%	5 Yrs @ 10%	0.76	1.9	N/A	65	21%	Metro Atlanta, GA
8299	Educational Testing	250	294	105	02/28/94	230	38%	7 Yrs @ 8%	0.78	2.2	0	30	6%	Southwest Florida
8299	Educ Testing/ Tutoring	250	294	87	01/31/94	230	38%	7 Yrs @ 8%	0.78	2.4	0	55	6%	Southwest Florida
8299	Auto Driving School	250	241	66	02/28/93	235	34%	7 Yrs @ 10%	0.98	3.6	0	40	N/A	New England
8351	Day Care Center	110	95	20	02/28/93	110	75%	5 Yrs @ 10%	1.16	5.5	0	18	N/A	New England
8351	Pre-School	119	240	62	12/31/92	111	54%	5 Yrs @ 8.5%	0.46	1.8	0	50	17%	Melbourne, FL
8399	Companion Agency	139	480	81	07/31/93	131	50%	5 Yrs @ 10%	0.27	1.6	0	0	0	Melbourne, FL
8721	Accounting Service	160	117	60	08/31/94	150	45%	5 Yrs @ 8%	1.28	2.5	0	75	3%	Southwest Florida
8721	Accounting Practice	160	120	60	07/31/94	150	45%	5 Yrs @ 8%	1.25	2.5	0	60	8%	Southwest Florida
8721	CPA Practice	147	97	59	07/31/92	120	100%	N/A	1.24	2.0	N/A	20	5%	Clearwater, FL
9999	Exporter	250	703	159	12/31/94	240	96%	4 Yrs @ 8%	0.34	1.5	0	45	N/A	Central Florida

APPENDIX 4

Sample Confidentiality Agreement

S Corporation
200 Main Square
Anywhere, USA
Attn: Mr. John Doe
       President

RE: *CONFIDENTIALITY AGREEMENT*

Dear Gentlemen:

In connection with our possible interest in purchasing S Corporation and/or its subsidiary, Sub. Inc. (individually and collectively the "Company"), you are furnishing us with certain information which is either non-public, confidential or proprietary in nature. The information furnished to us, together with analyses, compilations, studies or other documents prepared by us, or by our partners, directors, officers, employees, representatives, attorneys, accountants, financial advisors and other agents (individually and collectively the "Representatives"), which contain or otherwise reflect, such information or our review of, or interest in, the Company, are hereinafter referred to individually and collectively as the "Information." In consideration of the Company furnishing us with the Information, we agree that:

1. The Information shall be kept confidential and shall not, without the prior written consent of the Company, be

disclosed by us, or by our Representatives. Moreover, we agree to reveal the information only to our Representatives who need to know the Information for the purpose of evaluating the transaction described above, who are informed by us of the confidential nature of the Information and who shall agree in writing to be bound by the terms and conditions of this Agreement. The Company shall be named as a third-party beneficiary of the Agreement with our Representatives. We will be responsible for any breach of this Agreement by our Representatives.

2. Without the Company's prior written consent, we and our Representatives will not disclose to any individual or entity the Information, the fact that the Information has been made available, that discussions or negotiations are taking place concerning a possible transaction involving us and the Company, or any of the terms, conditions or other facts with respect to any such possible transaction (including the status thereof).

3. We shall keep a record of the Information furnished to us and of the location of such Information. The Information, except for that portion of the Information which consists of analyses, compilations, studies or other documents prepared by us or by our Representatives, will be returned to the Company immediately upon the Company's request, together with all copies thereof. That portion of the Information which consists of analyses, compilations, studies or other documents prepared by us or by our Representatives will be held by us and kept confidential and subject to the provisions of this Agreement, or destroyed by us upon the request of the Company. Such destruction shall be confirmed by us in writing.

4. This Agreement shall not apply to such portions of the Information which (a) are already or become generally available to the public through no fault or action by us or by our Representatives, or (b) become available to us on a non-confidential basis from a source, other than the Company or its Representatives, which is not prohibited from disclosing such portions to us by a contractual, legal or fiduciary obligation to the Company or its Representatives.

5. Without the Company's prior written consent, neither we nor any of our Affiliates (as hereafter defined) will for a period of one year from the date hereof either (i) directly or indirectly solicit for employment any person who is now employed by the

Company or any of its subsidiaries or (ii) employ any such person whether or not we or our Affiliates solicited such employment. The term "Affiliates" as used herein includes any individual or entity directly or indirectly, through one or more intermediaries, controlling us or controlled by or under common control with us.

6. For a period of one year from the date of this Agreement neither we nor any of our Affiliates will use any of the Information which is non-public in any business which is competitive to the business of the Company.

7. We understand that the Company has endeavored to include in the Information those materials which it believes to be reliable and relevant for the purpose of our evaluation, but we acknowledge that neither the Company nor its Representatives makes any representation or warranty as to the accuracy or completeness of the Information. The only representations or warranties for which the Company is responsible are those set forth in any definitive acquisition which the Company may execute.

8. If we are requested or directed in a judicial, administrative, or governmental proceeding to disclose any Proprietary Information, we will notify the Company as promptly as practicable so that the Company may either (a) seek an appropriate protective order or other relief or (b) waive the provisions of this Agreement.

9. In the event of a breach of any of the provisions of this Agreement or of any written agreement referred to in paragraph 1 hereof, the actual damages incurred by the Company will be difficult, if not impossible, to ascertain. Such damages will include (but not be limited to) (a) a loss of goodwill (including damage to the reputation of the Company and its shareholders, subsidiaries and other affiliates) and a loss of morale among employees of each of these entities; and (b) a competitive injury to the Company and its shareholders, subsidiaries and other affiliates. The parties hereto have agreed that in the event of a breach by us of any of the provisions of this Agreement or of any written agreement referred to in paragraph 1 hereof, the Company shall be entitled, in compensation for the Company's loss of goodwill, to receive from us the sum of $_____ as fixed and agreed liquidated damages, it being understood and agreed that such liquidated damages will not compensate for other damages or prejudice the Company's right to equitable relief as recited in paragraph 10 hereof.

10. We acknowledge that each of the provisions of this Agreement or of any written agreement referred to in paragraph 1 hereof is necessary to preserve the confidentiality of the Information provided pursuant to this Agreement and that a breach of any such provision will result in irreparable damage to the Company and its shareholders, subsidiaries and other affiliates, in an amount now impossible to calculate (except to the extent of the liquidated damages provided in paragraph 9 hereof). Therefore, in the event of any breach of any provision of this Agreement or of any written agreement referred to in paragraph 1 hereof, the Company shall be entitled (in addition to any other rights and remedies it may have at law or in equity) to have an injunction issued by any competent court of equity enjoining us and any other person from continuing such breach.

11. No failure or delay by the Company in exercising any right, power or privilege hereunder shall operate as a waiver thereof, nor shall any single or partial exercise thereof preclude any other or further exercise thereof or the exercise of any right, power or privilege hereunder.

12. This Agreement constitutes our entire agreement with respect to its subject matter, may not be amended, supplemented, waived or terminated except by a written instrument executed by the parties, and shall be governed by the internal laws of the State of _____. Each counterpart of this Agreement shall constitute an original against any party signing it.

Very truly yours,

B CORPORATION

BY: _____
       Name

TITLE: _____

Date: _____

Accepted

S CORPORATION

BY: _____
       Name

TITLE: _____

Date: _____

APPENDIX 5

Sample Letter of Intent

Dear S Corporation:

This letter[1] is intended to summarize the discussions between S Corporation and B Corporation and to constitute a non-legally binding Letter of Intent.[2] The discussions expressed in this Letter of Intent are intended to be embodied into a legally binding definitive agreement ("Definitive Agreement") to be signed by parties and which is subject to the approval of the respective boards of directors of the parties. Our discussions were as follows:

Purchase Price

Pursuant to the Definitive Agreement, S Corporation will sell all of its assets to B Corporation for $25,000,000.

Conditions to Closing

The consummation of the sale shall be subject to the satisfaction of the following conditions:

1. Substitute "document" for "letter" if the Letter of Intent is not expressed as a letter.
2. You may use the words "Agreement in Principle" instead of "Letter of Intent."

(a) the parties shall have executed on or prior to
_____, 199_ a Definitive Agreement containing
mutually acceptable provisions relating to, among other
things, representations, warranties, conditions, covenants,
and indemnification; and

(b) the boards of directors of both shall have approved the
Definitive Agreement; and

(c) a majority of the shareholders of S Corporation shall
have voted in favor of the Definitive Agreement; and

(d) the parties shall have received all required approvals
and consents from governmental authorities and agencies and
third parties.

General

Neither of the parties to this letter shall disclose to the public or to
any third party the existence of this letter or the proposed sale
described herein other than with the express prior written consent of the other party, except as may be required by law.

From and after the date hereof, upon reasonable prior notice
and during normal business hours, S Corporation will grant to B
Corporation and its agents, employees and designees full and
complete access to the books and records and personnel of S
Corporation. Except as may be required by law or court order, all
information so obtained, not otherwise already public, will be
held in confidence.

This Letter of Intent reflects certain major business terms
which are intended to be embodied into the Definitive
Agreement; it is understood that the Definitive Agreement will
contain many of the other terms and conditions which will have
to be negotiated and agreed to before the Definitive Agreement
can be finalized. Until the Definitive Agreement is finalized,
approved by the respective Boards of Directors (which approval
shall be in the sole subjective discretion of the respective Boards
of Directors), and properly executed, neither party shall have any
legally binding obligation to the other (whether under this Letter
of Intent or otherwise), including, but not limited to, a legal duty
to continue negotiations to reach such a Definitive Agreement,

and either party may discontinue negotiations at any time for any reason whatsoever.[3,4]

If the enclosed correctly expresses our understanding, please execute this letter where indicated below.

Very truly yours,

B CORPORATION

3. Consider adding the following in appropriate situations:

"In the event that either party brings suit to enforce any alleged legal obligations arising from this Letter of Intent, the other party shall be entitled to summary judgment and to be reimbursed for its attorney's fees and expenses."

4. In certain cases, the Letter of Intent may contain clauses, such as confidentiality provisions, which are intended to be legally binding. In such cases, add the following:

"Notwithstanding anything to the contrary contained herein, the provisions set forth in [identify place in Letter of Intent where provisions appear, e.g. "the third paragraph of page 2"] are intended to be legally binding upon the parties."

APPENDIX 6

Sample Agreement to Sell Assets for Cash

THIS AGREEMENT made as of the 1st day of May, 1994 by and among Albertson Medical Specialists, P.C., a Pennsylvania professional corporation ("AS"), Albertson Physical Therapy, P.C., a Pennsylvania professional corporation ("APT"), Jenkins-Michael Associates, a Pennsylvania general partnership ("J-R"; AS, APT and J-R are hereinafter referred to collectively as the "Companies"), Sara Ann Rubin, M.D. ("Sara"), Michael Daniel Rubin, M.D. ("Michael"), Kimberly Lageman, M.D. ("Kim") and Andrew Mortenson, M.D. ("Andrew"); Sara, Michael, Kim and Andrew are hereinafter referred to collectively as the "Shareholders"), and ClinCare Corporation, a Delaware corporation (the "Purchaser").

WITNESSETH:

WHEREAS, AS is engaged in the businesses of (i) providing orthopedic medical services and owning and operating an orthopedic medical practice and related activities in the Commonwealth of Pennsylvania and (ii) providing physical therapy services and owning and operating rehabilitation facilities and related activities in the Commonwealth of Pennsylvania (such activities set forth in clause (ii) hereof being hereinafter referred to as the "AS Business");

WHEREAS, APT is engaged in the business of providing physical therapy services and owning and operating a rehabilitation facility and related activities in the Commonwealth of Pennsylvania (such activities being hereinafter referred to as the "APT Business"; and together with the AS Business, the "Business");

WHEREAS, the Shareholders are holders of all of the common stock (the "AS Common Stock"), of AS, which shares constitute all of the issued and outstanding shares of capital stock of AS (all such shares of AS Common Stock held by the Shareholders being hereinafter referred to as the "AS Shares");

WHEREAS, the Shareholders are holders of all of the common stock (the "APT Common Stock"), of APT, which shares constitute all of the issued and outstanding shares of capital stock of APT (all such shares of APT Common Stock held by the Shareholders being hereinafter referred to as the "APT Shares");

WHEREAS, the Shareholders are the holders of all of the outstanding partnership interests (the "Partnership Interests") of J-R (the "Partnership");

WHEREAS, the Purchaser desires to acquire certain assets of the Companies relating to the Business as described in Section I(C)(i) hereof (the "Assets") and to assume certain liabilities and contractual obligations of the Companies relating to the Business as described in Section I(C)(ii) hereof (the "Assumed Liabilities"), and the Companies desire to sell or assign the Assets and to assign the Assumed Liabilities to the Purchaser, on the terms and subject to the conditions hereinafter set forth; and

WHEREAS, to induce the Purchaser to enter into this Agreement and perform its obligations hereunder, the Shareholders have agreed to make the representations, warranties, covenants and agreements of the Shareholders (including the indemnification and non-competition agreements) set forth herein.

NOW, THEREFORE, in consideration of the premises and the mutual covenants and agreements hereinafter set forth, and intending to be legally bound, the parties hereto hereby agree as follows:

SECTION I.
PURCHASE AND SALE OF THE ASSETS

A. *Purchase and Sale of the Assets.* Subject to the terms and conditions of this Agreement and on the basis of the representations, warranties, covenants and agreements herein contained, at the Closing (as hereinafter defined):

(i) The Companies agree to sell, assign and convey to the Purchaser or its designee and the Purchaser (or its designee) agrees to purchase, acquire and accept from the Companies, the Assets.

(ii) The Companies agree to assign to the Purchaser (or its designee) and the Purchaser (or its designee) agrees to accept and assume from the Companies, the Assumed Liabilities. The Purchaser (and the designee, if any) shall not assume and shall have no responsibility with respect to, and shall be indemnified as set forth in Section X hereof by the Companies and the Shareholders, jointly and severally, from and against, any and all liabilities or obligations of the Companies other than the Assumed Liabilities.

B. *Purchase Price and Non-Competition Price.* The purchase price (the "Purchase Price") for the Assets is $___*___, in cash. The consideration (the "Non-Competition Price") for the covenants not to compete made by the Shareholders in Section XI hereof is $___*___, in cash. The Purchase Price shall be paid by the delivery to the Companies at the Closing of certified or official bank checks in the following amounts: $___*___ to AS; $___*___ to APT; and $___*___ to J-R. The Non-Competition Price shall be paid by the delivery to each Shareholder at the Closing of a certified or official bank check payable to the order of such Shareholder in the amount of $___*___.

C. *Assets; Assumed Liabilities.*

(i) The Assets shall consist of the assets listed in Schedule I-(A) hereto, but excluding the assets listed in Schedule I-(B) hereto.

* Figures omitted.

(ii) The Assumed Liabilities shall consist of and shall be limited solely to the obligations and liabilities of the Companies listed in Schedule II hereto.

D. *Allocation.* The Purchase Price for the Assets (including the Assumed Liabilities assumed by the Purchaser (or its designee)) shall be allocated as set forth in Schedule III hereto. The parties hereto agree that the allocation of the Purchase Price is intended to comply with the allocation method required by Section 1060 of the Internal Revenue Code of 1986, as amended (the "Code"). The parties shall cooperate to comply with all substantive and procedural requirements of Section 1060 of the Code and any regulations thereunder, and the allocation shall be adjusted if, and to the extent, necessary to comply with the requirements of Section 1060 of the Code. Neither the Purchaser nor any of the Companies will take, or permit any affiliated person to take, for federal, state or local income tax purposes, any position inconsistent with the allocation set forth in Schedule III hereto, or, if applicable, such adjusted allocation. Each of the Companies and the Purchaser hereby agrees that it shall attach to its tax returns for the tax year in which the Closing shall occur an information statement on Form 8594, which shall be completed in accordance with allocations set forth in Schedule III hereto.

E. *Assignment.* The parties hereto acknowledge and agree that the Purchaser may designate a direct or indirect wholly owned subsidiary of the Purchaser to acquire the Assets and assume the Assumed Liabilities; provided, however, that all of the Purchaser's obligations hereunder shall not be affected by such designation by the Purchaser.

SECTION II.
REPRESENTATIONS, WARRANTIES, COVENANTS
AND AGREEMENTS OF THE COMPANIES
AND THE SHAREHOLDERS

The Companies and the Shareholders, jointly and severally, hereby represent and warrant to, and covenant and agree with, the Purchaser, as of the date hereof and as of the date of the Closing, that:

A. *Organization and Qualification.*

(i) AS is duly organized, validly existing and subsisting under the laws of the Commonwealth of Pennsylvania and has full corporate power and authority to own its properties and to conduct the businesses in which it is now engaged. AS is in good standing in each other jurisdiction wherein the failure so to qualify would have a material adverse effect on its businesses or properties. AS has no subsidiaries, owns no capital stock or other proprietary interest, directly or indirectly, in any other corporation, association, trust, partnership, joint venture or other entity and has no agreement with any person, firm or corporation to acquire any such capital stock or other proprietary interest. AS has full power, authority and legal right and, to the best of the knowledge of each of the Companies and each of the Shareholders, all necessary approvals, permits, licenses and authorizations to own its properties and to conduct the AS Business. AS has full power, authority and legal right to enter into and consummate the transactions contemplated under this Agreement. The copies of the articles of incorporation and by-laws of AS which have been delivered to the Purchaser are complete and correct.

(ii) APT is duly organized, validly existing and subsisting under the laws of the Commonwealth of Pennsylvania and has full corporate power and authority to own its properties and to conduct the businesses in which it is now engaged. APT is in good standing in each other jurisdiction where it is presently conducting business wherein the failure so to qualify would have a material adverse effect on its businesses or properties. APT has no subsidiaries, owns no capital stock or other proprietary interest, directly or indirectly, in any other corporation, association, trust, partnership, joint venture or other entity and has no agreement with any person, firm or corporation to acquire any such capital stock or other proprietary interest. APT has full power, authority and legal right and, to the best of the knowledge of each of the Companies and each of the Shareholders, all necessary approvals, permits, licenses and authorizations to own its properties and to conduct the APT

Business. APT has full power, authority and legal right to enter into and consummate the transactions contemplated under this Agreement. The copies of the articles of incorporation and by-laws of APT which have been delivered to the Purchaser are complete and correct.

(iii) J-R is duly organized and validly existing under the laws of the Commonwealth of Pennsylvania and has full partnership power and authority to own its properties and to conduct the businesses in which it is now engaged. J-R does not do business in any jurisdiction other than the Commonwealth of Pennsylvania. J-R has no subsidiaries, owns no capital stock or other proprietary interest, directly or indirectly, in any other corporation, association, trust, partnership, joint venture or other entity and has no agreement with any person, firm or corporation to acquire any such capital stock or other proprietary interest. J-R has full power, authority and legal right and, to the best of the knowledge of each of the Companies and each of the Shareholders, all necessary approvals, permits, licenses and authorizations to own its properties and to conduct the J-R Business. J-R has full power, authority and legal right to enter into and consummate the transactions contemplated under this Agreement. The copy of the partnership agreement which has been delivered to the Purchaser is complete and correct.

B. *Authority*. The execution and delivery of this Agreement by each of the Companies, the performance by each of the Companies of their covenants and agreements hereunder and the consummation by the Companies of the transactions contemplated hereby have been duly authorized by all necessary corporate or partnership action. This Agreement constitutes valid and legally binding obligations of each of the Companies, enforceable against each of the Companies in accordance with its terms, except as such enforceability may be limited by bankruptcy, insolvency, moratorium or other similar laws affecting creditors' rights generally and general principles of equity relating to the availability of equitable remedies.

C. *No Legal Bar; Conflicts*. Neither the execution and delivery of this Agreement, nor the consummation of the transactions contemplated hereby, violates any provision of the articles of incorporation or by-laws of either AS or APT or the agreement or certificate of partnership of J-R or any statute, ordinance, regulation, order, judgment or decree of any court or governmental agency or board, or conflicts with or will result in any breach of any of the terms of or constitute a default under or result in the termination of or the creation of any lien pursuant to the terms of any contract or agreement to which any of the Companies is a party or by which any of the Companies or any of the Assets is bound. No consents, approvals or authorizations of, or filings with, any governmental authority or any other person or entity are required in connection with the execution and delivery of this Agreement and the consummation of the transactions contemplated hereby, except for required consents to assignment of the contracts as set forth or cross-referenced on Exhibit C which, with the Purchaser's consent, the Companies are not obtaining.

D. *Financial Statements; No Undisclosed Liabilities.* The Companies and the Shareholders have delivered to the Purchaser schedules of revenues and expenses included in the tax returns for each of Companies for the years ended December 31, 1993, 1992 and 1991, which tax returns (hereinafter referred to as the "Financial Statements") have been prepared by Countz & Associates, the Companies' independent accountants. The Financial Statements are true and correct in all material respects and have been prepared using the income tax basis of accounting. The Financial Statements fully and fairly present the financial condition of each of the Companies as at the dates thereof and the results of the operations of each of the Companies for the periods indicated. None of the Companies and none of the Shareholders is aware of any material omissions in the Financial Statements. A true and correct copy of the Financial Statements is attached hereto as Exhibit D.

E. *Absence of Certain Changes.* Except as set forth in Exhibit E, subsequent to December 31, 1993, there has not been any (i) adverse or prospective adverse change in the condition of the Business, financial or otherwise, or in the results of the operations of any of the Companies or the Business; (ii) damage or destruction (whether or not insured) affecting the properties or business operations of any of the Companies; (iii) labor dispute or threatened labor dispute involving the key employees of any of the Companies or any resignations or threatened resignations of physical or occupational therapists, or notice that any employees of any of the Companies intend to take leaves of absence, with or without pay; (iv) actual or threatened disputes pertaining to the Business with any major accounts or referral sources of any of the Companies, or actual or threatened loss of business from any of the major accounts or referral sources of any of the Companies; or (v) changes in the methods or procedures for billing or collection of customer accounts or recording of customer accounts receivable or reserves for doubtful accounts with respect to any of the Companies.

F. *Real Property Owned or Leased.* A list and description of all real property owned by or leased to or by each of the Companies or in which each of the Companies has any interest is set forth in Exhibit F. All such leased real property is held subject to written leases or other agreements which are valid and effective in accordance with their respective terms, and there are no existing defaults or events of default, or events which with notice or lapse of time or both would constitute defaults, thereunder on the part of the Companies. None of the Companies and none of the Shareholders has any knowledge of any default or claimed or purported or alleged default or state of facts which with notice or lapse of time or both would constitute a default on the part of any other party in the performance of any obligation to be performed or paid by such other party under any lease referred to in Exhibit F. None of the Companies and none of the Shareholders has received any written or oral notice to the effect that any lease will not be renewed at the termination of the term thereof or that any such lease will be renewed only at a substantially higher rent.

G. *Title to Assets; Condition of Property.* Each of the Companies has good and valid title to the Assets it is transferring hereunder. Each of the Companies has the right, power and authority to sell and transfer the Assets it is transferring hereunder to the Purchaser (or its designee) and upon such transfer, the Purchaser (or its designee) will acquire good and valid title to the Assets, free and clear of all liens, charges, encumbrances, security interests or valid claims whatsoever. The Assets include substantially all properties and assets necessary for the operations of the Business consistent with its current operations, other than insurance, the telephone system, employees, permits and licenses, cash in excess of $25,000, the charts and records of Dr. Richard Sawbones and the Sawbones Receivables (as hereinafter defined), oral agreements with AssureCare and U.S. CareGuard and the Companies' names and logos. All such properties and assets are in good condition and repair, reasonable wear and tear excepted, consistent with their respective ages, and have been maintained and serviced in accordance with the normal practices of each of the Companies and as necessary in the normal course of business. None of the Assets is subject to any liens, charges, encumbrances or security interests. None of the Assets (or uses to which they are put) fails to conform with any applicable agreement, law, ordinance or regulation in a manner which is likely to be material to the operations of the Business.

H. *Taxes.* Each of the Companies has filed or caused to be filed on a timely basis all federal, state, local and other tax returns, reports and declarations required to be filed by it and has paid or adequately reserved for all taxes, including, but not limited to, income, excise, franchise, gross receipts, sales, use, property, unemployment, withholding, social security and workers' compensation taxes and estimated income and franchise tax payments, and penalties and fines, due and payable with respect to the periods covered by such returns (whether or not reflected on such returns), reports or declarations and all subsequent periods or pursuant to any assessment received by it in connection with such returns, reports or declarations so as to prevent any lien or charge from attaching to the Assets. All returns, reports and declarations filed by or on behalf of each of the Companies are true, complete and correct in all material respects. No deficiency in payment of any taxes for any period has been asserted by any taxing authority which remains unsettled at the date hereof, no written inquiries have been received by any of the Companies from any taxing authority with respect to possible claims for taxes or assessments and, to the knowledge of each of the Companies and each of the Shareholders, there is no basis for any additional claims or assessments for taxes. Since December 31, 1993, none of the Companies has incurred any tax liability other than in the ordinary course of business. For the prior three years, no tax return of any of the Companies has ever been audited and no written inquiries have been received by any of the Companies from a taxing authority with respect to a possible claim for taxes or assessments. None of the Companies has agreed to the extension of the statute of limitations with respect to any tax return. There are no assessments relating to the tax returns of the Companies pending or threatened. Each of the Companies has delivered to the Purchaser copies of the federal and state income (or franchise) tax returns filed by each of the Companies for the past three years.

I. *Permits; Compliance with Applicable Law.*

(i) *General.* Except as set forth on Exhibit I(i), none of the Companies, to its knowledge, is in default under any, and each has, to its knowledge, complied with all, statutes, ordinances, regulations, orders, judgments and decrees of any court or governmental entity or agency, relating to the Business or the Assets as to which a default or failure to comply might result in a material adverse effect on the Business. None of the Companies and none of the Shareholders has any knowledge of any basis for assertion of any violation of the foregoing or for any claim for compensation or damages or otherwise arising out of any violation of the foregoing. None of the Companies and none of the Shareholders has received any notification of any asserted present or past failure to comply with any of the foregoing which has not been satisfactorily responded to in the time period required thereunder.

(ii) *Permits.* Set forth in Exhibit I(ii) is a complete and accurate list of all permits, licenses, approvals, franchises, notices and authorizations issued by governmental entities or other regulatory authorities, federal, state or local (collectively the "Permits"), held by each of the Companies in connection with the Business. To the best of the knowledge of each of the Companies and each of the Shareholders, the Permits set forth in Exhibit I(ii) are all the Permits required for the conduct of the Business. All the Permits set forth in Exhibit I(ii) are in full force and effect, and, to the best of the knowledge of each of the Companies and each of the Shareholders, none of the Companies has engaged in any activity which would cause or permit revocation or suspension of any such Permit, and no action or proceeding looking to or contemplating the revocation or suspension of any such Permit is pending or threatened. There are no existing defaults or events of default or event or state of facts which with notice or lapse of time or both would constitute a default by any of the Companies under any such Permit. None of the Companies and none of the Shareholders has any knowledge of any default or claimed or purported or alleged default or state of facts which with notice or lapse of time or both would constitute a default on the part of any party in the performance of any obligation to be performed or paid by any party under any Permit set forth in Exhibit I(ii). The consummation of the transactions contemplated hereby will in no way affect the continuation, validity or effectiveness of the Permits set forth in Exhibit I(ii) or require the consent of any person. Except as set forth on Exhibit I(ii), the Companies are not required to be licensed by, nor are they subject to the regulation of, any governmental or regulatory body by reason of the conduct of the Business.

(iii) *Environmental.*

(a) To the knowledge of each of the Companies and each of the Shareholders, each of the Companies has duly complied with and the real estate owned by each of the Companies and the improvements thereon, and the real estate subject to the leases listed on Exhibit F and improvements thereon, and all other real estate leased by each of the Companies, and the improvements thereon (all such owned or leased real estate hereinafter referred to collectively as the "Premises"), are, to the knowledge of each of the Companies and each of the Shareholders, in compliance with the provisions of all federal, state and local environmental, health and safety laws, codes and ordinances and all rules and regulations promulgated thereunder.

(b) To the knowledge of each of the Companies and each of the Shareholders, each of the Companies has been issued, and will maintain until the date of the Closing, all required federal, state and local permits, licenses, certificates and approvals relating to (i) air emissions, (ii) discharges to surface water or ground water, (iii) noise emissions, (iv) solid or liquid waste disposal, (v) the use, generation, storage, transportation or disposal of toxic or hazardous substances or wastes (intended hereby and hereafter to include any and all such materials listed in any federal, state or local law, code or ordinance and all rules and regulations promulgated thereunder, as hazardous or potentially hazardous), or (vi) other environmental, health and safety matters.

(c) None of the Companies has received any notice of, and neither any of the Companies nor any of the Shareholders knows of any facts which might constitute, violations of any federal, state or local environmental, health or safety laws, codes or ordinances, and any rules or regulations promulgated thereunder, which relate to the use, ownership or occupancy of any of the Premises or of any premises formerly owned, leased or occupied by the Companies. The Companies are not in violation of any rights-of-way or restrictions affecting any of the Premises or any rights appurtenant thereto.

(iv) *Medicare and Medicaid.* Except as set forth in Exhibit I(iv), each of the Companies has complied with all laws, rules and regulations of the Medicare, Medicaid and other governmental healthcare programs, and has filed all claims, invoices, returns, cost reports and other forms, the use of which is required or permitted by such programs, in the manner prescribed. Except as set forth in Exhibit I(iv), all claims, returns, invoices, cost reports and other forms made by the Companies to Medicare, Medicaid or any other governmental health or welfare related entity or any other third party payor since the inception of the Business are in all respects true, complete, correct and accurate. Except as set forth in Exhibit I(iv), no deficiency in any such claims, returns, cost reports and other filings, including claims for over-payments or deficiencies for late filings, has been asserted or threatened by any federal or state agency or instrumentality or other provider or reimbursement entities relating to Medicare or Medicaid claims or any other third-party payor, and there is no basis for any claims or requests for reimbursement, except for claims for disallowances in the ordinary course. None of the Companies has been subject to any audit relating to fraudulent Medicare or Medicaid procedures or practices. Except as set forth in Exhibit I(iv), there is no basis for any claim or request for recoupment or reimbursement from any of the Companies by, or for reimbursement by any of the Companies of, any federal, district or state agency or instrumentality or other provider reimbursement entities relating to Medicare or Medicaid claims. Net revenues from the Medicare program represented approximately 50% of the net revenues of the APT Business and approximately 10% of the AS Business during calendar years 1991, 1992, 1993 and during the first five months of 1994, in each case with a plus or minus five percent variance. During 1991, 1992, 1993 and the first five months of 1994, the Companies had no revenues from the Medicaid program.

J. *Licenses.* None of the Companies produces or distributes any product, or performs any service under a license granted by another entity and has not licensed its rights in any current or planned products, designs or services to any other entities.

K. *Accounts Receivable; Inventories.* The accounts receivable of each of the Companies which are part of the Assets are in their entirety valid accounts receivable, arising in the ordinary course of business. On or before 180 days from the date of the Closing, the Purchaser shall collect at least $160,000 of such accounts receivable. The inventories and equipment of the Companies are on the whole merchantable (other than for obsolete or damaged inventory which on the whole is not material) and fully usable in the ordinary course of business consistent with the prior practice of the Business. The Companies shall have available to the Purchaser, and the Assets shall include, unrestricted cash and cash equivalents of at least $25,000.

L. *Contractual and Other Obligations.* Set forth in Exhibit L is a list and brief description of all contracts, agreements, licenses, leases, arrangements (written or oral) and other documents to which each of the Companies is a party or by which each of the Companies or any of the Assets is bound (including, in the case of loan agreements, a description of the amounts of any outstanding borrowings thereunder and the collateral, if any, for such borrowings); all of the foregoing being hereinafter referred to as the "Contracts." There are no material contingent obligations and liabilities of each of the Companies other than for lawsuits set forth on Exhibit AA. Neither the Companies nor, to the best of the knowledge of each of the Companies and each of the Shareholders, any other party is in default in the performance of any covenant or condition under any Contract and no claim of such a default has been made and no event has occurred which with the giving of notice or the lapse of time would constitute a default under any covenant or condition under any Contract. None of the Companies is a party to any Contract which would terminate or be materially adversely affected by consummation of the transactions contemplated by this Agreement. Except as set forth in Exhibit L, none of the Companies is a party to any Contract expected to be performed at a loss. Originals or true, correct and complete copies of all written Contracts have been provided to the Purchaser.

M. *Compensation.* Set forth in Exhibit M attached hereto is a list of all agreements between each of the Companies and each person employed by or independently contracting with such Company with regard to compensation, whether individually or collectively, and set forth in Exhibit M is a list of all employees of each of the Companies who are employed in the Business (except for Dr. Sawbones and Donald Lachman) entitled to receive annual compensation in excess of $20,000 and their respective salaries. The transactions contemplated by this Agreement will not result in any liability for severance pay to any employee or independent contractor of any of the Companies. None of the Companies has informed any employee or independent contractor providing services to any of the Companies that such person will receive any increase in compensation or benefits or any ownership interest in any of the Companies or the Business other than increases in the ordinary course.

N. *Employee Benefit Plans.* Except as set forth in Exhibit N attached hereto, the Companies do not maintain or sponsor, nor are they required to make contributions to, any pension, profit-sharing, savings, bonus, incentive or deferred compensation, severance pay, medical, life insurance, welfare or other employee benefit plan. All pension, profit-sharing, savings, bonus, incentive or deferred compensation, severance pay, medical, life insurance, welfare or other employee benefit plans within the meaning of Section 3(3) of the Employee Retirement Income Security Act of 1974, as amended (hereinafter referred to as "ERISA"), in which the employees of the Business participate (such plans and related trusts, insurance and annuity contracts, funding media and related agreements and arrangements, other than any "multi-employer plan" (within the meaning of Section 3(37) of ERISA), being hereinafter referred to as the "Benefit Plans" and any such multi-employer plans being hereinafter referred to as the "Multi-employer Plans") comply in all material respects with all requirements of the Department of Labor and the Internal Revenue Service, and with all other applicable law, and the Companies have not taken or failed to take any action with respect to either the Benefit Plans or the Multi-employer Plans which might create any liability on the part of the Companies or the Purchaser. Each "fiduciary" (within the meaning of Section 3(21)(A) of ERISA) as to each Benefit Plan and as to each Multi-employer Plan has complied in all material respects with the requirements of ERISA and all other applicable laws in respect of each such Plan. Each of the Companies has furnished to the Purchaser copies of all Benefit Plans and Multi-employer Plans. All financial statements, actuarial reports and annual reports and returns filed with the Internal Revenue Service with respect to such Benefit Plans and Multi-employer Plans are true and correct in all material respects, and none of the actuarial assumptions underlying such documents have changed since the respective dates thereof. In addition:

(i) Each Benefit Plan has received a favorable determination letter from the Internal Revenue Service as to its qualification under Section 401(a) of the Code;

(ii) No Benefit Plan which is a "defined benefit plan" (within the meaning of Section 3(35) of ERISA) (hereinafter referred to as the "Defined Benefit Plans") or Multi-employer Plan has incurred an "accumulated funding deficiency" (within the meaning of Section 412(a) of the Code), whether or not waived;

(iii) No "reportable event" (within the meaning of Section 4043 of ERISA) has occurred with respect to any Defined Benefit Plan or any Multi-employer Plan;

(iv) The Companies have not withdrawn as a contributing sponsor (partially or totally within the meaning of ERISA) from any Benefit Plan or any Multi-employer Plan; and neither the execution and delivery of this Agreement nor the consummation of the transactions contemplated herein will result in the withdrawal (partially or totally within the meaning of ERISA) from any Benefit Plan or Multi-employer Plan, or in any withdrawal or other liability of any nature to the Companies or the Purchaser under any Benefit Plan or Multi-employer Plan;

(v) No "prohibited transaction" (within the meaning of Section 406 of ERISA or Section 4975(c) of the Code) has occurred with respect to any Benefit Plan or Multi-employer Plan;

(vi) The excess of the aggregate present value of accrued benefits over the aggregate value of the assets of any Defined Benefit Plan (computed both on a termination basis and on an ongoing basis) is not more than $-0-, and the aggregate withdrawal liability of any of the Companies with respect to any Multi-employer Plan, assuming the withdrawal of any of the Companies from said Multi-employer Plan, is not more than $-0-;

(vii) No provision of any Benefit Plan or of any agreement, and no act or omission of any of the Companies, in any way limits, impairs, modifies or otherwise affects the right of the Companies or the Purchaser unilaterally to amend or terminate any Benefit Plan after the Closing, subject to the requirements of applicable law;

(viii) Except for a contribution of not in excess of $50,000 for the recently completed plan year, there are no contributions which are or hereafter will be required to be made to trusts for the prior fiscal year in connection with any Benefit Plan that would constitute a "defined contribution plan" (within the meaning of Section 3(34) of ERISA) with respect to services rendered by employees of the Companies prior to the date of Closing;

(ix) Other than claims in the ordinary course for benefits with respect to the Benefit Plans or the Multi-employer Plans, there are no actions, suits or claims (including claims for income taxes, interest, penalties, fines or excise taxes with respect thereto) pending with respect to any Benefit Plan or any Multi-employer Plan, or any circumstances which might give rise to any such action, suit or claim (including claims for income taxes, interest, penalties, fines or excise taxes with respect thereto);

(x) All reports, returns and similar documents with respect to the Benefit Plans required to be filed with any governmental agency have been so filed;

(xi) None of the Companies has incurred any liability to the Pension Benefit Guaranty Corporation (except for required premium payments). No notice of termination has been filed by the plan administrator (pursuant to Section 4041 of ERISA) or issued by the Pension Benefit Guaranty Corporation (pursuant to Section 4042 of ERISA) with respect to any Benefit Plan subject to ERISA. There has been no termination of any Defined Benefit Plan or any related trust by any of the Companies;

(xii) No Benefit Plan which is a Defined Benefit Plan subject to Title IV of ERISA has applied for or received a waiver of the minimum funding standards imposed by Section 412 of the Code; and

(xiii) None of the Companies has any obligation to provide health or other welfare benefits to former, retired or terminated employees, except as specifically required under Section 4980B of the Code. Each of the Companies has substantially complied with the notice and continuation requirements of Section 4980B of the Code and the regulations thereunder.

In connection with the transactions contemplated hereby, as soon as practicable in accordance with applicable laws and the plan documents, following the date of the Closing, the Shareholders shall cause the trustees of the Albertson Medical Specialists, P.C. 401(k) Profit Sharing Plan (the "Profit Sharing Plan") to offer to distribute the account balances in the Profit Sharing Plan of the Employees (as hereinafter defined) who are participants in the Profit Sharing Plan in accordance with the terms of the plan documents and any and all applicable laws, rules or regulations. AS shall have fully vested all Employees of any of the Companies in their account balances in the Profit Sharing Plan.

AS agrees that any contributions now due or that may become due to the Profit Sharing Plan shall be the sole responsibility of AS and shall be immediately paid, when due, by AS.

O. *Labor Relations.* To the knowledge of each of the Companies and each of the Shareholders, there have been no violations of any federal, state or local statutes, laws, ordinances, rules, regulations, orders or directives with respect to the employment of individuals by, or the employment practices or work conditions of, any of the Companies, or the terms and conditions of employment, wages and hours. To the knowledge of each of the Companies and each of the Shareholders, none of the Companies is engaged in any unfair labor practice or other unlawful employment practice and there are no charges of unfair labor practices or other employee-related complaints pending or, to the knowledge of each of the Companies and each of the Shareholders, threatened against any of the Companies before the National Labor Relations Board, the Equal Employment Opportunity Commission, the Occupational Safety and Health Review Commission, the Department of Labor or any other federal, state, local or other governmental authority. There is no strike, picketing, slowdown or work stoppage or organizational attempt pending, threatened against or involving the Business. No issue with respect to union representation is pending or threatened with respect to the employees of any of the Companies. No union or collective bargaining unit or other labor organization has ever been certified or recognized by any of the Companies as the representative of any of the employees of any of the Companies.

P. *Increases in Compensation or Benefits.* Except as set forth in Exhibit P, subsequent to December 31, 1993, there have been no increases in the compensation payable or to become payable to any of the Employees and there have been no payments or provisions for any awards, bonuses, loans, profit sharing, pension, retirement or welfare plans or similar or other disbursements or arrangements for or on behalf of such employees (or related parties thereof), in each case, other than pursuant to currently existing plans or arrangements, if any, set forth in Exhibit N. Except as set forth in Exhibit P, all bonuses heretofore granted to employees of any of the Companies have been paid in full to such employees. The vacation policy and the amount of accrued and unused vacation time for each Employee of each of the Companies is set forth in Exhibit P. Except as set forth in Exhibit P, no employee of any of the Companies who is employed in the Business is entitled to vacation time in excess of three weeks during the current calendar year and no employee of any of the Companies who is employed in the Business has any accrued vacation or sick time with respect to any prior period.

Q. *Insurance.* Each of the Companies maintains insurance policies covering the Assets and the various occurrences which may arise in connection with the operation of the Business. Such policies are in full force and effect and all premiums due thereon prior to or on the date of the Closing have been paid. Each of the Companies has complied in all respects with the provisions of such policies. A list and brief description of the insurance policies maintained by each of the Companies is set forth in Exhibit Q. There are no notices of any pending or threatened termination or premium increases with respect to any of such policies. The Companies have not had any casualty loss or occurrence which may give rise to any claim of any kind not covered by insurance (other than for the deductible) and none of the Companies nor any of the Shareholders is aware of any occurrence which may give rise to any claim of any kind not covered by insurance. Except as set forth in Exhibit Q, no third party has filed any claim against the Companies or the Business for personal injury or property damage of a kind for which liability insurance is generally available which is not fully insured, subject only to the standard deductible. All known claims against any of the Companies or the Business covered by insurance have been reported to the insurance carrier on a timely basis.

R. *Conduct of Business.* None of the Companies is restricted from conducting the Business in any location by agreement or court decree.

S. *Allowances.* Except as set forth in Exhibit S, none of the Companies has any obligation outside of the ordinary course of business to make allowances to any customers with respect to the Business.

T. *Patents, Trademarks, etc.* No patents, registered and common law trademarks, service marks, tradenames or copyrights constitute part of the Assets.

U. *Use of Names.* All names under which each of the Companies currently conducts the Business are listed in Exhibit U attached hereto. To the knowledge of each of the Companies and each of the Shareholders, there are no other persons or businesses conducting businesses similar to those of the Companies in the Commonwealth of Pennsylvania having the right to use or using the names set forth in Exhibit U or any variants of such names; and no other person or business has ever attempted to restrain any of the Companies or any of the Shareholders from using such names or any variants thereof.

V. *Power of Attorney.* None of the Companies has granted any power of attorney (revocable or irrevocable) to any person, firm or corporation for any purpose whatsoever.

W. *Accounts Payable, Indebtedness, Etc.* The accounts and notes payable and accrued expenses which are part of the Assumed Liabilities are in all respects valid claims that arose in the ordinary course of business. Since December 31, 1993, the accounts and notes payable and accrued expenses of each of the Companies have been paid in a manner consistent with past practices. The aggregate unpaid accounts payable and accrued expenses (excluding expenses constituting part of the Assumed Liabilities with respect to the Employees) of the Companies on the date of the Closing relating to Assumed Liabilities shall not exceed $5,000.

X. *No Foreign Person.* None of the Shareholders is a foreign person within the meaning of Section 1445(b)(2) of the Code.

Y. *Licensure, etc.* To the best of the knowledge of each of the Companies and each of the Shareholders, each individual employed or contracted with by each of the Companies to provide therapy services is duly licensed to provide such therapy services and is otherwise in compliance with all federal, district and state laws, rules and regulations relating to such professional licensure and otherwise meets the qualifications to provide such therapy services. To the best of the knowledge of each of the Companies and each of the Shareholders, each individual now or formerly employed or contracted by each of the Companies to provide professional services was duly licensed to provide such services during all periods prior to the Closing when such employee or independent contractor provided such services on behalf of any of the Companies. Each of the Companies, to the best of its knowledge, is in compliance with all relevant state laws and precedents relating to the corporate practice of licensed professions, and there are no material claims, disputes, actions, suits, proceedings or investigations currently pending, filed or commenced, or, to the best of its knowledge, threatened against or affecting the Assets or the Business relating to such laws and precedents, and no such material claim, dispute, action, suit, proceeding or investigation has been filed or commenced during the two-year period preceding the date of this Agreement relating to such laws and precedents, and none of the Companies is aware of any basis for such a valid claim.

Z. *Books and Records.* The books and records of each of the Companies are in all material respects complete and correct, have been maintained in accordance with good business practices and accurately reflect the basis for the financial position and results of operations of each of the Companies set forth in the Financial Statements. All of such books and records have been made available for inspection by the Purchaser and its representatives.

AA. *Litigation; Disputes.* Except as set forth in Exhibit AA, there are no claims, disputes, actions, suits, investigations or proceedings pending or threatened against or affecting any of the Companies, the Business or any of the Assets, no such claim, dispute, action, suit, proceeding or investigation has been pending or, to the best knowledge of each of the Companies and each of the Shareholders, threatened during the two-year period preceding the date of this Agreement and, to the best of the knowledge of each of the Companies and each of the Shareholders, there is no basis for any such claim, dispute, action, suit, investigation or proceeding. None of the Companies nor any of the Shareholders has any knowledge of any default under any such action, suit or proceeding. None of the Companies is in default in respect of any judgment, order, writ, injunction or decree of any court or of any federal, state, municipal or other government department, commission, bureau, agency or instrumentality or any arbitrator.

BB. *Location of Business and Assets.* Set forth in Exhibit BB is each location (specifying state, county and city) where each of the Companies (i) has a place of business, (ii) owns or leases real property and (iii) owns or leases any other property, including inventory, equipment and furniture.

CC. *Disclosure.* No representation or warranty made under any Section hereof and none of the information set forth herein, in the exhibits hereto or in any document delivered by any of the Companies or any of the Shareholders to the Purchaser, or any authorized representative of the Purchaser, pursuant to the express terms of this Agreement contains any untrue statement of a material fact by the Companies or the Shareholders or omits to state a material fact by the Companies or the Shareholders necessary to make the statements herein or therein not misleading.

SECTION III.
REPRESENTATIONS, WARRANTIES, COVENANTS AND AGREEMENTS OF THE SHAREHOLDERS

Each of the Shareholders, jointly and severally, hereby represents and warrants to, and covenants and agrees with, the Purchaser, as of the date hereof and as of the date of the Closing, that:

A. *Authority.* Such Shareholder is fully able to execute and deliver this Agreement and to perform his covenants and agreements hereunder, and this Agreement constitutes a valid and legally binding obligation of such Shareholder, enforceable against him in accordance with its terms, except as such enforceability may be limited by bankruptcy, insolvency, moratorium or other similar laws affecting creditors' rights generally and general principles of equity relating to the availability of equitable remedies.

B. *No Legal Bar; Conflicts.* Neither the execution and delivery of this Agreement, nor the consummation of the transactions contemplated hereby, violates any statute, ordinance, regulation, order, judgment or decree of any court or governmental agency, or conflicts with or will result in any breach of any of the terms of or constitute a default under or result in the termination of or the creation of any lien pursuant to the terms of any contract or agreement to which any such Shareholder is a party or by which any such Shareholder or any of his assets is bound.

SECTION IV.
REPRESENTATIONS, WARRANTIES, COVENANTS AND AGREEMENTS OF THE PURCHASER

The Purchaser hereby represents and warrants to, and covenants and agrees with, the Companies and each of the Shareholders, as of the date hereof and as of the Selling date of the Closing, that:

A. *Organization.* The Purchaser is a corporation duly organized, validly existing and in good standing under the laws of the State of Delaware and has full corporate power and authority to purchase the Assets, to conduct the business in which it is now engaged and to enter into this Agreement and consummate the transactions contemplated by this Agreement. The Purchaser is qualified as a foreign corporation in the Commonwealth of Pennsylvania.

B. *Authority.* The execution and delivery of this Agreement by the Purchaser, the performance by the Purchaser of its covenants and agreements hereunder and the consummation by the Purchaser of the transactions contemplated hereby have been duly authorized by all necessary corporate action, and this Agreement constitutes a valid and legally binding obligation of the Purchaser, enforceable against the Purchaser in accordance with its terms.

C. *No Legal Bar; Conflicts.* Neither the execution and delivery of this Agreement, nor the consummation of the transactions contemplated hereby, violates any provision of the certificate of incorporation or by-laws of the Purchaser or any statute, ordinance, regulation, order, judgment or decree of any court or governmental agency, or conflicts with or will result in any breach of any of the terms of or constitute a default under or result in the termination of or the creation of any lien pursuant to the terms of any contract or agreement to which the Purchaser is a party or by which the Purchaser or any of its assets is bound. No consents, approvals or authorizations of, or filings with, any governmental authority or any other person or entity are required in connection with the execution and delivery of this Agreement and the consummation of the transactions contemplated hereby, except post-Closing filings with respect to Medicare and Medicaid reimbursement and consent of the landlord of the premises at 2 Green Boulevard.

SECTION V.

[Intentionally Left Blank].

SECTION VI.
ADDITIONAL COVENANTS OF THE COMPANIES, THE SHAREHOLDERS AND THE PURCHASER

A. *Company Acquisition Proposal.* The Companies and each of the Shareholders covenant and agree that, from and after the date of this Agreement and until the Closing, none of them shall directly or indirectly (i) take any action to solicit, initiate or encourage any Company Acquisition Proposal (as hereinafter defined) or (ii) engage in negotiations with, or disclose any non-public information relating to any of the Companies or afford access to the properties, books or records of any of the Companies to, any person or entity that may be considering making, or has made, a Company Acquisition Proposal. The Companies and each of the Shareholders shall promptly notify the Purchaser after receipt of any Company Acquisition Proposal or any indication that any person or entity is considering making a Company Acquisition Proposal or any request for non-public information relating to any of the Companies or for access to the properties, books or records of the Companies by any person or entity that may be considering making, or has made, a Company Acquisition Proposal. For purposes of this Agreement, "Company Acquisition Proposal" means any offer or proposal for, or any indication of interest in, a merger or other business combination involving any of the Companies or the acquisition of any equity interest in any of the Companies or any portion of the Assets, other than the transactions contemplated by this Agreement.

B. *Goodwill; Publicity.* Each of the Companies and each of the Shareholders covenants and agrees that it or he, either before or after the Closing, will not make any untrue statement, written, oral or other, adverse to the interests of any of the Companies or the business reputation or good name of any of the Companies and that any and all publicity (whether written or oral) and, for a period of one hundred and twenty days after Closing, notices to third parties (other than employees of any of the Companies) concerning the sale of the Assets and other transactions contemplated by this Agreement, other than as required by law or disclosure to its lender for the real property located at 4204 Maryland Road, Willow Grove, Pennsylvania and to its insurer and accountants, shall be subject to the prior written approval of the Purchaser, which approval may be withheld in the sole discretion of the Purchaser. Notwithstanding the foregoing, the Companies and the Shareholders may disclose the transaction to senior executives of Community Hospital. The Purchaser agrees that any press release concerning the Closing hereunder shall be subject to the prior approval of the Shareholders, which such approval will not be unreasonably withheld.

The Purchaser agrees that, unless and until the Closing has been consummated, the Purchaser and its officers, directors, employees, agents and representatives will hold in strict confidence, and will not use any confidential or proprietary data or information obtained from any of the Companies or the Shareholders with respect to the Business or its financial condition, operation, contracts or other assets, except for the purposes of consummating the transaction contemplated by this Agreement.

The Purchaser agrees that, from and after the date of the Closing, the Purchaser and its officers, directors, employees, agents and representatives will hold in strict confidence and will not disclose to any person or entity the consideration paid to the Companies or the Shareholders or the financial terms of the leases contemplated hereby, except to its accountants, its insurers, any institutional lender from whom the Purchaser or any of its affiliates has, or may, borrow money and as may be required by law.

C. *Further Assurances.* Subject to the terms and conditions of this Agreement, each of the Companies and each of the Shareholders will use its or his reasonable best efforts to take, or cause to be taken, all actions and to do, or cause to be done, all things necessary or desirable under applicable laws and regulations to consummate the transactions contemplated by this Agreement; provided, however, that subsequent to the Closing, such efforts or actions shall be at no additional cost to the Companies or the Shareholders unless otherwise agreed to in writing by the Companies or the Shareholders.

D. *Correspondence, etc.* Each of the Companies and each of the Shareholders covenants and agrees that, subsequent to the Closing each of them will deliver to the Purchaser, promptly after the receipt thereof, all inquiries, correspondence and other materials received by any of them from any person or entity relating to the Business or the Assets.

E. *Books and Records.* Each of the Companies and each of the Shareholders covenants and agrees that, subsequent to the Closing, each of them shall give the Purchaser, upon reasonable prior notice and during normal business hours, access to the historical financial books and records of each of the Companies, to the extent such books and records are not included in the Assets, for a period of five years from the date of the Closing. Each of the Companies shall retain all such books and records in substantially their condition at the time of the Closing. Prior to the expiration of five years from the Closing, none of such books and records shall be destroyed without the prior written approval of the Purchaser or without first offering such books and records to the Purchaser.

F. *Discharge of Obligations.* Each of the Companies and each of the Shareholders covenants and agrees, subsequent to the Closing, to pay promptly and to otherwise fulfill and discharge all valid obligations and liabilities of each of the Companies which are not Assumed Liabilities hereunder when due and payable and otherwise prior to the time at which any of such obligations or liabilities could in any way result in or give rise to a claim against the Assets, the Business or the Purchaser, result in the imposition of any lien, charge or encumbrance on any of the Assets, or adversely affect the Purchaser's title to or use of any of the Assets.

G. *Delivery of Funds.* Subsequent to the Closing, the Companies and the Shareholders shall deliver on a daily basis any funds and any checks, notes, drafts and other instruments for the payment of money, duly endorsed to the Purchaser, received by any of them (i) comprising payment of any of the accounts receivable of the Companies constituting a part of the Assets and (ii) comprising payment of any amounts due from customers of the Companies or others for services rendered by the Companies, including pursuant to any provider agreements constituting part of the Assets.

H. *Tax Clearance.* APT will obtain the required bulk sales tax clearance certificates ("Tax Certificates") as mandated by §1403 of the Pennsylvania Fiscal Code (72 P.S. §1403).

I. *Employees.* As of the Closing, the Purchaser shall offer employment to all those persons employed by each of the Companies in the Business, each of whom is listed on Exhibit M hereto (all such employees, the "Employees"). As of the Closing, each of the Companies shall terminate the employment of all of the Employees. Nothing herein shall be deemed either to affect or to limit in any way the management prerogatives of the Purchaser with respect to the Employees who accept such offer of employment (including without limitation the right of the Purchaser to modify compensation or the right of the Purchaser to terminate the employment of any Employee), or to create or to grant to such Employees any third-party beneficiary rights or claims or causes of action of any kind or nature against the Purchaser or its affiliates. To the extent not inconsistent with applicable law, the Employees who accept such offer of employment shall be afforded employment at substantially the same compensation, seniority and benefit levels as such Employees currently enjoy; provided, however, that in all cases with respect to benefits such terms and conditions shall be, on the whole, consistent with the terms and conditions applicable to all other employees of the Purchaser, it being understood that the Employees shall be required to make the same contributions and payments in order to receive any such benefits as may be required of similarly situated employees of the Purchaser. Nothing herein shall prevent the Purchaser from terminating the employment of any such Employee at any time for any reason as determined by the Purchaser in its sole discretion; provided, however, that if the Purchaser should terminate the employment of any Employee within six months of the Closing, the Purchaser shall provide prior written notice of such termination to AS ten days before such termination. The Purchaser agrees to credit to each Employee hired by the Purchaser an amount of vacation time and sick, personal and disability days to the extent specifically set forth opposite such Employee's name in Exhibit M hereto. The Purchaser agrees that it will pay all premiums for COBRA benefits for any Employee who is denied coverage under the Purchaser's health insurance plan due to a "pre-existing" condition.

J. *Sawbones Receivables.* The Purchaser, for a period of six months from and after the Closing (the "Collection Period"), agrees to collect the accounts receivable generated by the business of Dr. Sawbones (the "Sawbones Receivables") and to pay the amounts so collected to AS on a monthly basis and deliver along therewith a statement reflecting the patient (and third party) which paid such accounts receivable and the amounts. The Purchaser agrees to use the same collection methods to collect the Sawbones Receivables as it employs to collect its receivables. Payments of accounts receivable shall be credited against the oldest receivable unless the patient or payor has directed otherwise. At the end of the Collection Period, the Purchaser agrees to return to AS all documentation in its possession with respect to the Sawbones Receivables and cease its collection efforts. Purchaser shall promptly give AS and its representatives, upon request, access to all of its books and records relating to the Sawbones Receivables. Purchaser shall have no right of set-off against any payments owed it under this Section VI(J).

K. *Support Services.* For a period of six months from the date of the Closing, the Purchaser agrees to provide to Dr. Sawbones support services consistent with those currently provided to Dr. Sawbones by AS including but not limited to billing, typing services and telephone services (including without limitation message taking and appointment making).

L. *Landlord Consent.* Each of the Shareholders and each of the Companies covenants and agrees to use his or its reasonable efforts to obtain any required consent of the landlord of the premises at 2 Green Boulevard to permit the Purchaser to occupy such premises in accordance with the terms of the sublease agreement attached hereto as Exhibit L-III.

M. *Medical Insurance Coverage.* Purchaser shall provide to Meg Flynn and Marsha Berger Grant, so long as each is an employee of Purchaser or an Affiliate thereof, at no cost, medical coverage for each person's husband or shall increase each person's compensation a sufficient amount to pay for such medical coverage and the additional taxes on the increased compensation.

N. *Phones.* The Companies and the Shareholders may use the phone system at the Green Boulevard Location consistent with their prior practice and the Purchaser shall pay for such telephone bills.

SECTION VII.
CLOSING

A. *Time and Place of Closing.* The closing of the purchase and sale of the Assets, as set forth herein (the "Closing") shall be held at the offices of Blank Rome Comisky & McCauley, Four Penn Center Plaza, Philadelphia, Pennsylvania, at 10:00 A.M., local time, on June 30, 1994. The parties agree that the collected revenues and expenses (other than the Assumed Liabilities) of the Business up to and including June 30, 1994 shall belong to the Companies.

B. *Delivery of Assets.* Delivery of the Assets shall be made by the Companies to the Purchaser (or its designee) at the Closing by delivering such bills of sale, assignments and other instruments of conveyance and transfer, and such powers of attorney, as shall be effective to vest in the Purchaser (or its designee) title to or other interest in, and the right to full custody and control of, the Assets, free and clear of all liens, charges, encumbrances and security interests whatsoever.

C. *Assumption of Assumed Liabilities.* At the Closing, the Purchaser (or its designee) shall deliver to the Companies such instruments as shall be sufficient to effect the assumption by the Purchaser (or its designee) of the Assumed Liabilities.

D. *Contracts and Books.* At the Closing, each of the Companies and each of the Shareholders shall make available to the Purchaser the Contracts and the books and records of each of the Companies constituting a part of the Assets.

E. *Additional Steps.* At the Closing, each of the Companies and each of the Shareholders shall take all steps required to put the Purchaser in actual possession and control of the Assets.

F. *Sales or Use Taxes.* Any and all sales or use taxes assessed in connection with this transaction shall be paid as specified by applicable law.

G. *Delivery of Funds.* The Companies agree to deliver to the Purchaser at the Closing a check in the amount of $25,000 representing the cash portion of the Assets.

SECTION VIII.
CONDITIONS TO THE COMPANIES'
OBLIGATION TO CLOSE

The obligations of the Companies to sell the Assets and otherwise consummate the transactions contemplated by this Agreement at the Closing are subject to the following conditions precedent, any or all of which may be waived by the Companies in their sole discretion, and each of which the Purchaser hereby agrees to use its best efforts to satisfy at or prior to the Closing:

A. *No Litigation.* No action, suit or proceeding against the Companies, the Shareholders or the Purchaser relating to the consummation of any of the transactions contemplated by this Agreement or any governmental action seeking to delay or enjoin any such transactions shall be pending or threatened.

B. *Representations and Warranties.* The representations and warranties made by the Purchaser herein shall be correct as of the date of the Closing in all material respects with the same force and effect as though such representations and warranties had been made as of the date of the Closing, and on the date of the Closing, the Purchaser shall deliver to the Companies a certificate dated the date of the Closing to such effect. All the terms, covenants and conditions of this Agreement to be complied with and performed by the Purchaser on or before the date of the Closing shall have been duly complied with and performed in all material respects, and on the date of the Closing, the Purchaser shall deliver to the Companies a certificate dated the date of the Closing to such effect.

C. *Opinion of Counsel.* The Companies shall have received an opinion of Smith & Rogers, counsel for the Purchaser, delivered to the Companies pursuant to the instructions of the Purchaser, dated the date of the Closing, in form and substance satisfactory to the Companies and their counsel, Blank Rome Comisky & McCauley.

D. *Leases.* The Purchaser's designee and J-R shall have entered into leases for the premises located at 200 Main Street, Anywhere, Pennsylvania (the "Main Street Location") and 1776 Independence Road, Philadelphia, Pennsylvania (the "Independence Location"), respectively, substantially in the form of Exhibits L-I and L-II. Furthermore, the Purchaser's designee shall have entered into a sublease agreement for the premises located at 2 Green Boulevard, Suite 22, Philadelphia, Pennsylvania (the "Green Boulevard Location"), substantially in the form of Exhibit L-III.

E. *Other Certificates.* The Companies shall have received such additional certificates, instruments and other documents, in form and substance satisfactory to them and their counsel, as it shall have reasonably requested in connection with the transactions contemplated hereby.

SECTION IX.
CONDITIONS TO THE PURCHASER'S
OBLIGATION TO CLOSE

The obligation of the Purchaser to purchase the Assets and otherwise consummate the transactions contemplated by this Agreement at the Closing is subject to the following conditions precedent, any or all of which may be waived by the Purchaser in its sole discretion, and each of which each of the Companies and each of the Shareholders hereby agrees to use their best efforts to satisfy at or prior to the Closing:

A. *Opinion of Counsel.* The Purchaser shall have received an opinion of Blank Rome Comisky & McCauley, counsel for the Companies and the Shareholders, delivered to the Purchaser pursuant to the instructions of the Companies and the Shareholders, dated the date of the Closing, in form and substance satisfactory to the Purchaser and its counsel, Messrs. Smith & Rogers.

B. *No Litigation.* No action, suit or proceeding against the Companies, any of the Shareholders or the Purchaser relating to the consummation of any of the transactions contemplated by this Agreement nor any governmental action seeking to delay or enjoin any such transactions shall be pending or threatened.

C. *Representations and Warranties.* The representations and warranties made by each of the Companies and each of the Shareholders herein shall be correct as of the date of the Closing in all material respects with the same force and effect as though such representations and warranties had been made as of the date of the Closing, and on the date of the Closing, each of the Companies and each of the Shareholders shall deliver to the Purchaser a certificate dated the date of the Closing to such effect. All the terms, covenants and conditions of this Agreement to be complied with and performed by each of the Companies and each of the Shareholders on or before the date of the Closing shall have been duly complied with and performed in all material respects, and on the date of the Closing, the Companies and the Shareholders shall deliver to the Purchaser a certificate dated the date of the Closing to such effect.

D. *Other Certificates.* The Purchaser shall have received such other certificates, instruments and other documents, in form and substance satisfactory to it and its counsel, as it shall have reasonably requested in connection with the transactions contemplated hereby.

E. *Sale of All the Assets.* All the Assets shall be sold to the Purchaser (or its designee) at the Closing.

F. *Lease Terminations.* J-R and each of AS and APT, as applicable, shall deliver to the Purchaser terminations of lease agreements for all those Assets listed in Schedule I-(A) which are leased to AS or APT by J-R and which Assets are being acquired by Purchaser.

G. *Leases.* The Purchaser's designee and J-R shall have entered into leases for the premises located at the Main Street Location and the Independence Location, respectively, substantially in the form of Exhibits L-I and L-II. Furthermore, the Purchaser's designee shall have entered into a sublease agreement for the premises located at 2 Green Boulevard, Suite 22, Philadelphia, Pennsylvania substantially in the form of Exhibit L-III.

SECTION X.
INDEMNIFICATION

A. *Indemnification by the Companies and the Shareholders.* From and after the date of the Closing and subject to this Section X, each of the Companies and each of the Shareholders, jointly and severally, shall indemnify and hold harmless the Purchaser from and against all losses, claims, assessments, demands, damages, liabilities, obligations, costs and/or expenses, including, without limitation, reasonable fees and disbursements of counsel (hereinafter referred to collectively as "Damages") sustained or incurred by the Purchaser (or its designee) (i) by reason of the breach of any of the obligations, covenants or provisions of, or the inaccuracy of any of the representations or warranties made by, any of the Companies or any of the Shareholders herein, or (ii) arising out of or relating to any liabilities or obligations of each of the Companies not assumed by the Purchaser (or its designee) hereunder, or (iii) any tax obligations or other liabilities resulting from the failure of any of the Companies to obtain Tax Certificates, or (iv) arising out of or relating to liabilities or obligations imposed upon the Purchaser by a third party due to any violations by the Companies of any federal, state or local statute, laws, ordinances, rules, regulations, orders, or directives with respect to the employment practices or work conditions of the Companies, or violation by the Companies of the terms and conditions of employment, wages and hours, or (v) arising out of or relating to the Profit Sharing Plan. Notwithstanding anything to the contrary, no indemnification shall be due pursuant to clause

(i) of this Section X(A) unless and to the extent that the aggregate Damages exceed $25,000 or with respect to any claim for Damages which is made or asserted by the Purchaser after the date on which the representation or warranty on which such claim for Damages is based expires as provided in Section XIII(B), and provided further, that in no event shall the Companies and the Shareholders be obligated to indemnify the Purchaser pursuant to clause (i) of this Section X(A) for an aggregate amount of Damages in excess of $1,800,000.

Notwithstanding anything to the contrary contained in this Agreement, neither the Companies nor the Shareholders shall be liable under the indemnification provisions of this Section X or otherwise have any liability for any misrepresentation or breach of warranty or covenant under this Agreement or otherwise have any liability in connection with the transactions contemplated by this Agreement to the extent that the existence of such liability, the breach of warranty or covenant or the falsity of the representation upon which such liability would be based is fully disclosed in this Agreement or in the Schedules attached hereto or is discovered by the Purchaser before the Closing; provided, however, that any such misrepresentation or breach of warranty or covenant so disclosed to the Purchaser by the Shareholders after the execution and delivery of this Agreement and prior to the Closing or otherwise discovered by the Purchaser shall not affect the right of the Purchaser to elect not to close the transactions contemplated by this Agreement as provided herein (it being understood and agreed that if, despite such right of the Purchaser to elect not to close by reason of the misrepresentation or breach so disclosed, the Purchaser nevertheless elects to close, thereby waiving such misrepresentation or breach, the Purchaser shall thereafter have no claim against the Companies or any of the Shareholders by reason of any such disclosed or discovered misrepresentation or breach of warranty or covenant).

B. *Indemnification by the Purchaser.* The Purchaser shall indemnify and hold harmless the Companies and each of the Shareholders from and against any and all Damages sustained or incurred by the Companies or any of the Shareholders (i) by reason of the breach of any of the obligations, covenants or provisions of, or the inaccuracy of any of the representations or warranties made by, the Purchaser herein, (ii) arising out of the Assumed Liabilities and/or (iii) arising from the Purchaser's conduct of the Business subsequent to the Closing.

C. *Procedure for Indemnification.* In the event that any party hereto shall incur any Damages in respect of which indemnity may be sought by such party pursuant to this Section X, the party from whom such indemnity may be sought (the "Indemnifying Party") shall be given written notice thereof by the party seeking such indemnity (the "Indemnified Party"), which notice shall specify the amount and nature of such Damages and include the request of the Indemnified Party for indemnification of such amount. The Indemnifying Party shall within 30 days pay to the Indemnified Party the amount of the Damages so specified.

D. *Recision, Punitive Damages.* It is specifically understood and agreed that in the event a misrepresentation or breach of warranty or covenant is discovered by the Purchaser after the Closing, the Purchaser shall not be entitled to a recision of this Agreement. In addition, the Purchaser shall not be entitled to recover consequential or punitive damages from the Companies or the Shareholders.

E. *Tax Benefits.* In the event that, notwithstanding the limitations contained in this Section X or elsewhere in this Agreement, the Companies or any Shareholder nevertheless becomes liable to the Purchaser under the provisions of this Agreement or otherwise, the Companies (and the Shareholders) shall be entitled to a credit or offset against any such liability of the value of any net tax benefit realized (by reason of a tax deduction, basis reduction, shifting of income, credits and/or deductions or otherwise) by the Purchaser in connection with the loss or damage suffered by the Purchaser which forms the basis of the Companies' or the Shareholders' liability hereunder. In addition, if any of the Companies or any of the Shareholders becomes obligated to indemnify Purchaser, the party so indemnifying, upon payment in full, shall be subrogated to all rights of the Indemnified Party with respect to all claims to which such indemnification relates.

F. *Exclusions.* Notwithstanding anything to the contrary contained in this Agreement or in the Bill of Sale executed pursuant hereto, there shall be excluded from the sale, transfer, conveyance and assignment hereunder, and the Assets shall not include, any debt, liability or obligation of, or claim against, any past or present shareholder, director or officer of the Companies, except as explicitly included in the Assets.

G. *Equitable Remedies.* With the exception of equitable remedies and except with respect to claims based on fraud, the indemnification provisions set forth in this Section X shall be the sole and exclusive remedy of the Purchaser with respect to any actions resulting or arising from the matters referred to in this Section X and, to the extent permitted by law, the Purchaser waives all other remedies available at law with respect thereto.

H. *Consents.* The Purchaser hereby waives its right to any claims it may have against the Companies and/or the Shareholders for their failure to obtain consents to assignment of any contracts (written or oral) which constitute part of the Assets.

I. *Accounts Receivable.* If the Companies and/or the Shareholders pay the Purchaser for uncollected accounts receivable as contemplated by the second sentence of Section II(K), then the Purchaser on a nonrecourse basis shall assign such uncollected accounts receivable to the Companies simultaneous to receiving the payment referred to in this Section X from the Companies and/or the Shareholders.

SECTION XI.
NON-COMPETITION AGREEMENT

Following the consummation of the transactions contemplated hereby, and in consideration thereof, none of the Companies and none of the Shareholders shall, subsequent to the date of the Closing and until seven years after the date of the Closing, directly or indirectly, (i) engage, whether as principal, agent, distributor, representative, investor, stockholder (except for passive investments of not more than 5% of the outstanding shares of any company listed on a national exchange or NASDAQ with shareholder equity exceeding $75,000,000), or employee of, or otherwise benefit from, any activity or business venture, anywhere within a fifty (50) mile radius of any location or facility where any of the Companies conduct the Business as of the date of the Closing, providing physical or occupational therapy, (ii) solicit or entice or endeavor to solicit or entice away from any member of the Purchaser Group (as hereinafter defined) any Employee, either on any of the Companies' or any of the Shareholders' own account or for any person, firm, corporation or other organization, whether or not such person would commit any breach of such person's contract of employment by reason of leaving the service of such member of the Purchaser Group, (iii) solicit or entice or endeavor to solicit or entice away any of the clients or customers of any member of the Purchaser Group, either on any of the Companies' or any of the Shareholders' own account or for any other person, firm, corporation or organization for the purpose of providing physical or occupational therapy services, or (iv) employ any person who was an Employee, or (v) at any time during such seven-year period, make any untrue statement, written, oral or other, adverse to the interests of any member of the Purchaser Group or the business reputation or good name of any member of the Purchaser Group. Following the consummation of the transactions contemplated hereby, and in consideration thereof, none of the Companies and none of the Shareholders shall, subsequent to the date of the Closing and for the term (either seven years if the tenant thereunder buys out the lease as contemplated thereunder or otherwise ten years) of the lease for the Main Street Location, lease any space at the premises at the Main Street Location to any person or entity, other than a member of the Purchaser Group, who is engaged in the practice of physical or occupational therapy; provided, however, that the Shareholders and the Companies shall not be bound by this provision in the event that the Purchaser or its designee, as applicable, exercises its option to terminate the lease for the Main Street Location pursuant to the terms of Paragraph 48 of such lease. Because the remedy at law for any breach of the foregoing provisions of this Section XI would be inadequate, each of the Companies and each of the Shareholders hereby consents, in case of any such breach, to the granting by any court of competent jurisdiction of specific enforcement, including, but not limited to, prejudgment injunctive relief of such provisions, as provided for in Section XIII hereof.

Notwithstanding the foregoing, it shall not be a breach of this Section XI for the Shareholders to engage in the practice of orthopedic medicine and the practice of psychiatry in connection with such medical practice.

In addition, notwithstanding the foregoing, the Companies and the Shareholders shall be permitted to provide consulting or medical services to inpatient rehabilitation facilities for compensation directly related to such services so long as none of the Shareholders expends more than twenty-five percent of his working time (the "Time Limit") providing consulting or medical services to inpatient rehabilitation facilities and the Companies or the Shareholders notify Purchaser in writing before providing such services. If any of the Shareholders does expend more than twenty-five percent of his working time providing consulting or medical services to inpatient rehabilitation facilities, then prior to exceeding the Time Limit in each instance he will first obtain written consent from Purchaser, such consent not to be unreasonably withheld by the Purchaser. Purchaser has been advised in writing that the Shareholders provide services to inpatient rehabilitation facilities at Community Hospital and at two nursing homes.

The parties hereto agree that if, in any proceeding, the court or other authority shall refuse to enforce the covenants herein set forth because such covenants cover too extensive a geographic area or too long a period of time, any such covenant shall be deemed appropriately amended and modified in keeping with the intention of the parties to the maximum extent permitted by law.

For purposes hereof, "Purchaser Group" shall mean, collectively, the Purchaser and its subsidiaries, affiliates and parent entities operating in the same lines of business.

SECTION XII.
BROKERS AND FINDERS

A. *The Shareholders' Obligations.* The Purchaser shall not have any obligation to pay any fee or other compensation to any person, firm or corporation dealt with by each of the Companies or any of the Shareholders in connection with this Agreement and the transactions contemplated hereby, and the Companies and each of the Shareholders, jointly and severally, hereby agree to indemnify and save the Purchaser harmless from any liability, damage, cost or expense arising from any claim for any such fee or other compensation.

B. *The Purchaser's Obligation.* Neither the Companies nor any of the Shareholders shall have any obligation to pay any fee or other compensation to any person, firm or corporation dealt with by the Purchaser in connection with this Agreement and the transactions contemplated hereby, and the Purchaser hereby agrees to indemnify and save the Companies and each of the Shareholders harmless from any liability, damage, cost or expense arising from any claim for any such fee or other compensation.

SECTION XIII.
MISCELLANEOUS

A. *Notices.* All notices, requests or instructions hereunder shall be in writing and delivered personally, sent by telecopy or sent by registered or certified mail, postage prepaid, as follows:

(1) If to the Companies or the Shareholders:

Albertson Medical Specialists, P.C.
1776 Independence Road,
Philadelphia, Pennsylvania

with a copy to:

Blank Rome Comisky & McCauley
Four Penn Center Plaza
Philadelphia, Pennsylvania

(2) If to the Purchaser:

ClinCare Corporation
1018 West Ninth Avenue
New York, New York

with a copy to:

Smith & Rogers
237 Main Street
New York, New York

Any of the above addresses may be changed at any time by notice given as provided above; provided, however, that any such notice of change of address shall be effective only upon receipt. All notices, requests or instructions given in accordance herewith shall be deemed received on the date of delivery, if hand delivered or telecopied, and two business days after the date of mailing, if mailed.

B. *Survival of Representations.* Each representation, warranty, covenant and agreement of the parties hereto herein contained shall survive the Closing, notwithstanding any investigation at any time made by or on behalf of any party hereto, for a period of two (2) years, except (a) for covenants and agreements contained in this Agreement which by their terms extend for more than two (2) years and (b) that nothing in the foregoing shall be deemed to diminish any Indemnitor's indemnification obligations to an Indemnitee respecting (x) any claim for Damages under Section X hereof for which notice to the Indemnitor has been given prior to the end of such two (2) year period, (y) the representations and warranties contained in Sections II(G), (H), (I)(iv) and (AA) and claims for common law fraud, each of which shall survive for the duration of the applicable statutes of limitations governing third-party claims made with respect thereto.

C. *Entire Agreement.* This Agreement and the documents referred to herein contain the entire agreement among the parties hereto with respect to the transactions contemplated hereby, and no modification hereof shall be effective unless in writing and signed by the party against which it is sought to be enforced.

D. *Further Assurances.* Each of the parties hereto shall use such party's reasonable best efforts to take such actions as may be necessary or reasonably requested by the other parties hereto to carry out and consummate the transactions contemplated by this Agreement; provided, however, that subsequent to the Closing, such efforts or actions shall be at no additional cost to the Companies or the Shareholders, unless otherwise agreed to in writing by the Companies or the Shareholders.

E. *Expenses.* Each of the parties hereto shall bear such party's own expenses in connection with this Agreement and the transactions contemplated hereby.

F. *Injunctive Relief.* Notwithstanding the provisions of Section XIII(G) hereof, in the event of a breach or threatened breach by any of the Companies or any of the Shareholders of the provisions of Section XI of this Agreement, each of the Companies and each of the Shareholders hereby consents and agrees that the Purchaser shall be entitled to an injunction or similar equitable relief restraining the Companies or the Shareholders, as the case may be, from committing or continuing any such breach or threatened breach or granting specific performance of any act required to be performed by the Companies or any of the Shareholders, as the case may be, under any such provision, without the necessity of showing any actual damage or that money damages would not afford an adequate remedy and without the necessity of posting any bond or other security. The parties hereto hereby consent to the jurisdiction of the Federal courts for the Eastern District of Pennsylvania and the Pennsylvania state courts located in such District for any proceedings under this Section XIII(F). The parties hereto agree that the availability of arbitration in Section XIII(G) hereof shall not be used by any party as grounds for the dismissal of any injunctive actions instituted by the Purchaser pursuant to this Section XIII(F). Nothing herein shall be construed as prohibiting the Purchaser from pursuing any other remedies at law or in equity which it may have.

G. *Arbitration.* Any controversy or claim arising out of or relating to this Agreement, or any breach hereof, shall, except as provided in Section XIII(F) hereof, be settled by arbitration in accordance with the rules of the American Arbitration Association then in effect and judgment upon the award rendered by the arbitrator may be entered in any court having jurisdiction thereof. The arbitration shall be held in the Philadelphia, Pennsylvania area.

H. *Invalidity.* Should any provision of this Agreement be held by a court or arbitration panel of competent jurisdiction to be enforceable only if modified, such holding shall not affect the validity of the remainder of this Agreement, the balance of which shall continue to be binding upon the parties hereto with any such modification to become a part hereof and treated as though originally set forth in this Agreement. The parties further agree that any such court or arbitration panel is expressly authorized to modify any such unenforceable provision of this Agreement in lieu of severing such unenforceable provision from this Agreement in its entirety, whether by rewriting the offending provision, deleting any or all of the offending provision, adding additional language to this Agreement, or by making such other modifications as it deems warranted to carry out the intent and agreement of the parties as embodied herein to the maximum extent permitted by law. The parties expressly agree that this Agreement as modified by the court or the arbitration panel shall be binding upon and enforceable against each of them. In any event, should one or more of the provisions of this Agreement be held to be invalid, illegal or unenforceable in any respect, such invalidity, illegality or unenforceability shall not affect any other provisions hereof, and if such provision or provisions are not modified as provided above, this Agreement shall be construed as if such invalid, illegal or unenforceable provisions had never been set forth herein.

I. *Knowledge.* Whenever used in this Agreement, the words "to the best of the knowledge of the Companies," or similar words, shall mean the knowledge or awareness which the Shareholders and Mr. Donald Lachman would obtain in the exercise of reasonable diligence or after due inquiry, it being understood and agreed that such knowledge or awareness of any or all of such persons, for purposes hereof, shall be attributed to the Company.

J. *Successors and Assigns.* This Agreement shall be binding upon and inure to the benefit of the successors and assigns of each of the Companies and the Purchaser, respectively, and the legal representatives and heirs of each of the Shareholders.

K. *Governing Law.* The validity of this Agreement and of any of its terms or provisions, as well as the rights and duties of the parties under this Agreement, shall be construed pursuant to and in accordance with the laws of the Commonwealth of Pennsylvania.

L. *Counterparts.* This Agreement may be executed in counterparts, each of which shall be deemed an original, but all of which taken together shall constitute one and the same instrument.

IN WITNESS WHEREOF, this Agreement has been duly executed by the parties hereto as of the date first above written.

Albertson Medical Specialists, P.C.

By: _____

    Name:

    Title:

Albertson Physical Therapy, P.C.

By: _____

    Name:

    Title:

Jenkins-Michael Associates

By: _____

    Name:

    Title:

_____

Sara Ann Rubin, M.D.

_____

Michael Daniel Rubin, M.D.

_____

Kimberly Lageman, M.D.

_____

Andrew Mortenson, M.D.

ClinCare Corporation

By: _____

(Schedules Omitted)

APPENDIX 7

Sample Agreement and Plan of Merger

[This agreement and plan of merger is an attachment to an agreement and plan of reorganization, which is similar in legal content to Appendix 6, except that the merger is tax free to those shareholders of Montour Bank who elect to receive common stock of Omega Financial Corporation. The following is an example of a forward triangular merger, i.e., Montour Bank, the target, is merged into a wholly-owned subsidiary of Omega Financial Corporation and does not survive the merger.]

THIS AGREEMENT made this ___ day of January, 1995 by and between MONTOUR BANK ("Montour"), a bank incorporated under the Pennsylvania Banking Code of 1965, as amended, and Montour Interim Bank ("NEWCO"), a newly formed bank under the Pennsylvania Banking Code of 1965, as amended, and a wholly owned subsidiary of Omega Financial Corporation ("Omega"), a Pennsylvania business corporation registered as a bank holding company under the Bank Holding Company Act of 1956, as amended. Montour and NEWCO are sometimes collectively referred to as the "Constituent Corporations."

BACKGROUND

Omega and Montour have entered into an Agreement and Plan of Reorganization of even date herewith (the "Reorganization

Agreement") which contemplates the merger of Montour with and into NEWCO (the "Merger") in accordance with the terms and conditions of the Reorganization Agreement and of this Agreement and Plan of Merger (the "Merger Agreement").

NOW, THEREFORE, in consideration of the mutual covenants and agreements herein contained and subject to the satisfaction of the terms and conditions set forth herein and in the Reorganization Agreement, and intending to be legally bound hereby, Montour and NEWCO do hereby agree as follows:

SECTION 1.
GENERAL

1.1 *Shareholder Approval.* This Merger Agreement shall be promptly submitted to the respective shareholders of the Constituent Corporations and, if approved by the vote or consent of the shareholders of each of them required by law, the Merger shall be made effective in the manner provided in Section 1.4 below.

1.2 *The Merger.* On the Effective Date, as hereinafter defined, Montour shall be merged with and into NEWCO under the Pennsylvania Banking Code of 1965, as amended, the separate existence of Montour shall cease, and NEWCO shall be the surviving bank (the "Surviving Corporation"), in accordance with this Merger Agreement.

1.3 *Name.* The name of the Surviving Corporation shall be changed to Montour Bank on the Effective Date, as hereinafter defined, and the location of its principal office shall be 1519 Bloom Road, Danville, Montour County, Pennsylvania.

1.4 *Effect of Merger.* On the Effective Date, the Surviving Corporation shall possess all the rights, privileges, powers, immunities, purposes and franchises, both public and private, and all the property (real, personal and mixed) and franchises of each of the Constituent Corporations. All debts due on whatever account to any of the Constituent Corporations, including subscriptions to shares and other choices in action belonging to any of the Constituent Corporations, shall be taken and deemed to be transferred to and vested in the Surviving Corporation without further act or deed. The Surviving Corporation shall thenceforth be responsible for all the liabilities and obligations of each of the Constituent Corporations, but the liabilities of the Constituent Corporations, or of their shareholders, directors or officers, shall not be affected; nor shall the rights of the creditors thereof or of any persons dealing with the Constituent Corporations, or any liens upon the property of the Constituent Corporations, be impaired by the Merger; and any claim existing or action or proceeding pending by or against any of the Constituent Corporations may be prosecuted to judgment as if the Merger had not taken place or the Surviving Corporation may be proceeded against or substituted in its place. Any taxes, penalties and public accounts of the Commonwealth of Pennsylvania claimed against any of the Constituent Corporations but not settled, assessed or determined prior to the Merger shall be settled, assessed or determined against the Surviving Corporation and, together with interest thereon, shall be a lien against the franchises and property, both real and personal, of the Surviving Corporation.

1.5 *Continuation in Business.* The Surviving Corporation shall continue in business with the assets and liabilities of the Constituent Corporations.

1.6 *Articles of Incorporation.* The Amended and Restated Articles of Incorporation (the "Articles of Incorporation") of the Surviving Corporation shall be as set forth in Exhibit "A" attached hereto and made a part hereof.

1.7 *By-Laws.* The Amended and Restated By-Laws of the Surviving Corporation shall be as set forth in Exhibit "B" attached hereto and made a part hereof.

1.8 *Directors.* On the Effective Date, the then Board of Directors of NEWCO, together with the four new directors appointed pursuant to Section 9.3 of the Reorganization Agreement, shall continue to serve as the Board of Directors of the Surviving Corporation until such time as their successors have been elected and qualified.

1.9 *Officers.* On the Effective Date, all persons who are executive or other officers of NEWCO, subject to the provisions of Section 9.3 of the Reorganization Agreement, shall remain as officers of the Surviving Corporation until such time as the

Board of Directors of the Surviving Corporation shall otherwise determine.

1.10 *Effective Date.* Subject to the terms and upon satisfaction of all requirements of law and the conditions specified in this Merger Agreement and the Reorganization Agreement including, among other conditions, receipt of the approval of The Board of Governors of the Federal Reserve Board, the Federal Deposit Insurance Corporation, and the Department of Banking of the Commonwealth of Pennsylvania, the Merger shall become effective, and the effective date of the Merger (the "Effective Date") shall occur, at the time of the filing of the Articles of Merger of the Constituent Corporations with the Secretary of State of the Commonwealth of Pennsylvania.

SECTION 2.
CONVERSION AND EXCHANGE OF SHARES

2.1 *Stock of NEWCO.* On the Effective Date, each share of common stock, par value $5.00 per share, of NEWCO issued or outstanding immediately prior to the Effective Date (except for shares owned by shareholders of NEWCO who duly assert dissenters' rights in accordance with this Merger Agreement and applicable law) shall, by virtue of the Merger and without any action on the part of the holder thereof, be automatically converted into and become one share of common stock, par value $5.00 per share, of the Surviving Corporation. From and after the Effective Date, each certificate which, prior to the Effective Date, represented shares of NEWCO shall evidence ownership of shares of the Surviving Corporation on the basis hereinbefore set forth.

2.2 *Stock of Montour.* Except as hereafter provided, on the Effective Date, each share of common stock, par value $5.00 per share, of Montour ("Montour Common Stock") issued and outstanding immediately prior to the Effective Date (except for shares owned by shareholders of Montour who duly assert dissenters' rights in accordance with this Merger Agreement and applicable law) shall, based on the election described in Section 5.2 of the Reorganization Agreement as to the type of consideration to be received by the holder thereof in exchange for all of his shares of Montour Common Stock (except as hereinafter provided), and by virtue of the Merger and without any action on the part of the holder thereof, be automatically converted into and become either (a) one-half share of the Common Stock of Omega, par value $5.00 per share (the "Omega Common Stock"), (b) $12 cash, (c) a combination of Omega common stock and cash under (a) and (b) above (collectively, the "Exchange Ratios"). Not more than forty-nine percent (49%) nor less than forty percent (40%) of the total number of outstanding shares of Montour Common Stock, as of the date hereof and immediately prior to the Effective Date, shall be converted into cash. In the event that holders of more than forty-nine percent (49%) of the total number of outstanding shares of Montour Common Stock elect to receive cash in exchange for Montour Common Stock, then that portion in excess of the maximum forty-nine percent (49%) non-stock consideration shall be distributed pro-rata in Omega Common Stock, at the rate of one-half share of Omega Common Stock for each share of Montour Common Stock, to those Montour share-holders who have elected to receive cash in exchange for their shares of Montour Common Stock and the amount of cash to be received by such shareholders in exchange for their shares of Montour Common Stock shall be appropriately reduced. In the event that holders of less than forty percent (40%) of the total number of outstanding shares of Montour Common Stock elect to receive cash in exchange for Montour Common Stock, then that portion of the required forty percent (40%) non-stock considera-tion that has not been selected shall be distributed, pro rata in cash at the rate of $12 for each share of Montour Common Stock, to those Montour shareholders who have elected to receive Omega Common Stock in exchange for their shares of Montour Common Stock and the number of shares of Omega Common Stock to be received by such shareholders in exchange for their shares of Montour Common Stock shall be appropriately reduced. The operation of the immediately preceding sentence is illustrated by the following example:

> Pursuant to the terms of Section 2.2 of this Merger Agreement, assuming that 418,080 shares of Montour Common Stock are outstanding, as of the date hereof and also immediately prior to the Effective Date, a minimum of 40 percent (or 167,232 shares) must be exchanged for cash. Assuming that all shareholders of

Montour make an election and that holders of 90 percent of the outstanding shares of Montour Common
Stock (376,272 shares) elect to receive Omega Common Stock, and the holders of 10 percent of the outstanding shares of Montour Common Stock (41,808
shares) elect to receive cash, then the minimum number of shares that must be exchanged for cash would
not be satisfied by the elections of Montour shareholders. As a result, pursuant to Section 2.2 of this Merger
Agreement, the difference between the minimum
number of shares that must be exchanged for cash and
the number of shares that actually elect to be so
exchanged (125,424 shares in this example) would be
exchanged for cash, on a pro rata basis among those
shareholders who elected to receive Omega Common
Stock, at the rate of $12 for each share of Montour
Common Stock. The number of shares of Montour
Common Stock to be exchanged for cash by each such
shareholder would be equal to the number of shares
held by him, multiplied by a fraction, the numerator
of which is equal to the difference between the minimum number of shares that must be exchanged for
cash and the number of shares that actually elect to be
so exchanged (125,424 shares in this example) and the
denominator of which is equal to the number of shares
which elected to be exchanged for Omega Common
Stock (376,272 in this example). Thus, each of the holders of the 376,272 shares of Montour Common Stock
who elected to receive Omega Common Stock in
exchange for their shares would receive cash, in lieu of
Omega Common Stock, at the rate of $12 per share in
exchange for 125,424/376,272 of their shares.

Any Montour shareholder who shall fail timely to make the
required election shall be deemed to have elected to receive
(i) Omega Common Stock, (ii) cash, (iii) any combination as
determined by the Board of Directors of Omega in its sole discretion. The elections deemed made pursuant to the immediately
preceding sentence shall be used in making the computations of
the type set forth in the above example.

From and after the Effective Date, each certificate which, prior to the Effective Date, represented shares of Montour Common Stock shall evidence ownership of either: (i) the number of shares of Omega Common Stock into which the shares of Montour Common Stock represented by such certificate shall have been converted, together with the right to receive any cash to which a Montour shareholder is entitled in lieu of the issuance of a fractional share, or (ii) the right to receive cash.

Notwithstanding anything to the contrary contained herein, in the event that the Average Price (as hereafter defined) of Omega Common Stock is more than $30, the Exchange Ratio of Montour Common Stock for Omega Common Stock shall be changed from one share of Montour Common Stock for one-half share of Omega Common Stock to one share of Montour Common Stock for the fraction of a share of Omega Common Stock obtained from the following formula: multiply .5 by a fraction equal to 30 divided by the Average Price; the result shall be rounded to two decimal points, with a third decimal point rounded upward if it equals .005 or more and ignored if it equals less than .005. "Average Price" as used herein shall refer to the mean average of the closing sale prices for Omega Common Stock (as quoted in the NASDAQ National Market System as reported by *The Wall Street Journal*) for the thirty business day period ending on the fifteenth business day next preceding the Effective Date. This paragraph shall not apply if, prior to the thirtieth business day ended on the fifteenth business day next preceding the Effective Date, Omega shall have made a public announcement of the intention to sell control of Omega to another entity, whether such sale be in the form of a merger, consolidation or sale of substantially all of the assets of Omega and its subsidiaries.

For purposes of computing the limitations on the number of outstanding shares of Montour Common Stock which elect cash pursuant to this Section 2.2, the amount of cash paid in lieu of fractional shares pursuant to Section 2.3 hereof and shares which exercise dissenters' rights pursuant to this Section 2.8 shall be included.

2.3 *Fractional Share Adjustments.* No fractional shares of Omega Common Stock shall be issued as a result of the Merger.

In lieu of the issuance of fractional shares, cash adjustments will be paid to the shareholders of Montour in respect of any fraction of a share of Omega Common Stock which would otherwise be issuable under this Merger Agreement. Such cash adjustment shall be equal to an amount determined by multiplying such fraction by the Average Price.

2.4 *Certain Adjustments.* In the event that Omega changes the number of shares of its common stock issued and outstanding prior to the Effective Date as a result of a stock split, stock dividend or similar recapitalization and the record date therefor shall be after the date hereof and prior to the Effective Date, the ratio under which Montour Common Stock may be converted into and exchanged for shares of Omega Common stock pursuant to Section 2.2 of this Merger Agreement shall be appropriately adjusted.

2.5 *Treasury Stock.* Each share of Montour Common Stock held as a treasury share immediately prior to the Effective Date, if any, shall thereupon and without notice be canceled.

2.6 *Exchange Agent.* At or prior to the Effective Date, Omega shall designate the Peoples National Bank of Central Pennsylvania in State College, Pennsylvania, to act as Exchange Agent to receive from the holders thereof certificates which immediately prior to the Effective Date represented Montour Common Stock and to exchange such certificates for certificates of Omega Common Stock and cash as herein provided.

2.7 *Exchange Procedure.* Promptly after the Effective Date, the Exchange Agent shall mail to each record holder, as of the Effective Date, of an outstanding certificate or certificates, which prior to the Effective Date represented shares of Montour Common Stock, a letter of transmittal (which shall specify how delivery shall be effected, and that risk of loss and title to such certificate or certificate shall pass only upon proper delivery of such certificate or certificates, together with a properly executed letter of transmittal, to the Exchange Agent at its address stated therein) and instructions for use in effecting the surrender of such certificate or certificates for exchange therefor. Upon surrender to the Exchange Agent of such certificate or certificates, together with such letter of transmittal, properly executed, the Exchange Agent shall, based on such record holder's election, as described in Section 5.2 of the Reorganization Agreement and in Section 2.2 of this Merger Agreement, exchange such certificate or certificates for: (a) shares of Omega Common Stock, (b) cash, or (c) a combination of Omega Common Stock and cash; and pay to any record holder receiving Omega Common Stock any payment due for a fractional share of Omega Common Stock. Until so surrendered, each outstanding certificate or certificates, which prior to the Effective Date represented shares of Montour Common Stock and which are thereupon exchanged for Omega Common Stock, shall be deemed for all purposes to evidence ownership of the number of shares of Omega Common Stock and the right to receive payment for any fractional share of Omega Common Stock into which the shares represented by such certificate or certificates have been changed or converted as aforesaid. Until so surrendered, each certificate or certificates outstanding, which prior to the Effective Date represented shares of Montour Common Stock, and which are thereupon exchanged for cash or any combination of cash and Omega Common Stock, shall evidence the right to receive cash and/or ownership of Omega Common Stock in which the shares represented by such certificate or certificates have been changed or converted as aforesaid; provided however, that no payment of cash shall be payable upon or in respect of any such certificate until it has been surrendered and exchanged as aforesaid.

2.8 *Dissenters' Rights.* Shareholders of Montour shall be entitled to exercise the rights of dissenting shareholders, with respect to this Merger Agreement, as provided in Sections 1222 and 1607 of the Pennsylvania Banking Code of 1965, as amended.

2.9 *Ownership of Stock of Surviving Corporation.* It is the intention of the Constituent Corporations that, immediately after the Effective Date, all of the outstanding capital stock of the Surviving Corporation shall be owned by Omega.

SECTION 3.
ADDITIONAL TERMS

3.1 *Conditions.* The obligations of the parties hereto to effect the Merger shall be subject to all of the terms and conditions contained in the Reorganization Agreement.

3.2 *Termination.* This Merger Agreement may be terminated and the Merger abandoned by the mutual written consent of the Boards of Directors of the parties hereto prior to or after the approval of the shareholders of the parties. If the Reorganization Agreement is terminated pursuant to the terms thereof, then this Merger Agreement shall terminate simultaneously and the Merger shall be abandoned without further action by the parties hereto.

3.3 *Amendment, Supplement or Waiver.* Any party to this Merger Agreement may, at any time prior to the Effective Date, by action taken by its Board of Directors or officers thereunto duly authorized, waive any of the terms or conditions of this Merger Agreement or agree to an amendment or supplement to this Merger Agreement by an agreement in writing executed in the same manner (but not necessarily by the same persons) as this Merger Agreement. No amendment, supplement or waiver of this Merger Agreement shall be binding unless executed in writing by the party to be bound thereby. No waiver of any of the provisions of this Merger Agreement shall be deemed or shall constitute a waiver of any other provisions hereof (whether or not similar), nor shall any waiver constitute a continuing waiver unless otherwise expressly provided. Furthermore, and not in limitation of the foregoing, each party's Board of Directors may authorize the amendment or supplementation of this Merger Agreement or waiver of any provision hereof, either before or after the approval by Montour's shareholders provided in section 5 of the Reorganization Agreement (and without seeking further shareholder approval), so long as such amendment, supplement or waiver does not result in a material change in the amount or form of consideration provided for herein.

3.4 *No Beneficiaries.* Nothing expressed or implied in this Merger Agreement is intended or shall be construed to confer upon or give any person, firm or corporation other than the parties hereto any rights or remedies under or by reason of this Merger Agreement, except as otherwise provided in Section 3.1 hereof, and, except as aforesaid, there are no third-party beneficiaries of this Merger Agreement.

3.5 *Assignment; Parties Bound.* No party hereto shall assign this Merger Agreement or any part hereof without the prior written consent of the other parties. Except as otherwise provided herein, this Merger Agreement shall be binding upon and inure to the benefit of the parties hereto and their respective permitted successors and assigns.

3.6 *Entire Agreement.* This Merger Agreement and the Reorganization Agreement constitute the entire agreement between the parties pertaining to the subject matter hereof and supersede all prior and contemporaneous agreements, understandings, negotiations and discussion, whether oral or written, of the parties, and there are no warranties, representations, covenants or other agreements between the parties in connection with the subject matter hereof except as specifically set forth herein or therein.

3.7 *Counterparts.* This Merger Agreement may be executed in two or more counterparts, each of which shall be deemed an original, but all of which together shall constitute one and the same instrument.

3.8 *Governing Law.* This Merger Agreement shall be governed by the laws of the Commonwealth of Pennsylvania applicable to contracts executed in and to be performed exclusively within the Commonwealth of Pennsylvania. The legal principle that ambiguities are construed against the drafter of a document shall not be applicable to this document.

WITNESS the signatures and seals of the Constituent Corporations on the day and year first above written, each hereunto set by its duly authorized officers and attested by its Secretary or Assistant Secretary pursuant to a resolution of the Board of Directors.

MONTOUR BANK

By: _____

(CORPORATE SEAL)   M. Ralph Campbell,
Chairman of the Board

Attest: _____

Charles I. Keiter,
Secretary

MONTOUR INTERIM BANK

(CORPORATE SEAL)   By: _____

Attest: _____

Index

Depreciation
    accelerated, tax savings from
        using, 25
    straight-line, financial statements'
        use of, 25
Directors
    auctioneer duty for, 131–32
    duty of candor for, 132
    liability insurance for, 197–98
Discount factor applied to cash
    flows, determining, 17–18
Discounted cash flow valuation
    method, 16–18
Discounted present value of inven-
    tory and receivables, 110
Dissenters' rights of appraisal, 102
Diversification of your wealth by
    sale of business to an ESOP, 137
Dividends, paying extraordinary, 35
Divorce, sale of business after, 4
Due diligence of buyer
closing date of agreement of sale as
        different from deadline for,
        169–70
    in conditions precedent for agree-
        ment of sale, 171
    eliminated upon agreement of
        sale, 78
    four rules for, 64
    questions sellers answer during,
        65–68
    speaking to key employees as
        part of, 41
    tips for surviving, 63–68
Dun & Bradstreet, information
    supplied to, 195
Duty of candor imposed on direc-
    tors, 132
Duty of fair dealing for control
    block holders, 133

Earnout, 152–58
    attorney's fees clause for, 156–57
    avoiding 100 percent, 152
    continuing seller's methods of
        accounting following, 154

control of business under, 152–53
defined, 3, 152
escrowing cash for, 156
exchanged following a merger or
    consolidation, 101
imputed interest to seller under,
    157–58
legal protections for seller under,
    153–54
litigation arising from, 156–57
maximizing, 155
negotiating the amount of, 154–55
negotiating the measurement
    period for, 155
not allowed in poolings, 125
protecting payment of, 156
Eastern Airlines' proposed acquisi-
    tion by Texas Air, 82–83
EBITDA (earnings before interest,
    taxes, depreciation, and amorti-
    zation) valuation method, 13–14
acquisition debt for buyer using,
    21–22
adjusted, 14
multipliers applied to adjusted,
    14–15
size of business related to size of
    multiplier of, 27
Employee stock ownership plan
    (ESOP)
    advantages of selling business to,
        137–38
    contributions to, tax deductibility
        of, 138
    optimal conditions of sale to,
        139–40
    to purchase your stock, 136–40
    tax deductibility of stock divi-
        dends paid to, 139
Employees
    advance written notice of plant
        closings and mass layoffs to, 180
    confidentiality about decision to
        sell from, 59
    hired by buyer, seller's indemnifi-
        cation against claims by, 177